Innovations in university management

Angelo Reynolds
School of Education
Ph.D.

Innovations in university management

by
Bikas C. Sanyal

UNESCO Publishing

International Institute for Educational Planning

The designations employed and the presentation of material throughout this review do not imply the expression of any opinion whatsoever on the part of UNESCO or IIEP concerning the legal status of any country, territory, city or area or its authorities, or concerning its frontiers or boundaries.

The IIEP is financed by UNESCO and by voluntary contributions from Member States. In recent years the following Member States have provided voluntary contributions to the Institute: Belgium, Canada, Denmark, Finland, Iceland, India, Ireland, Norway, Sweden, Switzerland and Venezuela.

Published by the
United Nations Educational, Scientific and Cultural Organization,
7 place de Fontenoy, 75700 Paris, France
Printed in France by Imprimerie Gauthier-Villars, 75018 Paris

Cover design by Blandine Cliquet
ISBN 92-803-1156-5
© UNESCO 1995   IIEP/ko'f

Preface

The subject of this book, *Innovations in University Management*, is a burning issue for the whole world to-day. Higher education around the world is going through a crisis.

Several factors – including financial scarcity, lack of relevance of contents and methods (in this age of rapid development of knowledge in general and of information technology in particular), unemployment and underemployment of higher education graduates, and public demand for accountability – are putting increasing pressure on the institutions to become cost-effective.

Moreover, we are observing a paradigm shift in the method of educational management where ministries are giving away more and more managerial responsibility to the institutions of higher education whilst retaining the regulatory and control functions for themselves.

These phenomena call for increased managerial competence among the senior officials of institutions of higher education.

In 1990, the *International Institute for Educational Planning* (IIEP), having foreseen these problems, launched an international research programme on the problems of higher education management at the institutional level to create a knowledge base on the methods of better utilization of existing resources.

International agencies including UNESCO, OECD and the World Bank, national governments and higher education institutions themselves have all recognized the need for improved managerial effectiveness, in order to make the best possible use of available resources and respond to changing social and economic needs.

The above-mentioned research focused on individual institutions as the unit of analysis for reasons mentioned earlier and aimed to increase understanding of the process of planning, introducing and implementing management innovations in institutions of higher education as well as to

Preface

identify factors associated with success or failure, explore ways of overcoming obstacles and problems, and suggest ways of improving institutional management.

The IIEP research began with an extensive literature review and creation of an information base, the writing of a series of papers on methodological issues and the preparation of 14 in-depth case studies on different types of innovations. The results of these activities were used to prepare a set of training materials for intensive training courses. The exchange of individual university experiences in managerial innovations in these training courses provided an additional knowledge base for IIEP.

This book attempts to synthesize all these results from the research and training programmes.

It should be emphasized that this work has been undertaken for the institutions of developing countries which have little access to information on an international scale, many of whom have requested the assistance of IIEP and UNESCO in overcoming difficulties and in participating in the debate taking place on institutional management. The present work is designed to respond to these requests. Emphasis has been placed on providing examples of good practice from around the world on different aspects of university management.

It will be observed that a process of sensitization of ministries and universities in developing countries to the need for improved management in higher education has already begun.

Not only has the IIEP project – with its information base, methodological papers, research studies and training activities – oriented part of its programme to this end but (as has been noted in this book), many agencies have been actively giving assistance in this field. The list is long but mention may be made here of the UNESCO Secretariat and its regional offices, the Association of African Universities (AAU), the Commonwealth Secretariat, the German Foundation for International Development (DSE), the United Kingdom Overseas Development Administration (ODA), the Swedish International Development Authority (SIDA), the World Bank (IBRD), Carnegie, Rockefeller, Soros and Ford Foundations, Norwegian Agency for International Development (NORAD), and the Netherlands Foundation for International Co-operation (NUFFIC).

Changes have begun to take place and it will not be for want of good will and help that universities will not be able to take their proper place as increasingly dynamic and respected partners in the socio-economic development of their countries.

Preface

However, the institutions of higher education will have to appreciate that changes must emanate from their own national and institutional contexts, in particular their attitudes and will to adapt to the needs and priorities set down in national plans and institutional missions.

It is our hope that the academic community and the institutional managers will derive tangible benefits from this synthesis.

Jacques Hallak
Assistant Director-General, UNESCO
Director, IIEP

Acknowledgements

I would like to express my gratitude to those who have offered their advice and assistance in writing this book. Special mention must be made of Jacques Hallak, the Assistant Director-General, UNESCO, and Director of IIEP at whose initiative I undertook the responsibility of directing the research project on higher education management. I must also acknowledge the assistance I have received from Joyce Collins at all stages of the project including the preparation of the information base, conducting the personal interviews and initial editing. Michaela Martin has provided invaluable assistance since she joined the project. Maureen Woodhall of the Institute of Education, University of London, helped me in designing the research proposal and N.V. Varghese of the National Institute of Educational Planning and Administration (NIEPA) New Delhi, helped me as a Resident Fellow of the Institute, in my early thinking and conceptualization of the project and prepared a list of literature on the subject. Douglas Windham (Distinguished Service Professor of the State University of New York, Albany, USA), Ulrich Teichler (Director of the Centre for Higher Education and Work, University of Kassel, Germany), Thierry Malan (Inspector-General of Educational Administration, Ministry of Education, France), Guy Neave (Director of Research, International Association of Universities), Geoffrey Caston (former Vice Chancellor of the University of the South Pacific), Manuel Crespo (University of Montreal), all have given me useful advice and comments on earlier drafts of the book. I must acknowledge the contribution made by the authors of the case studies and the methodological papers and those who offered their time in being interviewed at IIEP or responded to questions by correspondence. Without their inputs, the book could not have been written. They have been referred to throughout the text.

BCS
Paris, October 1995

Contents

Preface   v

Acknowledgements   ix

Part I.   **The research programme**

Chapter 1   The research programme, conceptual framework and structure   3

Part II.   **The external environment of higher educational institutions**

Chapter 2   The external environment of higher educational institutions in the late 1980s and early 1990s   17

Part III.   **Improving university management to meet changing needs**

Chapter 3   Mergers as a strategy to improve the efficiency and effectiveness of universities   51

Chapter 4   Overall university management reform   63

Chapter 5   Strategies adopted at national and institutional levels to improve overall university management   97

Contents

Part IV.	**Improving selected areas of university management**	
Chapter 6	Financial management	133
Chapter 7	Academic staff management	177
Chapter 8	Management of research and links with the economy	218
Chapter 9	Management of space	253
Chapter 10	Educational delivery systems	276
Part V.	**Prospects for improving management**	
Chapter 11	Taking stock: the prospects for improving institutional management in developing countries	297

Part I

The research programme

Chapter 1

The research programme, conceptual framework and structure

1. Rationale of the research programme

This report presents the results of an IIEP research project on *Improving the managerial effectiveness of higher educational institutions*, which began in 1990. It arose from the need for universities in developing countries to cope with the rapidly changing socioeconomic situations in which they found themselves, and was undertaken for the benefit of those institutions. They have little access to information on an international scale, and many of them have requested the assistance of IIEP and UNESCO in overcoming difficulties and in participating in the debate taking place on institutional management. These institutions often have no active associations or regional bodies, nor are they associated with the Organization for Economic Cooperation and Development (OECD), Paris, whose studies and analyses have considerably increased interest and debate and have provided much needed expertise to institutions. The present work is designed to promote a similar process in developing regions.

Almost everywhere, higher education institutions have been faced with demands for expansion of enrolments and improved efficiency. They have been forced to reduce expenditure per student, to seek new sources of funding and to improve the utilization of existing resources. At the same time, they have had to cope with increased diversification and new types of students, including adult learners, so as to meet the changing needs of the labour market. They have also been pressed to foster closer links with industry and to widen participation through the introduction of distance learning. All this implies a need to improve and change the mechanisms, techniques and styles of institutional management.

The implementation of innovation and change in institutional management, however, invariably faces obstacles. These include internal resistance, inadequate staff, lack of financial resources to make the change effective and inadequate time for planning. One purpose of the IIEP research programme was to establish what types of changes have occurred or are occurring in higher education management and to increase understanding of the process of planning, introducing and implementing management changes. The project tried to identify the factors associated with success or failure, to explore ways of overcoming obstacles, to suggest methods to improve management and to increase the responsiveness of higher education institutions to changing financial, economic and social pressures.

Caught between the pressures of social demands on the one hand, and demands for rationalization and accountability on the other, some universities have responded with quite radical attempts to shake up their management and increase productivity. Much ingenuity has been displayed, particularly in the developed countries, in countering criticism of the cosy and costly academic world by adapting the concept of strategic management to universities. Strategies have included year round teaching; shift or double intake systems; multiple campuses connected by satellite; the creation of 'entrepreneurial' universities; the establishment of revenue-earning industrial liaison units, technology centres and science parks; twinning and exchange arrangements.

However, in most developing countries, higher education remains too expensive an undertaking for them to be able to expand their systems as their development requires, and the funds for innovation are not available. What then can be derived from the experience of the last decade or so which can shed some light on the way higher education could most beneficially be organized and managed for the future? What, if anything, has really changed?

Some maintain that more cosmetic 'changes' have occurred rather than true reforms(1), for example, does not consider that a change from block grants to contractual engagements, together with increasing the proportion of financing by loan schemes, to be rational planning, nor likely to solve the problems of mass higher education. Furthermore, now it has been noted too that one dominant experience of the last 25 years has been the unexpectedly modest success of 'intentional change'(2). Substantial restructuring has occurred in several countries. While some have changed from a binary to a unitary system, others have done the opposite. Both have been aiming at the creation of more diverse and adaptive systems within a framework of government evaluation which, however, perversely encourages homogenization(3). Another paradox, pointed out within the context of Sweden but applicable in many countries, is that universities are asked both to adjust to demands of the labour market and also to create equal opportunities for all sections of society, i.e. to respond to and at the same time be independent of society.

Such contradictions may well perplex managers of relatively new higher educational systems, watching the swing of events and reading the conflicting opinions of academic and government 'experts' from much more developed systems. The present work intends to take the point of view of such an audience. What can be learnt? What management aspects are the most important for analysis and control both in the overall management of the institution and in the various constituent domains of finance, staff, research, space, links with industry and educational delivery?

2. Definitions

It will be useful to clarify from the start what is meant by 'Management'. Here it is proposed to adopt the generally used definition of 'planning, organization, leadership, control and development'.

The *higher educational institution* concerned is the *University*, "an institution of higher learning, participating in the evolution of knowledge which provides facilities for teaching and research, and authorized to hold examinations and grant academic degrees" (definition given by CEPES, European Centre for Higher Education, UNESCO). We are not generally concerned with specialized institutes or polytechnic-type institutions such as Fachhochschulen in Germany, although of course in the United Kingdom and Australia the binary line has been abolished and many former polytechnics have become universities.

Effectiveness is often, but not necessarily, used to refer to the conclusion of a goal-achievement evaluation, with all its limitations. *Success* is roughly equivalent to this sense. Although effectiveness can be construed more generally as referring to achieving an outcome that may not have been part of the aims of a programme, it always refers to some goal, even if not the original one; it is a means-end notion.

Efficiency goes beyond effectiveness by bringing in a reference to the amount of resources involved. It implies the absence of wastage in achieving a given output; it can be increased by increasing the output for a given input or by decreasing the input for a given output. It does not guarantee that the results are of any useful size or quality. For this reason, in many contexts, planners conventionally require that a social intervention must be both effective and efficient(4).

3. The content of the research programme

The research programme had several components: an information base, case studies, training materials and workshops.

a. The information base

The information base, which covers changes that have occurred in university management in a wide range of countries over 1989- 1994, was designed not only to assist the researchers in the IIEP programme, but also to be made available on request to university personnel, as a means of increasing awareness of the importance of good management and the different ways of addressing problems. This was particularly in the light of the poor state of university libraries in some developing countries and the general lack of up-to-date information on university management.

b. The case studies

Selected case studies were carried out to identify the factors and strategies associated with successful innovation and change, and the obstacles to be overcome.

Several types of innovation and change were chosen for particular study:

(i) *Change in the organization of institutions*
New forms of decision-making structures and information flows.
The merger of separate institutions, departments or units.
(ii) *Changes in financial management and resource allocation*
Devolved budgeting.
Resource generation.
(iii) *Changes in educational delivery systems*
From *semester* to *trimester*, from block to credit system, rationalization of curricula, double intakes.
(iv) *Changes in staff management, including staff development and appraisal*
(v) *Changes in the organization or funding of research, and development activities*

In total, 14 case studies and one desk study were carried out (see list of case studies in *Annex 1* to this Chapter, page 13).

c. Training activities

The IIEP included a module on institutional management in higher education in its Annual Training Programme. In addition, workshops composed of modules of three- to four-day sessions were held in the areas of:

- integrated institutional management;
- staff management;
- financial management;
- management of facilities and space;
- management of student flows.

The inclusion of a training element in the research programme required collection of information and self-analysis by the participants (which then became available as an input to the research) and enabled the selection of interesting experiences of improving management to be utilized as mini case studies for follow-up to the training. Participants were thereby encouraged to implement methods and techniques they had learned. The IIEP, in turn, was able to refine its teaching tools and improve its knowledge base.

The first workshop was held in Mauritius in September 1993, and included approximately 30 finance or planning officers and registrars from eastern and southern African universities. The evaluation confirmed the relevance of both the content and the approach taken and this volume contains material from some of the follow-up studies. The second workshop took place in Ghana in June 1994 for participants of English-speaking West Africa, and the third in Brunei in November 1994 for participants from South East Asia.

4. Objectives of the book

The objectives set for the book were to increase understanding of:

1. Trends in university management.
2. Factors contributing to successful management in an era of rapid socioeconomic and technological change.
3. Ways of improving efficiency, resource utilization and managerial effectiveness in higher educational institutions.

Analyses of the materials and workshop discussions suggested three broad conclusions:

Conclusion A. The external environment of higher educational institutions has changed rapidly and institutions have been slow to adapt. However, it is now generally accepted that efficient management is critical to the success and reputation of universities. This has only recently (the late 1980s) been acknowledged, and somewhat reluctantly by more traditional European higher educational institutions.

Conclusion B. In this era of rapid economic, social and technological change, good management must itself involve change. Managerial and educational reform is a continuing and integrated process. Changes in administration, in educational delivery methods, in staff, research, space and facilities management are necessarily interlinked. They constitute a cumulative adjustment process, which is best carried out as a joint co-operative endeavour by professional managers and academics and preferably should be proactive, not reactive.

Conclusion C. Management in different specific areas of the university (e.g. finance, staff, research, space, academic departments) requires co-ordination, control and accountability mechanisms and specific professional expertise. Only then can it contribute to overall good management and keep pace with other changes taking place elsewhere.

5. Conceptual framework

A great deal of research has been conducted in recent years on the management of higher educational institutions. To mention only a few major international programmes, we may cite the OECD IMHE research, that of the International Association of Universities, of the Institute of Management and Leadership of Universities (IGLU), of the Inter-American Organization of Universities and the Association of African Universities, as well as that of national research institutions such as the Centre for Higher Education Policy Studies at the University of Twente. Therefore a basis on which to build a conceptual framework exists, at least for developed countries, and for regions such as Latin America and Africa where quite a lot of work has been done.

As will be shown in *Chapters 2* and *4*, the management of higher educational institutions is strongly influenced by the prevailing external environment, and in the case of public and private subsidized institutions, above all by the type of government steering and control policies in place. The latter have, over time, been instrumental in the creation of specific management procedures and cultures (or non-management culture) within institutions. The conservative nature of universities and the need to introduce some external pressures to bring about changes in management is discussed in *Chapter 4*.

Some indications of socioeconomic conditions and government steering and control policies are therefore necessary to assist understanding of the way universities are managed. The review therefore begins in *Chapter 2* with these aspects, focusing on government steering and control policies, noting in particular any recent changes enacted. Such changes in management of the system have been used both to show trends in management and to classify countries into broad groups accordingly.

A major trend is *self-regulation and accountability*. This has been a topic for many authors such as Van Vught, Neave, and Kells(5). They have shown that certain governments, in adopting self-regulation policies, have changed the distribution of power and resources as well as the nature of funding and control. Where universities were previously largely autonomous, as for example in the USA and the United Kingdom, governments increased their own powers. However, conversely, where there had hitherto been strong central planning and control, government powers were reduced. Everywhere, university executive powers grew while those of the faculty diminished.

Self-regulation necessarily implies, in theory, a much more management-conscious university. Such an institution expends energy differently from those largely regulated by governments. It is more in control of and informed about the functioning of its organization, more aware of goals and markets, able to employ incentives, corporate in culture, more proactive in management and able to implement change throughout its organization. It has been described(6) as a cybernetic model: the system constantly adjusting and responding via a distributed rational decision-making system in numerous units. Cybernetic systems can run by themselves once overall direction is given, since organizational management is reinforced at all levels, (with a shared mission, information and feedback). There is a flat management hierarchy, with leadership exercised at many levels.

The conditions necessary for implementing self-regulation include an environment of trust and co-operation between government and universities, governmental oversight, external validation, staff time and resources, and improved managerial expertize (often given by special training programmes) to cope with increased information requirements, reporting, incentives and sanctions. The empirical evidence available suggests that such a mode of institutional management may be implemented either by centrally planned systems, where the greater autonomy offered to institutions provides an incentive to co-operate, or by previously highly autonomous systems, where financial constraints, competition and other factors eventually overcome initial resistance. The present research programme was not based on and did not support any particular model of steering and management. Self-regulation and accountability are still being developed in various forms. Mistakes have been made and the criteria for successful implementation are numerous. It would seem to be a model that has advantages in situations of mass higher education and in numerous institutions where governments have difficulties of control and wish to stimulate managerial effectiveness. This is discussed further in *Chapter 5* where the impacts of steering policies on institutional management are shown.

It is apparent that experiences of self-regulation are greatly influencing the thinking and policies of other countries. Some are now moving towards more self-regulatory systems, while others have expressed their intention to do so. Some centrally planned systems in both developed and developing countries are incorporating elements of self-regulation, while a number are actively seeking information about it by sending missions or staff abroad.

It was also necessary to deal with another government policy, closely linked with the capacity to implement 'self regulation and accountability'. This is the *rationalization of the system* by mergers of institutions and departments. This has been widely implemented in a variety of ways, and is discussed in *Chapter 3*. Merger policies have brought about large-scale managerial changes at the institutional level, for example in the computerization of information systems, the use of technology, centralization of planning, and the administration of services.

The analyses which follow on these two policies provide the basis for examining in *Chapter 4* their overall impact on institutional management. The types of changes adopted, the methods used and the obstacles encountered are analyzed in some detail on the basis of case studies and other empirical evidence. A broad overall approach has been taken, since, as stated in *Conclusion B* above, successful managerial reform has been acknowledged to be a continuing and integrated process, one change necessarily requiring changes elsewhere in the administrative or academic systems.

However, most universities seeking to initiate management change are concerned with its impact on specific domains, such as finance, staff, facilities, educational delivery, etc. *Part IV* of this book is therefore devoted to certain major areas of management. The conclusions drawn once more support the need for institutions to adopt an integrated management approach.

Part V of the book puts together the lessons learned, in particular what may be most useful in the difficult circumstances of developing countries, what needs to be done by governments and the universities themselves and what assistance might most usefully be provided by aid agencies.

6. Methodological issues

There are, of course, a number of issues to be considered as regards the methodology and approach chosen. They are as follows:

The information was gathered between 1990 and 1994 and covers for the most part only publications issued since 1987. The sources were journals, newspapers, books, direct correspondence, conferences and visitors. Some of these sources may not be considered academically unimpeachable, but there are difficulties when working at an international level. For example, even though a special effort was made to obtain information from developing countries, material from them is less rich in some areas, because of problems of language and low levels of publishing in some countries. Furthermore, in some other countries, such as the United Kingdom, change is taking place continually, and the information given may not include very recent developments.

In the case studies, not all areas could be covered. In most cases admissions, student welfare, maintenance of buildings and equipment, and educational delivery methods are not included. However, as workshops and training materials accumulate, a great deal of information on improving management techniques in the various domains will become available.

These difficulties can hardly be avoided when attempting research of a world-wide scope. The process of information analysis is usually assisted by national and regional associations of researchers or universities, but some of these publish a journal only once a year, if at all. This review may therefore be considered as a seminal paper on which developing country researchers may build. In spite of the inclusion of a good number of developing countries among the experiences analyzed, there may seem to be bias towards developed countries. If so, this may by no means be a total disadvantage: case studies undertaken show that management reform in developing countries has often been initiated by those having experience or knowledge of practice in quite a different environment. The dissemination of summarized and analyzed experiences of university reform incorporating elements of self-regulation and accountability is in urgent demand, as demonstrated by the flow of visiting university and Ministry personnel seeking information. The discussion in this review of the problems of managing change, the transferability and the feasibility of management methods are mainly oriented towards developing countries.

As to the classification (see *Chapter 2*), categorising particular country systems is always a sensitive and arguable procedure. Diversity is extreme and many cases are not clearly cut: institutional management in some countries may be very much more influenced by socioeconomic factors (e.g. in Eastern Europe at present), while in others, although the government may be managerially moribund, it remains formally in charge of planning, administration and control. Thus the classifications made here are broad and relatively simple. A balance had to be struck between a classification which allows readers to comprehend situations in general terms, according to environments and particular modes of steering and their actual impact on institutional management, and one which goes into considerable depth and nuances, requiring much explanation and reference to sources. The latter can usually only be attempted when dealing with two or three countries.

To conclude, it must be repeated that this is the beginning of a much larger endeavour. The immensely rich and broad range of experiences, analyses and lessons learned which are contained in this volume, can, it is hoped, nevertheless provide some of the inspiration, the strategies and the tools to help developing countries to solve their own problems and to establish more dynamic and better managed institutions.

Annex 1
List of case studies conducted in the IIEP research programme

Africa

Kenya   The management of double intakes: a case study of Kenyatta University.
Niger   Change from a block to a *credit* system at the University of Niamey.
Uganda   Implementation of change *to* improve the financial management of Makerere University.

Asia

China   Institutional merger in Hubei Province.
India   Management of innovation: a case study of the Birla Institute of Technology, Pilani.
Philippines   Change from a semester to a trimester academic calendar at the De La Salle University.

Latin America

Chile   Modernization of administration at the University of Concepción, Chile.
Mexico   Strategies to improve the rate of completion of degrees and reduce drop-out, Faculty of Engineering, UNAM.
Peru   Changes in research management at the Universidad Nactional Agraria, La Molina.

Developed countries

Australia   Amalgamation at the University of Sydney.
Restructuring of higher education in Australia. (desk study).
Belgium   Rationalization of curricula at the Catholic University of Leuven.
Finland   Improving managerial effectiveness at the University of Joensuu.
USA   Implementing a faculty assessment system: a case-study of the University of Pittsburgh.
United Kingdom   Managing budget deficits in higher education: the experience of the University of Edinburgh.

(Summaries of case studies have been placed throughout the text in box outlines. Information has of necessity been given in very succinct form and readers may refer back to the full reports for more details: references are given).

References

1. Eicher J.C. "The financial crisis and its consequences for European higher education" In *Higher Education Policy,* Vol. 3, No. 4, 1990.

2. Kerr C. "A critical age in the university world, accumulated heritage versus modern imperatives" In *European Journal of Education*, Vol. 22, No. 2, 1987.

3. Lynn Meek V. et al. "Policy change in higher education" In *Higher Education*, Vol. 21, No. 4, 1991.

4. Scriven H, "Evaluation Thesaurus", Sage Publications, London, United Kingdom, 1991.

5. Van Vaught Frans. *Self-regulation in higher education*, Jessica Kingsley, London, 1992.

6. Middlehurst R. and Elton L. "Leadership and management in higher education" in *Studies in Higher Education*, Vol. 17, No. 3, 1992.

Part II

The external environment of higher educational institutions

Chapter 2

The external environment of higher educational institutions in the late 1980s and early 1990s

The 1980s was nowhere a comfortable decade for institutions of higher education. Many of them had been fairly small scale institutions catering to relatively small segments of society and the economy within a fairly predictable funding and demand environment, and found themselves expected to provide 'mass' higher education (not only full time, but also continuing and distance programmes) in a situation of financial constraint and competition for resources.

Demands on management in these two situations are vastly different. The extent and manner of adaptation to these demands were influenced by:

(i) changes in the external environment such as economic pressures, technological development, social demand, political ideology, etc.;

(ii) the type of government steering policy adopted. Some systems were sheltered from the full force of external impacts, while others suffered severe impacts but were subject to so much government regulation that they were able to make only limited adjustments. Yet others were required to develop their managerial capacities so as to meet set norms and performance indicators, report in some detail and compete with fellow institutions for funds.

This chapter will attempt to trace along a continuum the types of steering policies adopted, ranging through those which have implemented self-regulation and accountability, those in transition, those which have announced a policy of self-regulation but have met obstacles, to systems under centralized management, some of which may also have introduced elements of self-regulation which are compatible with their centralized administration, planning and control.

Four broad types are recognized, each of which will cover some rather diverse situations which nevertheless have managerial policies in common that have had an impact on the functioning of institutions.

1. Institutions most open to impacts from the outside, i.e. largely autonomous and self-regulatory within a broad framework of accountability. These are to be found in the USA (greater use of free market incentives and relatively light state regulation), and in the Netherlands (and Flemish Belgian institutions), Canada, Australia and the United Kingdom (under state guidelines and subject to more rigorous accountability measures)(1). These will be classified under the term *self-regulation and accountability implemented*. 'Regulation' has been defined as the informed and periodic process through which a system, institution, programme or procedure is attuned over time to expectations (intentions, standards, norms) through choices and actions judged by the regulator(s) to be needed as a result of formative or summative evaluation. (Kells, 1992).

2. Institutions where governments have already decreed a policy change to a more self-regulatory type of system and certain elements have been implemented, with the co-operation of higher educational institutions. These are classified as *self-regulation in transition*. They are to be found mostly in the Nordic countries. A few other countries (e.g. Singapore, Philippines, Nigeria, Algeria) might arguably also be put in this classification, but the changes there are so recent that their impact on institutional management has not been fully analyzed and can be seen only in specific domains (e.g. research management in Singapore).

3. Those where governments have announced a policy change but problems and obstacles in implementation have been encountered. Perhaps only a few elements have been introduced, such as greater institutional autonomy, evaluation or strategic planning. Examples are seen in certain Latin American and Eastern European countries. These will be classified *self-regulation in difficulty*.

4. Institutions under direct *centralized planning and control*, as seen in many developing countries and some continental European ones (e.g. France, Italy, Austria, Germany). Specific governments may have introduced elements of self-regulation compatible with their centralized systems.

This classification will be used throughout the report so that readers may place experiences within their contexts.

1. Self-regulation and accountability implemented

A recent OECD research programme has noted signs of a move towards a knowledge-intensive economy (2). The service sector accounts for nearly 70 per cent of all employment in many of the OECD countries and is now being reinforced by the trend in manufacturing to knowledge-based products and processes. There is strong pressure for better quality and shorter product life- cycles, with fewer routine and unskilled jobs; the pace of change is likely to quicken. Educational policy makers are responding by emphasising institutional diversification in order to achieve the appropriate mix of educational outcomes for the emerging knowledge-intensive economy. A major issue is how important a role to give to the market – as supreme arbiter and indicator of change – and how much 'steering' is necessary on the part of the government. The choice of path chosen is evidently a political one. OECD nations seem to be generally aware, however, that to ensure the best chances of development within the present economic climate, mass higher education will have to be provided so that imparts are not only the requisite core curricula but also 'higher order thinking skills', previously thought necessary mainly for top level professionals.

(i) USA

The highly diversified and market-oriented system of autonomous public and private institutions in the *USA* is under close scrutiny. Federal and state legislatures and executives – and the American people – have become more critical of higher education, objecting to its cost and to the high loan default rates. The criticism is that self-regulation has become self-serving.

Governance structures have increased in size and complexity with more multi-campus institutions, consolidated governing boards and co-ordinating bodies for master planning. States have become more efficiency conscious: fiscal audits have expanded to review institutional and administrative performance and ensure tighter control so as to reduce misuse of funds.

While some public universities have administrative control over internal budget allocation, staff policies and academic programmes, others are subject to various forms of state regulation. One researcher found four models of steering or control, i.e. (a) state agency, with institutions having no responsibility for financial and staff decisions, (b) state control, (c) state aide and (d) corporate, with independent institutions receiving state funds only via student grants. The second and third are the most prevalent(3).

For the American system as a whole, control is exercised largely by accreditation and evaluation procedures. These have been a long-standing practice, with consumers, perhaps rather more than governments, requiring information on institutional performance. Accreditation is voluntary but almost all institutions undergo the process to establish their status and because federal loans and grants are awarded only to students attending accredited colleges. Mechanisms, like the system, are extremely diverse and enable research institutions to pursue academic excellence, while community colleges can emphasize open access and education for the masses, with each judged accordingly. The main method of institutional evaluation is the six regional inter-state accreditation bodies which undertake institutional evaluation, at ten-year intervals, aiming at the control of minimum quality standards. The accreditation process includes self-assessment of mission, governance and administration, educational programmes, faculty and staff, library and other learning resources, student services, physical and financial resources, and special educational programmes. This is followed by study visits by a commission composed of external peers. These six regional agencies, in the face of mounting criticism, have recently agreed to draw up new standards of evaluation, emphasising what students have learned, and to make their reports public(4).

Apart from this, State bodies approve new academic programmes, which allow for innovation, such as in Missouri a *value-added approach*, or Ohio a *selective excellence programme*. In addition, some fifty professional accreditation bodies, organized in the Council of Post-Secondary Accreditation, undertake periodic evaluation of specific courses and programmes (medicine, law, engineering, business, etc.). Several private organizations (e.g. the American Council of Education, Carnegie Foundation) carry out rankings of institutional performance, which are used by students wishing to choose suitable institutions.

Considerable federal and state investment has been made in computerization and information systems. EDUCOM was founded in 1964 as a non-profit consortium of higher education institutions to facilitate the introduction, use and management of information technology in higher education and to promote co-operative efforts among the institutions. However, it was as late as 1985 before some consensus emerged about the scope and opportunities for investing in campus computing and communications infrastructure. It was then realized that information technology could revolutionize a whole range of administrative, management and service functions. Decision support systems in computer networks are now in operation in most universities.

It can be seen that apart from the ten year institutional review, the evaluation/control system is largely academic. However, the question is now being asked whether this can continue. Problems have emerged, such as excessive administrative costs, fees increasing faster than inflation, and misuse of funds, leading to public and government demands for assurance that universities are both efficient and effective in serving students and society(5). Implementation of new regulations on accountability appears to have been postponed for the time being, but these will be directed particularly at the quality of curricula and staff, the promotion system and the way fees are calculated(6).

Characteristics: Highly diversified, market-oriented and autonomous system with a pervasive management culture, use of computer networks and information systems, voluntary accreditation but only ten-yearly overall institutional evaluation linked to funding incentives, i.e. managerial accountability is not strong.

(ii) Canada

In Canada each province is responsible for its own higher educational institutions. The public universities enjoy broad administrative autonomy even though 80 per cent of funding comes from the government. A period of austerity began in the 1990s when university budgets remained static or were reduced, forcing a change to a more managerial attitude on the part of institutional administrations. In Ontario and Quebec, assessment is decentralized to intermediate associations of universities, which have agreed to minimal norms for assessment. Universities can start new programmes without government approval but in that event no funding will be given. Provincial governments steer by policy announcements, by control of new courses and evaluation, and also by incentive formula funding. The Quebec government, for example, grants a lump sum for each degree gained in order to improve output efficiency rates, while research universities receive more funds according to the number of Ph.Ds produced(7), (8).

Characteristics: State steering, but broad university administrative autonomy, decentralized university association assessment linked to funding incentives.

(iii) United Kingdom

The United Kingdom, which was one of the most liberal systems, has now become one of the most strongly steered and controlled in the developed world(9). This has been accompanied by severe financial constraints; the unit of resource per student has fallen by 22 per cent over the period 1989-1993(10). Changes in organization have been too numerous and rapid to describe in detail at this stage, but readers will, as in the case of other countries, find more detail in subsequent chapters dealing with finance, staff, space and research management. Government action has been interpreted by some academics as an attack on higher education(11).

Degree standards in British universities have long been maintained by a system of external examiners, while professional associations have influenced the content of courses. Enrolments are restricted and steered by grant funding, though universities may take full fee-paying students as they see fit(12).

The reinforcement of entrepreneurial management, together with a list of performance indicators for resource allocation within universities was proposed by the Jarratt Committee as early as 1985. The Department of Education and Science (now Department for Education) then Paper felt that the development of performance indicators was necessary to secure *value for money*, and by 1987 the number of indicators defined had risen to 37, many of them being indicators of costs(13), (14). With this in mind, two major grants were given in the 1980s by the University Grants Committee to assist computerization, one to the University of Bradford and the other to the University of Aston. Subsequently 19 universities and colleges formed a consortium to use the most advanced computer systems for the improvement of top level management under the Management and Administrative Computing Initiative. This covers finance, student records, estate management, research contracts and payroll and personnel records in a single system, and uses a common data format in to generate reports across the system for use by the Higher Education Funding Council, and in grant applications(15). In parallel to this work, the University Grants Committee introduced in 1985 a new funding model which separated the funds for teaching and research activities. The funding of research was partially related to perceived research performance, and by 1993 this had evolved into a full-blown research assessment procedure whereby universities are ranked according to a complex formula (see *Chapter 8*).

The issue of quality was taken up in 1990 by the universities themselves. The Committee of Vice-Chancellors and Principals set up an Academic Audit Unit (now the Division for Quality Audit of the Higher

Education Quality Council) to scrutinize the mechanisms universities have in place to maintain quality. Audit teams receive documentation from institutions and visit them to examine methods of course review, the teaching and learning process, student assessment and classification procedures, staff development, training, appraisal and incentives and methods of feedback and enhancement processes.

In addition, assessment of teaching quality is carried out by the Higher Education Funding Council, following pilot schemes in 1992 and 1993. Institutions carried out self-assessments and had to provide indicators of performance, including entry qualifications, market share, course applications, cost per student, completion rates, student degree results and employment statistics. Institutions claiming to provide an 'excellent' education automatically receive assessment visits and a sample of others are also visited. Three quality rankings of excellent, satisfactory and unsatisfactory are awarded, and inform funding(16). The system has been heavily criticized and satirized in the universities, and the Government has undertaken to review it in consultation with them.

It will be noted that though university associations set up their own evaluation mechanisms, these were not considered sufficient for use in allocating funds. The situation is still very fluid and a vigorous debate is taking place on how to assess educational quality in an acceptable way(17), (18). Recent over-expansion (an 11 per cent increase in student numbers instead of the 7.3 per cent budgeted for in 1993) has caused the Ministry to propose tilting the HEFC role more to active planning(19).

Characteristics: Rapid change, strong Government steering and control, performance indicators and investment in management information systems, inter-institutional comparisons and rankings, formulae funding, recent emphasis on quality audit.

(iv) Netherlands

In *the Netherlands*, as in the United Kingdom, the government led the way in initiating change designed to increase the efficiency and effectiveness of universities. After two retrenchment operations in the early 1980s (which included a shorter four-year curriculum, reduction in the number of full-time professors, higher teaching loads and lower subsidies to students) a new steering philosophy was outlined, involving more university managerial autonomy in return for accountability and for quality. Under the 1985 law on university policy-making and planning, each university had to publish a planning document as a basis for discussions with the Ministry of Education. A cycle of policy/budget/evaluation reports was to take place over three years.

Reports can lead to changes in policy, while policy changes or evaluation can change the budget. Funding for teaching and research were separated and based on formulae and output. However, universities still have no right to decide on enrolment numbers or standards.

The universities' own national association (VSNU) was, after negotiation with the government, given responsibility for setting up a system of quality assurance. It succeeded in convincing the Ministry not to use the outcomes for funding purposes, at least not for the time being. The VSNU turned the assessment procedure into one which sought improvement rather than just control. It was tested during 1988-1990 and includes self-assessment, followed by a peer visit and report to which a written reply is made by the university. Departments can decide whether they wish to implement the recommendations, and have an interest in doing so since they will be evaluated again in five years' time. The Government Inspectorate for Higher Education ensures that the evaluation is carried out and makes additional studies on special subjects such as teacher training courses, study loads, student selection procedures, etc.(20). Reports comment on strengths and weaknesses, educational methods, the structure and organization of programmes, and conditions in the university, but do not attempt to make any rankings.

The universities themselves in 1981 formed a Foundation for University Administration Automation to co-ordinate analyses and system designs for staff, finance and students. In 1983 they agreed with the Ministry of Education on an Information Statute for the supply of basic data. In 1990 interest shifted towards information for planning and accountability: information is supplied as much as possible through existing periodic reports(21).

Academics co-operated fully because peer evaluation was acceptable and feedback appreciated(22). The 'Dutch model' is considered to be a success and has been adopted by Belgian Flemish universities and some Latin American countries. However, the government would like to see more attention given to accountability and university executive level management. Talks are taking place on the mode and objectives of the second round of assessments and universities have been requested to give feedback on follow-up action to evaluations. The Dutch are also working on the development of hard and soft statistical indicators, but as yet not much is normative.

*Characteristics:*Strong Government steering, combining aspects of traditional planning and control with self regulation, the university association having responsibility for implementation which includes improvement, not just control. Co-operation in computerization. The Government considers accountability too weak.

(v) Australia

The unification of the higher education system in Australia had many elements of the United Kingdom and Netherlands changes but its main feature was wide-scale amalgamation of institutions. This was not only for educational reasons, but also to enhance control. The government believed that reform could be accomplished only within larger units and required universities to be more responsive to its plans. Moreover, some of the larger institutions themselves wanted more autonomy in staff and resource management. What occurred was a restructuring in which institutions have to compete for status and resources via formula funding and incentive schemes. The government increased resources for higher education, in particular for computer networks, and encouraged rapid expansion of enrolments, bringing down unit costs.

In this situation, quality assurance has been a major concern. The procedure chosen was of a voluntary and university-led type. The government established a Committee for Quality Assurance in 1992 with a fund amounting to two per cent of total expenditure on higher education for rewarding institutions that "demonstrably enhanced quality". Guidelines were set. Only half the universities could benefit and no university was to receive more than five per cent of its existing budget. The emphasis was to be on outcomes rather than procedures and was to involve research, teaching and service to the community (the latter is an aspect not considered in most assessment schemes). Whole universities, not individual departments, were to be assessed(23), (24).

The national committee carrying out these assessments includes a representative of the Vice-Chancellors' Committee, academic organizations, students and business groups. Each university submits a report of only 20 pages, to be followed by a visit from the national committee which will look in the first instance at overall profiles of management practice, composition of the student population and competence of graduates. Subsequent evaluations in the following years will concentrate on teaching, then research and community services. Where grants are made, their effect is followed up. This approach is considered to have the advantages of greater simplicity and clarity and treats universities as organic entities, not just a collection of departments. Accountability is also ensured by university annual reports and institutional profiles (submitted with requests for funding) which are monitored annually by the Higher Education Committee and by financial audit.

Characteristics: Strong government steering by formula funding and quality assessment linked to funding incentives, investment in computer networks and amalgamation implemented by universities.

(vi) New Zealand

Rather similar policies have been adopted in New Zealand, where universities are subject to regimes of reporting and monitoring and have been forced to absorb rises in costs. However, the changes met greater resistance from the academic community and resulted in a long series of consultations, the universities arguing that policies were far too driven by economic considerations. Nevertheless, the process is continuing, in particular with the merger of colleges of education with universities.

From the above, it can be seen that although these countries are all characterized by self-regulation and accountability, there are some major differences in the pressure exerted by governmental steering and accountability measures (the USA universities so far experiencing less) and in the details laid down, the extent and rapidity of change and the spirit of government-university co-operation (those universities losing some degree of autonomy expressing more reluctance to change). However, in all cases, steering strategies were backed up by support in the form of expertise and extra funding for incentives, training initiatives or staff changes, and investment in computers and information technology, buildings, etc. Additional, sometimes very substantial, means to carry out change were made available.

2. Self-regulation in transition

A feature of the Nordic countries has been their stability and strong welfare systems, in which education is considered to be of major importance. There is little or no private higher education and the state systems are highly centralized. Admissions, curricula, and some other matters may still be decided through extensive parliamentary machinery and regulations. These countries were not under such severe economic pressure in the 1980s as, say, the United Kingdom, and were therefore able to adopt more gradualistic and proactive approaches to bring about the change in higher education which they could foresee would be necessary in the mid-1990s.

(i) Finland

This was particularly the case in *Finland*. Government policy decreed regional institutions in areas where the population is low and the system has a surplus capacity of student places. Efficiency has not been high, with a graduation rate of one graduate per teacher per year(25). The government prepared for change by appointing certain institutions to conduct pilot projects in specific areas such as management, decentralized budgeting and educational delivery. In 1988 legislation to increase the powers of university decision-making bodies was passed and a dialogue between the Ministry and universities on their 5 year plans, profiles of strengths and use of resources was instituted. In 1992 the funding system was changed to one of lump-sum budgets based on an output formula. There is a performance evaluation component in the budget, indicators are kept simple and there are as yet no quality aspects. The traditional evaluation processes continue; for example, the Academy of Finland evaluates disciplines by peer review at the rate of eight per year, and the Council of Higher Education Departments also evaluates research and teaching by discipline. The universities themselves have adopted a variety of approaches to evaluation, and most use it in some form.

A national computerized database was created for which information is collected annually. It contains quantitative data on performance and costs (13 indicators). These are used primarily for planning by university decision-makers and also by the Ministry of Education, but other persons may gain access.

However, financial pressures have now begun to have their toll. The higher education budget for 1993 has been cut by eight per cent in real terms. More cuts are expected in 1994 and 1995. The total amount of State higher education budget reductions in three years will be, according to present estimates, about 15 per cent. In Autumn 1992 the Ministry of Education also published a programme for the structural development of the Finnish higher education system. Its long-run aim is to make the higher education system more effective and efficient, and to improve conditions for high quality research.

The reform of public administration will be implemented in an environment different from that anticipated in the planning stages of the change. The Finnish public sector has been used to growing budgets and tight centralized control, whereas the relaxation of political and bureaucratic control is now felt to be the strategy which will lead to a gradual improvement of efficiency in all public organizations. In the higher education sector, small institutions will be merged and some activities, departments or faculties will be closed. The universities have been offered the opportunity to do all this independently. They had to make the painful decisions on their own terms by January 1993 or let the government undertake the restructuring for them(26).

In Norway, from 1987 onwards, the government set up several commissions and initiated measures designed to improve productivity and quality without increasing resource inputs. All institutions were to introduce strategic planning and reporting of results in 1990 which a small office at the Ministry of Cultural and Scientific Affairs would oversee. The main aim of universities was stated to be education and teaching, not research. The January 1990 Act gave greater self-government to higher educational institutions, the general ethos being inspired by the Dutch model. This Act went into some detail as regards university management; for example, university senates were to become steering committees of only 9 to 13 members, and each department was to have a critical mass of 20 staff and to develop stronger leadership.

    (ii)   Sweden

Sweden began rather earlier with a policy which aimed at enhancement of the self-steering capacity of institutions and departments. In 1987 it changed the former line to a broad programme budget thus giving more discretion to universities. It also opened them up to outside influence by stipulating that each Board of Governors was to contain a majority (6 out of 11) of external members. Responsibility for Informatics Centres was given by the National Council to regional universities. The University of Uppsala specialized in management and produced the first systems for salaries and student registration which were adopted by most universities. A National Centre of Super Computers was created and universities were connected to it in a network. At present most universities have their own information systems which allow management to decide which data to produce for their needs(27).

The National Board of Universities and Colleges launched a project on institutional and departmental self-evaluation, initiated by a series of workshops at which institutions were invited to reflect by means of simulation exercises on ways and means of trimming budgets. Departments, for a number of years, have had to prepare annual reports for their faculty board. In several Swedish universities, self-evaluation has thus become part of the annual budgetary process, while other evaluation work is linked with institutional planning processes(28). In June 1990 a Council for the Renewal of Undergraduate Education was established to decide on and fund experimental projects in institutions. A further reform in 1993 abolished the National Board and its functions were divided amongst the Ministry of Education, an evaluation agency and a National Audit Unit. Sweden is now moving towards an explicit system of quality control under which institutions are asked for a description of quality assurance processes. A new funding system covering a budgetary period of three years has been introduced under which high quality is to be rewarded and the annual collection of data at the central level is being kept to a minimum(29). The Government still appoints Vice Chancellors and members of the Governing Boards but the latter are now responsible for the internal structure of governance, for financial planning, and for the appointment of staff. The Universities and Colleges have formed their own National Association for Higher Education and the choice of style of university management is being debated(30).

Characteristics: Gradual change to greater university managerial autonomy steered by governments, with university co-operation in pilot projects.

3. Self-regulation in difficulty

a. Eastern Europe

A cost-effective managerial philosophy has begun to spread to Eastern Europe where, due to centralized planning traditions, lack of the requisite economic framework and a profound long-lasting recession, its implementation meets many obstacles. There is agreement on the need for more autonomy and modern management methods but not on how they can be made to work. The EEC Tempus Programme to support university development has received more than 1,300 proposals from institutions, and at the same time the World Bank has created a "Catching up with Europe Development Fund" which has similar objectives. The problem is how to establish the priority areas which will have the greatest multiplier effects on the system as a whole.

(i) Russia

In the Russian Federation, large universities now have control over their budgets and are free to formulate their own specialized programmes. Enterprises are asked to pay for their graduate employees and for research. However, graduates are not in as great demand as formerly and so far, industrial sponsorship is nowhere near meeting the shortfall in government funding for research. Industry has realized that it is cheaper to do the research work oneself. According to the new (1992) Russian legislation, universities have exclusive control of their land, buildings and equipment and have the right to choose State or local sources of financing and to enter into joint ventures with foreign firms. However, since there are many small over-specialized institutions, it is expected that, as in other European countries, a large number of mergers and closures will take place. The trend is therefore towards decentralization, diversification and partial student/employer supported education. Diversification will consist of State and local structures as well as industry/university conglomerates.

Some business groups and banks, who are the largest clients for qualified personnel, are already participating in policy making. A private higher educational sector is also beginning to emerge.

(ii) Bulgaria

In *Bulgaria* the situation is somewhat similar. In November 1989 the management of higher education institutions was decentralized: they may manage their material and financial resources and recruit staff. Funding is obtained from contracts with the State and other employers for the finance of the number of students needed. Institutions alone have to set enrolments and decide on types of course. In addition they may earn funds from research, training, foreign students and production activities and establish endowment funds(31).

(iii) Ukraine

The *Ukraine* has announced that a new structure of higher education is to be created together with a system of accreditation to allow greater institutional autonomy.

(vi) Estonia

In *Estonia* there is still considerable uncertainty, severe budget constraints and proposals for restructuring. Meanwhile, the universities declared themselves in 1992 to be autonomous, although there is as yet no legislation to legitimize this.

(v) Poland

Poland has plans to reform its educational system, which will incorporate decentralization, more autonomy, development of the private sector and redefinition of standards in order to adapt to European systems of higher education (32). The September 1990 legislation covered reform of academic career structures, and granted autonomy regarding internal organization, curricula and the election of Rectors and Deans. However, there is no evaluation system as yet. Government steering is effected by allocation of funds but this, due to the excessive rigidity of a traditional line item budget, is hampering change. For example, staff funds are allocated according to student numbers and any savings cannot be spent on other items(33).

(vi) Romania

Romania's university system is concentrated in the capital (80 per cent) and larger cities. However, a diversity of second-level higher educational institutions have been created, and under a new law permitting the creation of small enterprises (less than 20 people) private sector institutions have also recently been established. Their quality will be supervized by an Accreditation Commission, funded on the lines of the American Board for the Accreditation of Engineering Education.

(vii) Hungary

Hungary has experienced a less abrupt transition from a centrally planned to a market economy. Its higher education system enrols only 14 per cent of the age cohort. The Hungarian Rectors' Conference has emerged out of the collapse of the previous association and is co-operating with the Ministry and World Bank in Project Universitas to restructure the higher education network. It is proposed to create regional centres around universities, concentrating management and developing common facilities(34). Accreditation and self assessment of course content have been introduced(35).

(viii) Czech and Slovak Republics

In *Czechoslovakia* the 1990 Act on Higher Education guaranteed academic freedom and autonomy, with Rectors and Deans elected by their respective Senates. In the *Czech Republic* a new 1993 Act on Higher Education clarified the mission of the desired 'research university' and a 5 year plan (1992-97) was designed in which it was stipulated that 20 per cent of revenue should be generated from private sources. The Slovak Republic established a Council of Higher Education composed of elected representatives of universities as well as an Accreditation Committee to evaluate teaching and research quality(36).

Reports from the Eastern European countries indicate that large proportions of graduates (as many as 50 per cent) are unable to find work, enrolments have declined, support from industry is low, salaries have not been paid for some months, and universities are engaged in crisis management. A few have been able to benefit from a boom in demand for business and foreign language courses. Under the circumstances, little research is being done as yet on change in individual institutional management except for a few reports from Central Europe.

Characteristics: Government desire for change expressed in legislation is impeded by the poor economic situation; many reform proposals are still unclear; contract funding has been adopted in the East European systems.

b. Central and Latin America

Recent literature emphasizes the problems of mass social demand; decline in quality; the fact that students cannot afford to study full time; and staff salaries so low that good academics leave or take second and third jobs. At the same time, the power of teacher and student unions causes any change to be highly politicized.

Governments have set limits to their expenditures and have reduced the pressure of social demand by allowing the growth of private institutions, of which there are now large numbers, usually offering the cheaper types of education. A wide variety of structures exists: autocratic, bureaucratic, collegial, political, organized anarchic and entrepreneurial(37), (38). However, the social and political framework has not so far favoured management change, although the need for improvement is acknowledged, and despite growing competition from the private sector. For state institutions, government bureaucracy is a major problem. Universities are not free to establish budgets or intervene in salary scales, so that institutions deal only with minor current expenses. However, some governments have begun to put forward proposals to abandon incremental budgeting, to lessen isolation and to institute evaluation as an instrument of policy. Traditionally most higher education systems in Latin America have been equipped with an accreditation type of evaluation by which newly founded institutions or newly created programmes receive official approval after meeting minimum quality standards. It is conducted either by a ministerial body, by an autonomous body at the university or by a buffer type organization. However, new types of evaluations are being established which aim at comparability or improvement. These are not without their problems, and in Venezuela, university evaluation is being contested(39).

(i) Mexico

The Government of *Mexico* has attempted to steer its university system towards more regulated expansion, institutional evaluation, closer links with the productive sector and differential salary scales for academics. However, with few exceptions, public universities follow a rigid traditional organization. Attempts to enrol students in new technology fields have failed and the interests of pressure groups have so far proved stronger than State rhetoric(40). The results of very recent initiatives are not yet available, including the 1989 National System which grants incentive bonuses to 30 per cent of staff in each institution, and the 1989 National Commission for Evaluation of Higher Education. The 1990 and 1992 institutional evaluations found that few universities could give complete information and most were descriptive and not analytical(41). The government now proposes a National System of Evaluation as from 1993 which will cover institutions, sub-systems and programmes by peer review.

(ii) Chile

Chile's Committee to reform the law on higher education in 1991 proposed to reinforce autonomy and self-regulation by setting up a buffer National Council of Higher Education to accredit new universities and supervise the existing ones. The Dutch model was suggested for evaluation. Student loans or grants would be given and a Fund for Institutional Development would provide incentives to improve quality. The legislation to enforce these proposals had not yet been approved by 1993. Resistance is strong: the private universities do not want obligatory evaluation, public universities do not want to share funds with the private sector and linking performance to the budget frightens them. University staff are accustomed to leaving management to the government(42).

(iii) Other countries in Latin and Central America

Similar attempts have been made in *Colombia*, *Argentina*, *Bolivia*, *Brazil* and *Ecuador*, where the Ministry of Education is conducting a major project on decentralization in the 17 public and private universities in the country, assisted by IBRD. The introduction of inter-institutional differentiation and greater autonomy was shelved in Brazil and the government is adopting a policy of piecemeal and incremental change, which will take longer and be more expensive. In Cuba a decentralization process was initiated to give more flexibility in curricula and the use of teachers. But heads of institutions hesitated to take decisions and the latest report is that decentralization has not been a success in this context(43). Nevertheless Cuba is continuing to merge institutes and faculties and to increase activities to generate revenue.

Despite problems at the national level, in this region there are individual institutions which have taken management initiatives, as will be seen in the subsequent chapters. Furthermore, funds have been made available for computers and information systems in some large universities (e.g. UNAM, Mexico, Sao Paulo and others in Brazil), providing tools to assist progress towards greater efficiency.

*Characteristics:*Government desire for change as shown by policy, evaluation systems and investment in computerization, has been impeded by traditional bureaucracy, politicization and lack of a management culture among academics.

4. Centralized planning and control

a. Western Europe

Continental Europe (*France, Italy, Belgium, Austria, Portugal, Germany,* and *Greece*)

In these countries, Ministries of Education generally prescribe budgets, student admissions and fees, buildings and size of staff. They also validate courses and set the formal structure of university management. Initiatives to improve efficiency therefore usually come from Governments. There are exceptions, and some relatively autonomous institutions do exist. Notable examples are the French *grandes écoles* which are in some cases privately funded, and are administered by Directors and representatives of the funding authority and of the students. Even apart from these, the extent of centralized control is in some cases decreasing. For example, the 1989 Italian law gave universities control over appointments and teaching methods and an autonomous National Committee for Evaluation has been established. Portugal also enacted a law on university autonomy in 1988, but this is limited by the need to negotiate a 5 year contract fixing expansion targets and staffing levels, with the Government.

(i) France

France's system of four-year contracts has been in force since 1989; they allow for the participation of municipalities and business enterprises in university decision-making. A recent critique of the French management system observed that although universities had just elaborated four-year plans, this had to be done within the framework of annual budgetary appropriations by the Government. Accounting procedures were said to be archaic, and to allow for little analysis of real costs. Much time is wasted getting around regulations, and centralized staff management creates rigidity(44).

However, improvements are being sought through the National Evaluation Committee, which is independent of political and administrative structures, and placed under the authority of the Head of State. Its explicit role is to provide more transparency in French higher education and to issue qualitative information on higher education institutions, including both universities and *grandes écoles*. Every eight years, it appraises the major activities and the functioning of institutions: research, initial and continuing education, management, governance and institutional policy. The CNE also examines the state of art in a particular discipline. It decided to adopt a pragmatic approach in gathering written information, which is complemented by expert visits. A methodology indicating the basic information to be furnished by the institutions, the Ministry or national research bodies was worked out by the French Conference of University Presidents(45). External experts – national and foreign academics, researchers and representatives from industry – form the committee for each institution. They study the documentation provided and visit the institution for discussions. Their report is then submitted for comment to the head of institution and ultimately published. The CNE has been operational for eight years or so and has evaluated most of the higher education institutions in France. It has accumulated considerable experience in institutional evaluation and is currently reconsidering its methodology before moving on to a second phase of return visits to assess progress(46).

The Ministry and universities have co-operated over computerization. By 1988 two information systems had been introduced, one for finance and the other for courses, with access to a common data base associated with a guarantee of autonomy for each individual department in its own sphere of responsibility. The new technologies have not yet made their full impact; lack of training has delayed implementation(47). In 1992, 85 institutions were grouped under GIGUE (Group for Computerized Management) to study and develop computerized systems for staff management, etc. A project SISE (system of student records) will enable reliable information on students and their progress to be produced. Old norms are to be replaced by a more flexible and precise analytical system (SANREMO) for the allocation of resources and funds. Basic running costs are to be calculated on standard criteria(48).

Meanwhile, the first surveys by a new body, the Observatory of Higher Education Costs, attached to the Ministry of Education, have been released, giving the first global costing of courses per student(49). A recent report states that the system of fixing the exact number of posts in four year contracts is to be abolished so as to give more flexibility; seven new universities are to opt out of the national framework for a period and will be able to change their internal decision-making structures(50).

(ii) Germany

Discussions have begun in *Germany* about new ways of steering higher educational systems, while increasing institutional managerial autonomy(51). The State governments have called for more competition in higher education but are not willing to transfer power and responsibility to institutions. In 1988 the West German Rectors' Symposium defined a set of performance indicators to evaluate outcomes, stating that they preferred objective data to peer review, but only four universities have so far published any data. They have been assisted by the Hochschul-Informations System (HIS) – the national software house for administrative computing for higher education, which has developed two types of software: an adaptable mainframe based system for central administration, and a personal computer based system for use by decentralized units such as departments or projects.

However, the cost of reunification has imposed constraints and budget cuts, including reductions in study places and plans to introduce tuition fees. The need for greater effectiveness is keenly felt, and six states have funded programmes to improve the quality of teaching so as to increase efficiency, through such measures as shorter duration of programmes, lower drop-out rates, curriculum reform, and innovative teaching methods(52).

(iii) Belgium

In *Belgium*, the government has paid little attention either to university management or to autonomy: universities function as decentralized public services and there is little direct government intervention. They have, however, been deeply affected by continual cuts in funding since 1975, while at the same time being expected to cope with expansion. In 1989, the country was federalized; the Flemish and French universities have since then begun to go in separate directions, the Flemish tending to follow the Dutch reforms(53).

Other systems remain largely unchanged as governmental and academic bureaucracies. For example, in Greece all decisions need ministerial approval and the creation of new posts, appointment of staff and implementation of budgets have to follow a complex bureaucratic process. There is very little managerial responsibility in universities (54). In Austria decision-making power lies at the top with the government and at the bottom with the Professors, who are appointed by the President and over whom the Dean has no direct authority(55).

Characteristics: Interest in new ways of government steering has been expressed by a number of countries in Continental Europe, though there has so far been little significant progress towards self-regulation, except perhaps in France. The French and German governments have funded the development of information systems but these have not brought about managerial changes.

Most of the centrally planned and controlled systems of higher education are, however, to be found in developing regions.

b. Asia

This region, containing some of the richest and some of the poorest of countries, has sought solutions in co-operation with the productive sector, emphasizing technology and science. It has also seen the development of a private sector, which has greatly expanded the supply of higher education (*China, India, Pakistan* and *Vietnam* are recent examples). However, where private education has spread widely, this has usually been at the expense of quality (*Thailand*, Indonesia, *the Philippines*). The use of new technologies has made progress in India, Thailand, China and the South Pacific, but the impact is so far small. Countries whose investment in higher education has been high, such as the *Republic of Korea, Malaysia* and *Thailand*, are now seeing the results in the form of qualified manpower. In other countries, public sector spending on higher education has had to be restrained before the basic level of provision could be achieved(56, (57).

The bureaucratic and centralized nature of public administration, with the lack of an autonomous management culture in public institutions, has presented major problems, which often persist even in a very dynamic business environment. Some examples which may be quoted are: Republic of Korea, "authoritarianism and centralization are blamed for low staff morale and brain drain"(58); India: "[the 1986] reforms have tended to increase government control of universities and resulted in waste of time in obtaining approval of even minor matters. The State has shown little interest in ensuring efficient functioning, allowing student growth while allocations for maintenance are made on an ad hoc basis";(59) Thailand: "the major obstacles to good management include an over-bureaucratic system, lack of qualified professors and a limited budget"(60).

(i) India

Some governments have been quite aware of the deficiencies of their centralized bureaucracies, but nevertheless seem unable or unwilling to implement any radical or wide-scale reform. India is one example. The 1986 New Policy on Education officially encouraged decentralization and the involvement of client groups in higher education but the structures to accomplish the change do not exist(61). As in Latin America, teaching staff frequently have second jobs and are not interested in the management of the university. Political, trade union and other interests pull in different directions, and many teachers are available for only half the working day. Vice Chancellors may be appointed and dismissed on political grounds and in any case may have to spend a lot of their time visiting government offices to accelerate payment of financial allocations. (The situation in Pakistan and Bangladesh is somewhat similar). The Indian plan for autonomous departments has only been implemented in a few institutions and the general opinion is that the New Policy on Education has failed to make much impact(62). Nevertheless, the Government is continuing to press for change and recently announced (1993) two big concessions to assist universities in income generation: (i) whatever income they are able to generate will no longer be deducted from the government/state grants given to them; (ii) 100 per cent tax exemption will be given to industry for donations made to universities. The only condition is that such generated income should not be used for salaries. A UGC Committee is looking into the financial management of universities and intends to propose some flexible norms to guide management, particularly as regards ratios for non-teaching staff. Control of quality is being tightened; some 55 State universities and 3,000 colleges have not been found fit because they lack basic facilities.

(ii) China

China is another example. During the last decade, reforms have frequently been announced, but few have brought much change(63). In August 1992 the State redefined its role as a sharing of responsibilities between the centre and the institutions. The centre was to lay down the principles, carry out macro planning and evaluate quality, while the institutions were to introduce and revise courses, decide on admissions and research, hire staff and generally manage themselves(64). But university Presidents remained under party committee guidance, and their staff remained state employees, most of them staying in the same institution until they retire. In addition, though institutions may take fee-paying students, they are still given an enrolment quota for such students. Moreover, while a few technical institutions may be earning substantial amounts from research and training contracts and from printing and computer services, the underlying major problem of high unit cost remains. Improvements have been made by mergers, broadening educational programmes and organizing institutional networks to share facilities and materials, but these do not affect the expensive monolithic nature of higher educational institutions which offer services such as hospitals and schools to their staff and families.

(iii) Pakistan

Pakistan has taken the first tentative steps towards self-regulation by transferring responsibility for higher education to provincial governments; universities will be allowed to acquire industrial and agricultural assets and negotiate foreign assistance(65).

(iv) Hong Kong

Hong Kong has taken a major step towards self regulation: the government recently established a quasi-public accrediting system for higher education, embodying a mix of regulatory principles applied in other countries, including internal self-assessed validation of programmes and external review by international experts.

(v) Philippines

In the *Philippines*, 85 per cent of the higher education sector is private and has its own Fund for Assistance to Private Education. The Governing Boards of public institutions are appointed by the President of the country and these approve the programmes, budget and staff appointments. Control is exercised through the budget which provides 80-90 per cent of the total institutional funding. The movement towards self-regulation in state institutions has been active far longer than in many of the other nations, yet its implementation has suffered delay because of the lack of a stable, national policy commitment by the government. Accrediting agencies are, however, already functioning(66).

The wealthier countries, particularly the so-called Newly Industrializing Countries (NICs), have chosen the path of strong governmental steering, in some cases adjusting their systems to particular industries and scientific fields(67). The Republic of Korea, Taiwan and Singapore retained a tight grip on access with only the best entering science and engineering. Malaysian and Indonesian higher education remains very centralized. In Indonesia, the relevant Government Department (DGHE) monitors the performance of all institutions, even though many of them are private. It also appoints Rectors and Deputy Rectors and regulates admissions. Goals are set by the National Planning Board.

Characteristics: Tight government control and bureaucracy; attempts at change have been impeded by socio-political factors in some countries; a lack of management culture and expertise among academics.

c. Sub-Saharan Africa

The African region has been particularly hard hit by the world economic crisis, the fall in primary commodity prices and the consequences of structural adjustment. It is recognized as having serious financial and management problems in higher education. Social demand seems insatiable but universities produce too many graduates of dubious quality and relevance and generate too little new knowledge and direct development support(68). During the 1980s many governments came to recognize that too high an enrolment combined with imbalance in disciplines are causing problems of low quality, unemployment and unrest, in addition to being increasingly difficult to fund.

Generally, university management has been occupied with trying to contain this situation, while in some cases palliative have been attempted. Examples are the reduction of unit costs by encouraging students to live off campus (Ghana, Uganda, Tanzania), rationalization of courses (Ibadan and Ife in Nigeria), bookshops and cafeterias as self-financing enterprises (Uganda, Zambia), student loan schemes (Botswana, Ghana, Kenya, Lesotho, Malawi, Rwanda, Zambia, Zimbabwe), and payment of academic staff by lecture output (Uganda). Such measures, though useful, evidently are not enough to arrest the decline in quality of teachers, buildings, equipment and maintenance. Some universities in the region heavily depend on donor assistance for their very survival (e.g. Mozambique).

In this situation, where little or no increase in budgets can be expected, a major drive is now being undertaken to improve management efficiency. National governments, universities, the Association of African Universities and aid agencies are all taking part. Most of the universities in the region have been visited by AAU study teams and are to draw up strategic plans according to which aid from donor agencies can be targeted.

A systematic attempt to rationalize and improve quality is being made in Nigeria, where higher education is confronted with under funding and decreasing quality, while social demand for higher education has resulted in a doubling in student numbers from 1980 to 1989, when there were over 300,000 students. The reform programme was aimed at the consolidation and rehabilitation of existing institutions rather than further expansion. Universities were to be motivated by formulae funding, covering course balance, enrolments, student/staff ratios, and staff quality. Greater efficiency in resource utilization was made a criterion of eligibility for rehabilitation loans. The Federal Ministry of Education set national minimum standards for both academic programmes and whole institutions, with evaluation by visitation panels established by the Ministry in collaboration with the National University Commission (NUC). The panels consist of a chairman, a university representative, a ministry official, a military/civilian and a legal expert. They collect information, check files and conduct interviews at the institutions(69). Attention is paid to finance, administration, services, research, teaching and personnel. Their reports are submitted to the Government, and are subsequently used for resource allocation. The recommendations are published, together with the response of the government(70). Out of 836 undergraduate programmes examined in this way between March 1990 and June 1991, only 185 qualified fully for accreditation and met all requirements in terms of academic content, staffing and physical facilities. Seventy-nine were denied accreditation and 572 received interim accreditation only.

Other governments have also recently turned their attention to attaining a more rational management of higher education. Ghana, in 1989, initiated a programme aiming at cost-effective courses, relevant and integrated programmes and private sources of finance. Zambia's 1989 White Paper set out the expenditures to be met by fees, and established norms for student/staff ratios and administrative and support staff. In 1993 the Government proposed a modest enrolment decline and the introduction of a student loan scheme. Kenya has also set staffing norms. Mauritius launched its Tertiary Education Development Plan in 1993: all institutions form part of a network sharing a range of educational functions working on a modular and credit system. The plan envisages expansion of access, a broad based education and the use of distance methods for teachers' courses.

Private higher education is beginning to receive some encouragement: Kenya has experienced rapid growth of this sector and controls quality through a Commission for Higher Education. In Zimbabwe, a new Africa University is being built by the United Methodist Church. However, the level of economic development is such that private education cannot expect to flourish to the same extent as in Asia or

Latin America. Thus improvement of public university management is considered as a particularly critical target area by donor agencies.

*Characteristics:*Strong government control but until recently little interest or assistance given to improving university management apart from Ghana and Nigeria, which have invested in computers and information systems. Attempts at improving efficiency now being made in other countries.

d.   Arab States

Reports suggest that higher educational systems in the Arab world remain traditional with little attempt to innovate on the part of governments or institutions(71). The problems of mass higher education are to be seen in most countries of the region; in Algeria, Yemen, Morocco, Tunisia, the Arab Republic of Egypt and Iraq, a secondary school certificate allows enrolment in the arts, though high grades are needed to enter faculties of medicine and engineering(72). Failure rates of around 50 per cent at the end of the first year are a serious problem, compounded by the tendency of failed students to hold on to their places in order to retain subsidized transport, meals and rooms. It is acknowledged that the traditional universities cannot cope with the necessary changes, since they lack capable administrators, sound planning, and clear objectives(73). Faculties have little autonomy, since staff are managed by the Ministry and budgets extrapolated from previous years.

Most articles on higher education in the Arab States refer to excessive centralization. In Iraq, the Ministry determines faculty workloads, programmes of study and dates of examinations, as well as funding and policy. In Egypt, the number of enrolments is decided by the Supreme Council of Universities, which also makes the regulations for admissions(74). If anything, government control has recently increased, and admissions policies have been tightened. Measures were taken in Kuwait to strictly enforce university entrance and staff regulations. In Tunisia, scholarships are to be awarded only to students who achieve a satisfactory grade after their first year. Jordan, in 1986 established direct government control in order to reform administrative structures and staff recruitment. The pressure of social demand is being reduced by the establishment of private institutions. In Egypt, the first of these opened in 1989 and has obtained contributions from industry. Efforts are being made in Egypt and Tunisia to channel secondary school leavers into two-year technical schools, but higher education confers status, and students are responding only slowly to the demand for technicians.

Tunisia has also adopted a policy to expand technical education by creating higher institutes of technology. In July 1989 the Tunisian system was rc-organized so as to become more autonomous and diversified. As an incentive for efficiency, funds were to be distributed according to norms, and universities were encouraged to seek other sources of revenue. A student loan scheme was also to be developed. More radically, in Algeria the Ministry decided in 1990 to decentralize all responsibilities except for budget allocations. It is not yet known how these two reforms have fared within a traditional environment and against teacher resistance to change.

The Egyptian Ministry of Education has created a Centre for Higher Educational Reform (CHER) to provide an information service, to conduct studies on educational conditions and to train faculty in new technologies for education, thus forming a basis for modernization(75). The Sudan has recently established new regional universities in order to expand higher education, and has strengthened the executive level management of universities by the addition of a Deputy Vice Chancellor and a post of Chairman of the Council(76).

Characteristics: Strong government control and traditional bureaucracy, weak executive level university management and lack of management expertise and culture. However, government has recently expressed a desire for change in several countries.

5. Conclusions

There has been a clear trend towards "self-regulation and accountability" in the developed countries, for the following reasons:

- the sensitivity and resistance of universities in some countries to ceding autonomy in spheres where this was traditional;
- the inability of governments to monitor in every detail management, academic programmes, or the standard of teaching;
- the desirability of the university itself becoming involved in the assessment of socio-economic needs, especially at the local level;
- public funding constraints require that universities make their own efforts to save money and generate income, rather than always looking to the government to solve problems;
- in principle, management efficiency requires that those immediately using resources should ensure their maximum use and be accountable for them.

43

In line with this trend, many countries have seen the government curtail student grants and allowances and institute loan schemes, insisting that the student must also take personal responsibility for his role in the higher education system.

The policy of "self-regulation and accountability" was introduced both in previously largely autonomous (United Kingdom) and in centrally planned and controlled systems (Netherlands and the Nordic countries). In the latter the universities were more ready to cooperate, since they appreciated the reduction of state regulation, whereas in the autonomous systems the burdens of greater accountability were often resented. It is quite feasible for centrally planned systems to change to more self-regulatory management, though it may take longer.

A major problem for the developing countries, however, is that their universities lack the resources and the staff to take on the responsibilities of management, so that self-regulation could only realistically be seen as a long-term goal towards which institutions would work. The design of appropriate budgeting, control and accountability mechanisms would have to be undertaken by the Government (as in France), which would also have to equip university managements for their new tasks.

It was intended that the IIEP research programme should assist universities in developing countries to carry out such change by providing a base of knowledge about innovative university management in various domains. The routes that universities in developing countries might take to increase efficiency would probably be different from those in developed countries. It is for them to devise locally adapted cost-effective higher education for themselves. The following chapters indicate differing routes and strategies, in both developed and developing countries, showing what can be done, given the will at the institutional level.

This chapter has shown that government policy plays a major role in bringing about change. There has been one overriding feature of recent developments in government policy for all types of system. Everywhere there has been a much greater will to shape higher education so as to support socio-economic development. Everywhere this has involved more active intervention in the way universities are managed, and also in what is taught and how it is taught. This is often achieved directly by the insistence on such matters as efficiency and productivity; career-oriented courses; credit/modular programmes; open and distance higher education; applied R&D; technology transfer and knowledge diffusion. More indirect methods include formulae funding, incentives and sanctions.

References

(1) Van Vught, Frans. "Autonomy and accountability in government/university relations". Paper presented to World Bank Seminar on improvement of higher education in developing countries, Kuala Lumpur, July 1991.
(2) Bengtsson, J. 1993. "Labour markets of the future: the challenge to educational policy makers". In *European Journal of Education*, Vol.28, No.2,
(3) Volkwein J. "State regulation and campus autonomy". Higher Education: Handbook of Theory and Research 1987 Agathon Press, New York
(4) *Times Higher Education Supplement*, 4 February 1994
(5) Hodges, L. "The quality debate". In *Times Higher Education Supplement*, 26 February 1993.
(6) *Times Higher Education Supplement*, 17 December 1993
(7) Crespo, M. Discussion IIEP November 1992.
(8) Smoreav, R. "University evaluation in Canada". In *IGLU*, 2 April 1992.
(9) Kogan, M. "The British case". In *La Evaluacion Academica*, Vol.1, documents of the Columbus Project on university management. UNESCO, Paris, 1993.
(10) *Times Higher Education Supplement*, 3 December 1993
(11) Kogan, Maurice et al. 1983. *The attack on higher education*, Kogan Page, London.
(12) CVCP/UGC (1986), *Performance indicators in universities*. A first statement by the Joint CVCP/UGC working group.
(13) CVCP/UGC (1987), *Performance indicators in universities*. A second statement by the Joint CVCP/UGC working group.
(14) Schuller T. (1990), "Performance measurement in higher and continuing education". In Chris Bill and Duncan Harries (eds), *World Yearbook of Education, 1990: Assessment and Evaluation*. London: Kogan Page.
(15) *Times Higher Education Supplement*, 14 September 1990
(16) *Times Higher Education Supplement*, 1 January 1993, and *United Kingdom Higher Education Digest*, Issue 14, Autumn 1992.
(17) Warren, J. "Learning as an indicator of educational quality". In *Studies in Higher Education*, Vol.17, No.3, 1992.
(18) Hadley, T. and Winn, S. "Measuring value added at course level: an exploratory study". In *Higher Educational Review*, Vol.25, No.1, Autumn 1992.
(19) *Times Higher Education Supplement*, 3 December 1993
(20) Kalkwijk, J. "The Dutch Inspectorate of Higher Education". Paper presented to EAIR 13th Forum, September 1991.
(21) Schutte F. "Impact of information policy on university management". Paper for CRE Colombus Meeting, January 1991

(22) Ackerman, H. "The Dutch case". In *La Evaluacion Academica*, in Columbus Project Documents on University Management, Vol.1. UNESCO, Paris, 1993.
(23) *Times Higher Education Supplement*, 27 September 1993.
(24) Williams, B. "The rise and fall of binary systems in two countries and the consequence for universities". In *Studies in Higher Education*, Vol.17, No.3, 1992.
(25) Kivinen, O. and Rinne, R. "Investment in higher education: the Finnish experience". In *Higher Education Policy*, Vol.5, No.2, 1992.
(26) Holtta, S. and Pulliainen, K. *Improving managerial effectiveness at the University of Joensuu, Finland*, IIEP, Paris, 1992.
(27) Furstenback J. "Computerized management in Swedish universities CREaction" No. 95 1991/1
(28) Dahllöf, Urban, "Evaluation of higher education in Sweden". In Vinayagum Chinapah (ed), *Evaluation of higher education in a changing Europe*. A report from the UNESCO Seminar held in Stockholm, May 1990.
(29) Sizer, J. et al. "The role of performance indicators in higher education". In *Higher Education*, Vol. 24, No.2, September 1992.
(30) Brandstrom D. and Franke Wiberg S. "Steering Higher Educational systems in Europe: case of Sweden". In *Higher Education in Europe*, Vol. XVII No. 3 1992
(31) Hristo, A. "Higher education in Bulgaria under conditions of transition to a market economy". Paper for CEPES Meeting, Plovdiv, November 1990.
(32) Mission report of the CEC Task Force Human Resources to Central and Eastern Europe (22 May-1 June 1991), CEC document of 17 September 1991.
(33) Information in Higher Education in Europe, Vol XVIII No 1 1993
(34) Kozma, T. "Steering higher education; Hungary". In *Higher Education in Europe*, Vol. XVII, No.3, 1992.
(35) Lajos T. Perspectives, "Hopes and Disappointments". In *European Journal of Education*, Vol. 28, No. 4, 1993
(36) Pisut J. "Higher Education Reforms in the Slovak Republic". In *European Journal of Education*, Vol. 28, No. 4, 1993
(37) Samoilovich, D. "Transformation through institutional development: a valid option for the Latin American university?" In *Ideas en Ciencias Sociales*, Vol. 3, No. 6, 1987.
(38) Mignone, E.F. "University enrolment in Latin America, risks and prospects". In *Revista Interamericana de Desarollo de Educacion*, Vol. 32, No.102, 1988.
(39) Albornoz O. "Steering Higher Education: Venezuela" In *Higher Education Policy*, Vol. 6 No. 4, 1993
(40) Kent, R. "Higher education in Mexico: from unregulated expansion to evaluation". In *Higher Education*, Vol.25, No.1, 1993.
(41) Casillas, J. "The impact of evaluation processes on higher educational systems". In *IGLU*, No. 2, April 1992.

(42) Samoilovich, E. *Evaluation of quality in higher education in different socio-economic contexts*. Report of UNESCO Round Table, Geneva, 1992.
(43) Trista Perez B. *Report to IIEP*, 22 July 1991.
(44) Gusatz, M. "Seven handicaps of universities". In *Le Monde*, 4 April 1991.
(45) Comité National d'evaluation (1988). "Méthodologie de l'évaluation". In *Bulletin du CNE*, No. 6, May 1988.
(46) Staropoli, André (1988), "The Comité National d'Evaluation: Preliminary results of a French experiment". In *European Journal of Education*, Vol. 22, No.2.
(47) Bouchet R. "Impact of information technologies on university administration". In *International Journal of Institutional Management in Higher Education* 1988.
(48) Courtois G. "La gestion des établissements à l'heure de l'informatique". In *Le Monde*, 12 May 1992
(49) *Times Higher Education Supplement*, 26 February 1993.
(50) *Times Higher Education Supplement*, 26 November 1993
(51) Van Vught, F. "Flexibility production and pattern management". In *Higher Education Policy*, Vol. 4, No. 4, 1991.
(52) Berendt B. "Widening access to universities while improving the quality of teaching?" In *Higher Education in Europe*, Vol. XVIII No. 1 1993.
(53) Wielemans W. and Vanderhoeven A. "Market impact and policy drift". In *Neave G. (ed.) Prometheus Bound*, 1991 Pergamon, Oxford
(54) Saitis, C. "Development and reform of university administration in Greece". In *International Journal, Institutional Management in Higher Education*, 1988, Vol. 12, No. 1.
(55) Pratt J. "Creating a binary policy in Austria". In *Higher Education Quarterly*, Vol. 47 No. 2, Spring 1993.
(56) Faraj, A. "Higher education and economic development in South Asian countries". In *Higher Education Review*, Vol. 21, No.1, 1988.
(57) Dias, M.A. "Trends and challenges in higher education: a global approach" Paper for 2nd UNESCO- NGO Collective consultation on higher education, April 1991.
(58) *Times Higher Education Supplement*, 14 February 1990.
(59) Nanjundappa, D. "University finances". In *University News*, 20 October 1989.
(60) Bovornsum, V. and Fry, G. "Higher education and Thai development". In *Higher Education Policy*, Vol.4, No. 2, June 1991.
(61) Rao, T. "Planning and management for excellence and efficiency in higher education", Paper of Indian Institute of Management, 1991.
(62) Saxena, R. "Governance of Indian universities". In *Higher Education*, Vol. 20, No. 1, July 1990.
(63) Robinson, J. "Stumbling on two legs: education and reform in China". In *Comparative Education Review*, Vol. 35, No. 1, February 1991.
(64) Huo Yiping " Higher Education in China: Problems and Current Reforms". In *Higher Education Policy* Vol. 6 No. 4, 1993.

(65) Siddiqui, M. "Programme for reform of university education", Paper, Academy of Educational Planning and Management, Islamabad, August 1990.
(66) Cooney, R. and Paqueo Arrezoz. "Higher education regulation in the Phillipines". In *Higher Education Policy*, Vol. 6, No. 2, 1992.
(67) Singh, J. "Higher education and development: the experience of four NICs in Asia". In *Prospects*, Vol. XVI, No. 3, 1991.
(68) Habte, A. "Support for Sub-Saharan Africa – where does the World Bank stand?" In *Higher Education Policy*, Vol. 2, No. 2, 1989.
(69) *Times Higher Education Supplement*, 12 April 1991.
(70) UNESCO (1990), "Evaluation procedures used to measure the efficiency of higher education systems and institutions". New papers on higher education studies and research 1.
(71) Bubtana, A. "Perspectives and trends of Arab higher education", Paper for 2nd UNESCO NGO Collaborative Consultation on Higher Education, April 1991.
(72) Abou Chacra, R. "Problems of higher education in Arab States". In *Prospects*, Vol. XVI, No. 3, 1991.
(73) Moustafa, M. "Faculty development plan for Arab universities". In *Higher Education Policy*, Vol. 5, No. 4, 1992.
(74) Clark B. and Neave G. *Encyclopaedia of Higher Education*, Pergamon Press, Oxford 1992.
(75) Shann M. "Reform of Higher Education in Egypt" in *Higher Education Policy*, Vol. 24, No. 2, September 1992.
(76) Forojalla S. "Recent Proposals for reform of higher education in Sudan: Problems and Prospects". In *Higher Education Policy*, Vol. 5 No. 4, 1992.

Part III

Improving university management to meet changing needs

This Part is devoted to:

Chapter 3: Mergers as a strategy to improve the efficiency and effectiveness of universities

The use of mergers as a government strategy to rationalize systems of higher education has been noted in *Part II*. Here it is dealt with in some detail. Case studies from a developing centrally-planned country *China* and from a developed self-regulated system *Australia* are used as illustrations, together with experiences described in the literature.

Chapter 4: Overall university management reform.

Actual trends in overall university management are analyzed according to the classifications defined in *Part II*, along with a brief outline of the evolution of innovation theories. Case studies and experiences from both developed and developing countries show that some common approaches have been widely used to achieve more efficient management.

Analyses in both chapters highlight certain significant issues, i.e.:
- the status of the initiator(s) and the extent of their power;
- the role of leadership;
- the extent of information circulation and participation of various university or external groups;
- capacity for efficient planning, co-ordination and evaluation;
- additional resources made available, and incentives offered;
- problems encountered and how they were dealt with;
- the degree to which objectives were achieved.

These issues are also examined in *Part IV* which deals with specific areas of university management.

Chapter 5: Strategies adopted at national and institutional levels to improve overall university management

This chapter summarizes the information given in *Chapters 2, 3* and *4* about the range of strategies that have been used in varying contexts, in order to show what kinds of changes occurred under particular steering policies. The full impact of such policies on institutional management can only be discerned when the most important aspects of management have been examined, (i.e. finance, staff, space, research), and this is the objective of *Part IV* of the report.

Chapter 3

Mergers as a strategy to improve the efficiency and effectiveness of universities

1. The role of mergers

Mergers of various kinds have been a rather general feature of recent efforts to improve the effectiveness of higher educational institutions. Most experience has so far been reported from those self-regulating systems in which government policy has dictated reforms to be implemented by individual institutions themselves, such as the United Kingdom, the Netherlands and above all, Australia. However, for countries in transition to self-regulation, such as the Nordic, there have also been reports of merging of small institutions, while for the Eastern European countries ("self-regulation in difficulty"), reform plans are being made which will involve both mergers and closures. The only report of mergers in Latin America so far is from Cuba.

In systems under centralized planning, many of which are of the open admission type, there are few reports of mergers and rather more about the establishment of multi-campus institutions, as in France and Italy. An exception to this is China, where the rationalization and expansion of higher education is now a major preoccupation. The case study from Hubei Province, China, describes a pilot project on merging two technical institutions which was designed to provide the government with guidelines for further rationalization measures(1). Such lessons from experience should be of benefit to many managers in higher education, particularly since, as will be noted from the studies, there are many procedures, conditions and problems that are commonly encountered in mergers, wherever the institutions are and whatever types they happen to be. Before considering these common features, it would be useful to distinguish the varying roles that mergers can play.

2. Mergers at the national level

The aims of mergers at this level have been manifold. They can, for example, be used to expand (as in Australia) or contract (as in the United Kingdom in the 1970s) the supply of higher education. A study by Miriam Henry shows that the many goals of restructuring envisaged in the Australian reforms (including better quality of teaching and research, expansion, equity, efficiency and accountability) generated support from a variety of groups(2). At the institutional level, however, some distortions and contradictions occurred which now require remedial action if the reforms are to be successful. The national purpose of mergers is generally to use them as one of the strategies for achieving better control of the system so as to ensure that it serves integrated education and macro-economic policies. Mergers are intended to improve control and management, and also to improve the supply and quality of education in the various disciplines.

(a) Control and management

It was the view in the Australian reform that a lesser number of institutions (it eventually fell to 35), would be much more economically and effectively administered and controlled than the previous 71. The work would be transferred to university central administrations who would be in charge of managing their diverse units and campuses.

(b) Supply of education

In the United Kingdom and the Netherlands, the main aim of mergers at this level was to rationalize the supply of higher education in the various disciplines. For example, in the Netherlands the number of locations offering the same degree was much reduced. Exchanges of specialization between departments took place in order to establish centres of excellence and a regional co-operation procedure was implemented to share facilities between departments in different universities (Law of Task Redistribution, February 1984). Unit costs were cut by 30 per cent from 1983 to 1989(3). Most of the merging of institutions in the Netherlands concerned the technical and vocational colleges so as to concentrate equipment and facilities. By July 1987, 314 out of 348 such institutions had merged into 51, only 34 remaining untouched. The largest merger involved 19 institutions(4).

Avoidance of duplication within a geographic region has been given some emphasis in the subject-specific reviews carried out in the United Kingdom. These reviews were designed to see how national needs for training could best be satisfied by the system, and were carried out by questionnaire surveys and site visits. It was found that the notion of critical mass or minimum size was important, but that this varies widely by subject. Some subjects (e.g. Physics) should be taught at all large population centres. The review of Sociology, for example, produced maps of the location of teaching departments and made suggestions as to which might co-operate in teaching, research, seminars and library acquisitions, and also those which might be closed. Often departments in universities which were sited close together and serving the same region were selected for closure (e.g. the transfer of Swansea's Geology Department to Cardiff)(5). This review showed that mergers can take place not just between entire institutions but also between departments, and that co-operation short of merger can consist of the sharing of teaching and research staff or services, an example being the sharing by the University of Oxford and the former Oxford Polytechnic of lectures and library purchases and facilities.

3. The Institutional level

This brings us to consider mergers from the viewpoint of institutions, whose primary motives may differ somewhat from those set out in national educational policies. They may be induced to merge by possibilities of increased funding (in Australia, they were given additional funds for computers, telecommunications, relocation and early retirement), increased power and prestige, and economies of scale. Negatively, they may be compelled to do so by threats of bankruptcy or closure, or by legislation.

The ways in which they can merge, as a whole, in particular domains or simply by affiliation, are illustrated in the study by Michael Taylor of the University of Sydney(6). This university acts as an academic sponsor to a new university in the suburbs, and has also amalgamated with five colleges, two of which were completely incorporated while three others retained a certain degree of autonomy though they had to adopt the administrative procedures of the university. The colleges at some distance away still have to do much of their own administration. Student records and enrolments are centralized, accounts integrated and library catalogues are held on the same computer network.

The concept of parent or sponsor institution is by no means new. The Universities of London and Wales have always been federal bodies composed of institutions with their own Senates, governing boards and academic programmes, which co-exist under a central authority responsible for carrying out strategic planning, acting as a funding focus and managing common provision of some services. However, as in the above description of Australian experience, here too the farther the institution is from the centre, the more responsibilities have to be delegated(7).

New institutions are springing up under multi-sponsorship, e.g. the Milton Keynes College was to become a polytechnic in a joint venture with the former Leicester Polytechnic and the Open University(8), while the University of Sussex and the former Brighton Polytechnic have created a new inter-institutional Institute of Engineering, which is to combine all their teaching and research activities in this domain, although this is considered to be a 'link' not a merger, and *was not to affect the institutional identity of either party*(9).

Norway has developed a variation of the parent institution concept. Special emphasis was put on the spread of regional colleges, which co-operated in an ad hoc fashion with certain universities for particular programmes. Formal co-operation agreements are being established (e.g. the University of Bergen and five regional colleges) to decentralize Masters' courses in the core disciplines of secondary school teachers. Training is given to college staff at Ph.D level and joint research programmes are conducted(10).

Another type of merger aims at developing a regional network. One example of this took place in East Anglia (United Kingdom), where two institutions merged to form a polytechnic while four other colleges opted for association but with independent management, their funds being channelled through a central administration. Negotiations were going on (1991) with other colleges to complete the network. Local industry was very interested in obtaining all types of training close at hand and a company offered a 125 acre site near Chelmsford to enable the polytechnic to concentrate at least some of its activities on to one cheaper campus(11). The disappearance of the binary system in the United Kingdom has given an impetus to mergers of polytechnics and colleges in order to create institutions worthy of the name of a university and able to compete with older institutions. One such is the University of Greenwich (established in 1992) which as the Thames Polytechnic at the end of the 1980s merged with several colleges to become an institution of 13,000 students on seven large sites spread over south east London and Kent.

It has been suggested by some that the motives for merger ought to be primarily academic(12): to consolidate or to rectify weaknesses, to open new markets and to provide a strong base for research and consultancy. This was recognised in Bahrain, where the Polytechnic and the University recently merged because neither was viable alone. However, this proved to be a difficult undertaking, because of their different missions and structures. Mergers in the academic field alone are relatively easy to negotiate, and are taking place in some numbers at the international level, being increasingly necessary for languages, business management and new technology. The first part of the course may be in one country and the final year in another, or a university may open a campus on the site of another in a different country, enabling the sharing of some staff and services costs. Academic motives have been behind some highly innovative schemes for co-operation and sharing which were not envisaged by government policy at all.

Both the Australian and the Chinese studies carried out for the IIEP research programme show that the institutions had similar goals and that these were mainly academic. Both wanted a broader range of disciplines and increased options, higher quality of academic staff and increased research and services capabilities. They expected eventually to make savings by means of central administration of enrolments and services and economies of scale in some courses, though these would not materialize for some years. The main immediate beneficiaries were firstly staff, who received training, and in some cases promotion and research funding, and secondly students who would be able to select from a broader range of options and graduate from an institution of higher prestige. However, since one study was carried out in a centrally-planned system and the other under self-regulation, the processes were somewhat different, though they had to deal with similar issues. Brief outlines are given below.

a.   Merger in China(13)

The Chinese higher education system was seen to be suffering from the effects of a previous policy under which large numbers of small uneconomic specialized institutes were built. Since the problem was at the system level, initiatives to solve it emanated from the top. The Ministry decided to undertake several pilot merger projects in order to gain experience and set down the guidelines for subsequent action. The procedure adopted was a formal governmental one involving the Central Ministry, provincial planning and education authorities, leading academics and administrators from national universities and the chief executives of the two institutes involved.

The process took six years from the initial top-level meeting in the Province in 1984, followed by the work of the Task Force set up to plan the merger, the recruitment of key personnel in 1985, construction of facilities and retraining of staff throughout the period 1984-1990, until eventually the first enrolments were made under the new name in 1990. A top-level academic from a national university was recruited for day-to-day leadership and almost half the faculty were sent for re-training in leading universities while others were given in-service courses, in particular in foreign languages. Transfers of higher quality academics and administrators were arranged with a leading University of Technology. In addition, the Provincial Government made considerable additional capital funding available.

There were problems of delay in the co-ordination of all the government agencies involved and some friction between the groups of staff from the two former institutions. Not all staff could be housed on campus in the first instance and had to be transported. More seriously, the high rate of inflation reduced the value of the funds made available for construction and buildings could not be completed as planned. This was a major factor in certain target ratios not being reached, since enrolment could not expand as rapidly as foreseen. However, the quality of staff and facilities improved, unit costs in constant prices started to fall and the student:teaching-staff ratio rose from 3.6 in 1984 to 7.9 in 1990. It is expected that these trends will continue. In addition, whereas the two original institutions were very weak in research work, the present institute now undertakes national and provincial level projects as well as work for local enterprises under contract. However, though a success, such a merger required considerable capital resources which the provincial government could not easily fund for more numerous mergers.

b. Merger in Australia(14)

The impetus for amalgamation in Australian higher education was given by legislation, which set the minimum size of an institution as 5,000 full-time equivalent students. The institutions themselves negotiated the necessary mergers, and most took place between a relatively large university and two or more small colleges.

The case study of the University of Sydney reflects the short experience of amalgamation which began in 1988 and had to be formally completed by January 1990 though it is acknowledged that the process will linger on for a number of years. The university was approached by four colleges offering a wide range of courses and by a conservatorium of music. All their programmes were compatible with the disciplines in the university. Negotiations were conducted with these colleges to work out Heads of Agreement, covering the status of the joining institution; participation in governance; guarantees for staff against loss of salary or redundancy; reciprocal rights of access to resources; the operation of accounts and the ownership of assets and liabilities. These draft agreements had to be approved by the institutional governing bodies, after which Consolidation Implementation Committees were set up for each institution to work out details. It eventually transpired that four of the institutions remained much as they were, i.e. college or conservatorium, but the Institute of Nursing Studies became a faculty of the university and its Director became a Dean. The major disputes concerned the extent of independence to be allowed to the colleges, and the status of staff. In the event, two of the three former Principals could not be reconciled and resigned or retired. The staff hierarchy (was fortunately similar,) at least at lower levels, but the title of Professor was not automatically conferred upon senior college staff, and was denied to some.

The government made available special funding for computers, libraries, telephones, early retirement and relocation. Centralization of student records and enrolment has taken place, as well as integration of accounts, though the more distant colleges have to do some of their own accounting. It was not expected to make any economies for the first three years though thereafter savings on administration should be made. The University of Sydney is now on three campuses as much as 50 kilometres away from each other, but eventually one college will transfer to the main campus. Benefits to the college staff have been considerable, including promotion to a university post, sabbatical leave and research funding, which were not available previously.

Comparison of these two experiences, in China and Australia, shows similarities in the impetus for the merger (the government), in the substantial additional resources that had to be made available, in the long period before substantial benefits are expected, and in the way that special incentives had to be given to the staff (training in China and university status in Australia). The role of the new chief executive and new staff was critical in China for the success of the merger after the planning had been completed at top level, whereas in Australia the vital role in planning was played by the Negotiation and Consolidation Implementation Committees, involving the senior staff of the institutions and no one from the government. The Australian experience, in the initial phase at least, has more of the characteristics of a takeover while the Chinese created an entirely new institution.

A considerable literature already exists on the Australian amalgamation. Most of these studies describe only the first couple of years of merger and are rather non-committal about economies and efficiency, but concerned about low staff morale. An example is the University of New England which amalgamated with one college nearby, which was integrated into the central campus, and another 250 kilometres away(15). The former college Principals became Deputy Vice Chancellors and other high-level administrative staff were assigned similar duties. Services staff and their equipment were transferred to the central campus. However, heads of existing departments were asked to resign and a reselection process was carried out for heads of new departments. Budgets were devolved to four academic budget centres, each headed by a Dean with administrative staff. The disadvantages found are that administration takes much longer and more high grade administrative assistance has to be given to Deputy Vice Chancellors. Many people were overworked and while staff had expected that amalgamation would give rise to a new high quality university reflecting the values of all three institutions, those of the colleges are felt to have been cast aside. Low morale of staff has emerged as a key issue, and the latest report from this university is that it is seeking separation from the distant college.

Low morale of staff seems to be rather a pervasive feature of the Australian experience. The 1989 Report of the Task Force on Amalgamation stated that difficulties in some cases were due to fears that one institution would be dominated by another and that it would lose its distinctive ethos. Taylor reports that the University of Sydney, being larger and much more prestigious, was able to impose its policies and practices on amalgamating colleges, whereas at the University of West Sydney, which was composed of three rather similar institutions, no one of them could be reconciled to loss of autonomy.

Other general evaluations have been more optimistic than some of the individual university reports. In the opinion of one author, though multi-campus institutions pose special organizational and communication problems and some combinations may not survive, many seem to be operating smoothly with new structures and communication technology to link campuses for committee meetings and teaching. The role of senior management has been strengthened and there is a new competitive and entrepreneurial approach to industrial co-operative ventures and the generation of revenue(16).

The prospect of long-term success is borne out by some earlier Australian experience. As long ago as 1981, many teachers' colleges were amalgamated, and have since thrived. In Western Australia in 1982, what is now the Edith Cowan University emerged as a polytechnic on the amalgamation of three teachers' colleges. In the short term, this cost a great deal of money for new buildings, the new administration, communications and the upgrading of staff. It took three or four years before economies began to appear. One of the six campuses was sold to another university so as to obtain the money to build and re-build. One campus was converted into a conference and residential short course centre which brings in revenue. All the separate campuses now use one big library, while purchasing is done centrally. Since the merger was between teachers' colleges, the ethos did not change, but only one set of programmes is now taught at all four campuses and there is joint development of audio-visual methods. With funds from the government, a two-way telecommunications system for all campuses has been set up so that a lecture on one campus can be received on another. Twenty-four electronic classrooms have been set up in all parts of the State using the satellite to transmit courses given at Perth. The university considers its merger to have been the cornerstone of its long-term success, and expects to be 30 per cent privately funded by the year 2000(17).

Experience in the United Kingdom suggests that mergers facilitate the introduction of strategic planning, a more powerful role for the Vice Chancellor as Chief Executive, internal restructuring and other measures to improve management. One study which attempted to evaluate the effects on management is that between two colleges of the University of London. It was felt that the new administrative system led to greater transparency of management. The number of committees was kept small and a joint planning committee was established to reconcile academic plans with financial constraints. The College set up a new senior administrative team and used the services of a consultant on team work and the roles of heads of departments. Five years on, in 1990, it was concluded that the merger had unleashed a wave of creativity and a management process which is more conscious of reconciling academic objectives with increasing efficiency(18).

4. Mergers at the departmental level

It has been noted that mergers between institutions have generally also entailed internal restructuring and merging of departments: the University of New England was one example given from Australia. But this has also taken place without amalgamation with another institution, in order to rationalize administration and make economies, and for academic reasons such as grouping activities of the same nature in one unit. An example comes from the University of Surrey (United Kingdom), which amalgamated all its activities in the field of education into one Department of Educational Studies (including the former Institute for Educational Technology, the Centre for Adult Education, and the Audio

Visual Aids Unit). The aim was to save money. There were, however, no new premises or facilities and staff could not easily be moved closer together. The staff were the main resource and the best use had to be made of them. The new Department had to reduce its work with the teaching professions and extend that with industry. Perhaps the biggest change was the establishment of a range of joint appointments (18 in all) with providers of similar programmes who could attract funds more easily than the university(19).

Such internal reforms have also taken place in universities in developing countries. They have had a variety of aims, often intended to start the university off on a much more dynamic track. For example, in Ouagadougou, Burkina Faso, in order to overcome resistance in certain institutes to expansion of enrolments, 14 institutes or schools were regrouped into nine entities – five large faculties and four specialized institutes. At the same time the government provided three additional large lecture theatres. Enrolments since the change in 1988 have increased by 30 per cent and the cost per student has declined(20). The University of Bangui is also now undertaking mergers of Faculties, with the aims of greater orientation of students to scientific and professional programmes, creation of short courses for nurses, paramedics and technicians, and improving the quality of teaching, continuing education and research capabilities(21).

5. Characteristics of mergers

(a) In most countries the primary impetus to merger has come from government policy. Sometimes, however, and especially in the United States, institutions have merged to create a larger resource base and greater prestige for competition in the market for students and research funds.

(b) The goals of institutional mergers have been diverse and wide ranging. The emphasis in national policy has been on control, effectiveness, rational coverage and efficiency, whereas institutions have tended to stress academic quality improvements.

(c) Mergers should be viewed mainly as a long-term strategy and should therefore be accompanied by development plans. They may, however, also present considerable short-term financial opportunities through the sale of land, buildings and other assets.

(d) Geographic and academic propinquity are important factors for the success of an institutional merger, though distance can to some extent be overcome by technology.

(e) The differing ethos of institutions has been a serious obstacle in some cases, the obvious examples being differing emphases on teaching and research, pure and applied research, practical and theoretical work, postgraduate, undergraduate and sub-degree teaching. However, it has been argued that the greater the difference, the more potential there is for innovation and diversification(22). In actual experience, the staff of former polytechnics and colleges merged with universities have sometimes felt that the value of their work has been overlooked in the new institution; some United Kingdom polytechnics refused to merge with universities for this reason. Long-term experience from mergers of teacher training colleges in Australia shows that mergers of institutions in the same field of work offer more benefits from economies of scale, in production of teaching materials, use of new technology, short courses and distance learning.

(f) Bearing in mind (d) and (e) above, it has been the practice for varying lesser degrees of association to be envisaged for institutions which are at a distance or have a specialized role or ethos: sponsorship, affiliation, accreditation, franchising, consortia. These types of linkage permit institutions to retain their independence while joint teaching, research and service activities can be organised more effectively, e.g. library networks, franchising courses, consortia for continuing education. These forms are becoming more popular and can be relatively easily adapted to changing needs(23). Most disagreements in initial negotiations concern the extent to which units can retain their independence.

(g) In any type of merger, the general rule has been to centralize strategic planning, financial control, fund raising and provision of services. However, since the merging institutions had previously been accustomed to responsibility for decision-making, it has often been possible to devolve many management responsibilities to the component units, with the allocation of a lump sum budget.

(h) The anxieties and sensitivities of staff have been a particular problem and have been alleviated by regular communications and consultations, re-training and opportunities for promotion or upgrading of status. It is often particularly important to maintain a balance in status between the senior administrators of the institutions, as both the Chinese and the Australian case-studies show. All staff need assurances that they will have not less favourable conditions, that any early retirements will be voluntary, and that there will be possible benefits.

References

(1) Min Weifang, A *case study of an institutional merger in Hubei Province, People's Republic of China*, IIEP, Paris, 1992.
(2) Henry, M. The *restructuring of higher education in Australia*, IIEP Research Report No. 99, Paris, 1994.
(3) *Times Higher Education Supplement*, 24 February 1989.
(4) Goedegebuure L.; Lynn Meek, "Restructuring higher education: a comparative analysis between Australia and the Netherlands". In *Comparative Education* Vol. 27, No.1, 1991.
(5) Hoare, A. "Reviewing the reviews: the geography of university rationalization in higher education". In *Higher Education Quarterly*, Vol. 45, No. 3, Summer 1991.
(6) Taylor, M., *Amalgamation at the University of Sydney, Australia: the institutional viewpoint*, IIEP, Paris, 1994.
(7) Fielden, J. "Merged structures". In *Higher Education Newsletter* No. 2, Price Waterhouse, April 1992.
(8) *Times Higher Education Supplement*, 4 October 1991.
(9) *Times Higher Education Supplement*, 17 April 1993.
(10) Lerheim, M. "Norway: the role of universities in a decentralized system". In *Higher Education Management*, Vol.1, No.3, November 1989.
(11) *Times Higher Education Supplement*, 10 May 1991.
(12) Dale, T. "Merging higher educational institutions: lessons learned from Australia". In *Higher Education Newsletter* No. 2, Price Waterhouse, April 1992.
(13) Min Weifang, idem.
(14) Taylor, M., idem.
(15) Teacher, B. "Trans-binary amalgamations in Australia: a college perspective". In *Higher Education Review*, Vol.23, No.1, 1990.
(16) Harman, G. "Institutional amalgamations of the binary system in Australia". In *Higher Education Quarterly*, Vol.45, No.2, Spring 1991.
(17) Lawrence, B. Deputy Vice Chancellor, Edith Cowan University, Perth. Visit IIEP, June 1992.
(18) Wedderburn, D. "Reflections on the merger of Royal Holloway and Bedford Colleges 1981-85". In *Higher Education Quarterly*, Vol. 45, No. 2, Spring 1991.
(19) James, D. "Merging educational groups". In *Higher Education Quarterly*, Vol. 45, No. 3, Summer 1991.
(20) Traore, S. *Etude de fusion à l'université d'Ouagadougou*, IIEP, Paris, 1991.
(21) Dolingo, M. *Programme of action for the rationalization of the University of Bangui*, IIEP, Paris, 1991.
(22) Goedegebuure, L. *Mergers in higher education*, Uitgeverij Lemma, Utrecht, 1992.
(23) Pritchard R. "Mergers and linkages in British Higher Education".In *Higher Education Quarterly*, Vol. 47, No. 2 Spring 1993.

Chapter 4

Overall university management reform

This chapter begins the analysis of management change within institutions. *Section 1* briefly outlines the basic characteristics of structure and management of universities a decade or so ago. *Section 2* recounts the major trends in the evolution of theory. *Section 3* attempts to describe the present state of university management and the kinds of changes that have actually been implemented in decision-making structures, classified by type of regulatory system.

1. The basic characteristics of universities

A decade ago, Burton Clark pointed out that since the basic purpose of higher education institutions was and still is the creation and dissemination of knowledge, the organizational unit and focus of attention for individual academics is their discipline and the professional community to which they belong, rather than their institutional affiliation(1). This traditional feature of the profession has been further reinforced by the fact that academics need nowadays to be increasingly involved in their subjects in order to keep up with rapid knowledge expansion.

Using much the same arguments, Mintzberg classified higher education institutions as professional bureaucracies with a decentralized and fragmented structure and wide diffusion of decision-making power(2). The advantages and disadvantages of the departmental structure and 'loose coupling' were listed by Weick(3) as follows:

a. Functions

- it allows some portions of the organization to persist while others change;
- it provides many independent sensing mechanisms;
- it is good for localized adaption, one element can be swift and economical to adapt as compared to the whole;

- the whole system can sustain greater mutation and innovation;
- any breakdown in one element can be sealed off;
- it gives more self-determination to actors;
- it should be more efficient since co-ordination takes time and money.

b. Dysfunctions

- it is a non-rational system of fund allocation;
- it is incapable of being used as a means of overall change;
- any beneficial mutation cannot easily be diffused;
- there is some duplication in administration, negotiation, etc.

Thus even before economic and policy constraints forced universities to try to improve their management, theorists were pointing out the unsuitability of university structures for efficient institutional management and for bringing about overall changes.

In line with this, another basic feature of institutions of higher education was the ambiguity of and conflict among the variety of goals towards which academics were working. As opposed to business enterprises in which everyone is ultimately committed to the basic goal of making profits, in universities research or scholarship (often involving individually defined goals) usually takes precedence over teaching and services (with goals usually defined by the institution). As to the actual decision-making processes, much literature in the 1980s was devoted to classifying the models then prevailing. As late as 1985, some theorists still felt that because of departmental autonomy, the 'organized anarchy model' was appropriate to universities, with their problematic goals, fluid participation and unclear problem-solving procedures. Others argued that a 'political' model was more appropriate, since the university consisted of conflicting interest groups and coalitions involved in bargaining and negotiation. Decision-making could be viewed as a largely political process with individuals and groups defending their vested interests.

However, the most commonly supported model of decision-making in higher education institutions was the 'collegiate' one, in which most decisions are made by the whole community. Thus decision-making was usually committee-based, both at central and at faculty/department level, and according to a consensus reached among colleagues. One of the main sources of power within a university was membership of an influential committee with access to resources of expertise, plant, equipment and funds. However, it is evident that the collegial structure does not respond well to external pressures, since it generally lacks speedy decision-making, clear responsibility of individuals, ruthlessness to outsiders and maintenance of group discipline.

Given the vastly increased external pressures on universities in the 1980s, academics therefore turned their attention to finding solutions, both in theory and in practice.

2. The evolution of theoretical thinking as regards organizational change and management

In the early 1980s, researchers were already looking into the conditions which might be most conducive to organizational change. According to Nordvall, some type of instability was necessary as a stimulus in addition to the change being profitable and compatible(4); Rutherford *et. al.* suggested that a predisposition to change was created when operations were distorted and when some kind of external pressure was exerted or incentives offered(5). They considered that prescriptive pressure was ineffective except when it directly threatened survival. Continuing this line of thought, Wurzberg, in considering institutional capacity for adaptation, pointed out that tradition and past practice created vested interests, and most universities, being large, were more subject to inertia(6). The most propitious time for change is when they are knocked off balance by external events.

Examples of this were the mergers between institutions which occurred in the Netherlands and Australia. Survival was the objective; institutions had to continue to be eligible for funds and yet at the same time maximize independence. The Dutch HBOs (technical institutes) tended to choose mergers that would make them more dominant at supra-regional level while in Australia, colleges sought university status on the best terms negotiable and even the geographically isolated looked for some kind of association within a university structure.

Becher and Kogan have also dealt with this subject(7). For them, a basic precondition is that some driving force should open up cracks in the system into which elements from the environment may flow and create a potential for movement. It may take place in a normative or operational mode but the process will be ineffective until adjustments have taken place in both modes. 'Coercive' change is resented but more and more (as we have seen in *Part II*) the central authorities are taking this course, in addition to 'manipulative' strategies, which offer incentives. Where there is some element of negotiation, the participants are likely to feel under greater obligation to carry out the change or may be convinced that it is a new and more effective means to an accepted end. A further discussion of theory in conjunction with experience will be found in *Chapter 5* where the results of analysis of overall institutional changes are examined.

Parallel with research on the impetus to change, a great deal more thought was being given to how university management could be improved, much of which derived from the business management literature. Certain concepts were tried out because they seemed to attack one of the basic problems of university management, how to clarify institutional objectives as a basis for subsequent systematic managerial action.

During the mix-sixties, the Planning, Programming and Budgeting System (PPBS) was imposed on all Californian state agencies including higher education institutions. It prescribed a rather complex linear procedure for setting up an institutional mission with detailed quantifiable targets to be implemented through annual budget allocations(8). However, because of its complexity and high staff and computing costs, PPBS was quickly succeeded by the Management by Objectives approach which was also based on the assumption that the lack of clearly stated institutional goals was a major obstacle to increased institutional effectiveness. Goals were first to be clarified by the academic community and then expressed quantitatively as standards of performance both for the institution and for individual staff members. MBO was followed during the mid-seventies by the zero-based budgeting approach(9), which required that the goals of an organizational unit should determine the budget and not the budget the goals to be achieved(10). This was applied successfully in only a few instances.

The search continued, and by the end of the seventies, the concepts of strategic planning and management were developed. Strategic planning is more appropriate when there are unknowns, opportunities and threats, since the concept requires an institution to develop widespread capability among staff to participate in planning. The key to planning strategically is environmental scanning at two levels: institutional and departmental. Faculty and administration are usually well-informed processors of qualitative information but a university-wide information system is important to provide control. The steps taken, for example, in some American universities were:

(1) Review of mission.
(2) Determination of salient strengths.
(3) Comparison with market trends.
(4) Deployment in the future.
(5) Intended strategy(11).

The hypothesis was that such planning and management is better able to cope with the present trends of de-regulation and accountability, of diversification of programmes to meet socio-economic demands and the introduction of new technologies, of the need for a long-term strategy for research in a period of scientific and technological revolution, and the creation of a public image in an era of increasing competition for funds and students(12).

Another major area of theoretical thinking in the 1980s concerned the possibility of higher educational institutions adopting a more entrepreneurial type of management. There was some evidence from the commercial sector that organizations with an external focus tended to be much more capable of managing change than those that were internally focused, of which higher education institutions are classic examples. In line with this, it was increasingly suggested that heads of institutions should have stronger powers, and better support for financial and other resource management, to enable them to function as chief executives. Similarly, it was suggested that committee systems should be replaced by management executive groups in order to permit quick decisions in times of crisis.

The most recent articles(13) argue that no one model can fully describe the nature of decision-making in such a complex organization. A number of decisions are entirely made by administrative fiat (the bureaucratic model); others depend on the professional judgment of the individual academic, or are made through committees uniting academics and external representatives (the collegiate model), while the top executive decisions may be closer to the political model.

Part II highlighted another of the demands made by governments: quality assurance. Here it was thought that the total quality management (TQM) experience in the service sector could provide some helpful hints. TQM is characterized by team work, systematic analysis of the problems, and the intensive use of information to achieve continuous improvement of services. It is participative and stresses the need for staff development(14). It has been characterized as a never ending journey towards organizational improvement, the routes varying according to the needs of the institution. Researchers have pointed out the complementarity of strategic planning, which involves mainly senior staff and is cyclical over the medium and long term, and TQM as a continuous process based on the management responsibility of all staff, whose decisions are based on up to date data to obtain immediate results(15). Another recent managerial improvement concept is 're-engineering', which involves periodically breaking the old and creating an entirely new organizational structure to meet new needs. There are elements of all these concepts in university management practice.

To summarize this brief review of theory, it is evident that there have been quite marked changes in thinking on higher educational management in little more than a decade, viz.

1. The major trend has been an increasing acknowledgment of the need to strengthen overall institutional management and to make it more businesslike, while retaining a decentralized structure with its considerable advantages in a teaching and research institution. Various means to accomplish this have been:
    - conversion of the post of Vice-Chancellor/Rector into Chief Executive;
    - centralizing power in an executive group of key departmental managers;
    - streamlining decision-making by line management and merging departments;
    - establishing procedures of accountability at each level of the university structure, with the basic units becoming cost centres;
    - providing training in management, particularly as regards finance, staff and physical facilities.
2. A parallel trend was the clarification of goals and basic directions for institutional development, for example in mission statements. Strategic planning emphasized proactive adaptation to environmental change as a basic requirement for institutional effectiveness and survival in a competitive environment.
3. Latterly, the need became apparent to integrate measures to ensure quality.

As can be seen from the references, most of this theoretical work has been done in relation to systems where universities have autonomy within a framework of accountability. Little has come from higher educational institutions in developing countries or from systems under direct governmental planning and control. It seems to be the general view that government planning and funding has encouraged universities in the latter countries to feel little responsibility for management.

3. Trends in university management

In this section, some of the reactions of higher education institutions to the pressures exerted on them are given, together with an overview of the type of changes generally adopted within the different classified contexts.

(a) Self-regulation and accountability implemented

It seems to be the case that higher educational institutions are now generally considered to be responsible for their own fate, whether within a free market public and private system or the regulatory framework of a mainly state public system. The literature shows that some institutions reacted defensively by retrenching or merging, while others launched out in new directions as entrepreneurial universities, changing their management structure and embarking on new revenue earning activities, public relations and marketing exercises, etc. The IIEP research programme was particularly interested in the latter type and how such change was brought about.

(i) USA

Management of *United States* universities has been described as typically a federation of hierarchical layers, having a blend of bureaucratic, collegial and market characteristics(16). The top level of President (who is much occupied with fund-raising and public relations), and the Vice-Presidents for academic affairs, personnel and research, provide leadership and meet frequently to discuss management. The University Board's task is usually limited to review. Recently more of the top administrators are specialist managers and non-academics, unlike their European counterparts. Market-sensitive criteria are used, such as student enrolment by course, external funding generated and cost of programmes. Schools usually have their own internal governance to deal with admissions and academic co-ordination, under a Dean. An analysis of the federal structure has been made by Bruce Johnstone, who reported that 41 out of the 50 states in the USA. have organized their public universities into a total of 58 multi-campus systems (covering 7 million students) whose 'system-wide administrations' are headed by a President and Governing Board(17). Their responsibilities have been listed as leadership, resource allocation, programme and research assessment, policies for admissions and students, information, public relations, support services and business management. The importance of information in such a management system is paramount: the State University of New York's Office of Institutional Research, Planning and Policy Analysis, maintains 25 data bases. It handles all reports required by legislation and for internal purposes. In present times of relative austerity, the system-wide administrations have played a critical role in maintaining long-term integrity; they provide a buffer against political interference, set targets for economies and give guidance on common approaches. The main and persistent problem is to keep such central administrations lean.

The strategic planning concept was first implemented in the USA and experience there has shown that such planning cannot by itself overcome weak communication and protective behaviour in universities. So far it appears that only marginal benefits have been achieved from setting priorities, and that what is needed in most cases is not large-scale solutions but small pervasive gains. One researcher, describing the solutions to the management problems of his own very large institution, maintained that straightforward attacks on specific problems often fail, and that a successful strategy would be one which included strategic thinking; constraints on resources; individual and group empowerment; incentives, recognition and rewards; and small gains achieved by people improving their own efficiency(18). Good departmental management has therefore been emphasised and reinforced. Each unit's plan now includes a situational analysis, using such performance indicators as normal teaching load, research, use of technology and support services. Units that maintain good records are treated more sympathetically when new funding is available. Staff whose publications receive favourable reviews are allocated more time for research; excellent teaching is given awards, and salary increments have been extended to give a wider range than before. Higher pay is given to departmental heads to emphasize the importance of good management. Such changes were carried out after open discussion and presentation of information: each unit had to defend its record on the performance indicators(19).

As was the case with strategic planning, United States universities were the first to experiment with the Total Quality Management concept. A survey conducted in 1992 showed that 23 institutions had implemented TQM in some form. At the Virginia Commonwealth University, there were doubts about its applicability, and the President established a Quality Council as a monthly forum to impart information; two pilot projects were undertaken on computing and personnel services, in order to gain confidence (20). Oregon State University chose to attempt to increase its computing and administrative efficiency by the use of TQM team-work methods. Results included a decrease in the cost of maintenance, a 50 per cent cut in the time for preparation of the budget and improvement of the computer delivery network. The problems included resistance by middle management to diminution of its control, and scarcity of time for team-work. TQM is even harder to implement in academic areas with individualistic teaching staff, and it was recommended that institutions might try pilot projects in service areas first(21).

(ii) United Kingdom

In the *United Kingdom* university management changed in the late 1980s, in response to Government measures. Vice-Chancellors became more like American university Presidents, sometimes spending half their time on external relations, the creation of mission statements, and negotiation with the public and private providers of funds. Pro Vice-Chancellors have been created with roles similar to Vice-Presidents. Policies generally adopted include: mission statements, overall planning of resources and accountability, line management, departments as self-managing cost centres raising their own research money, and measurement of output with a range of evaluation mechanisms(22). The use by government agencies of performance indicators has naturally filtered down into institutional management. Some newer institutions, working with modular systems, have adopted basic units other than departments, such as schools of study or course teams. Management structures are more devolved, with fewer units and committees but with the addition of corporate management teams to take the key decisions. Collective collegial decision-making has been reduced for the institution as a whole but is still found at department level(23).

However, it has been noted that some of the mission statements contain empty phrases like "serving the needs of the economy", and few have managed a genuine concentration of efforts(24). The implementation of strategic management has therefore posed some problems. One United Kingdom university adopted specific criteria of excellence, closing programmes which were not attracting high ability students; here the key decision-maker was the Vice-Chancellor, supported by special advisory groups on budgetary and academic planning. Other universities not so severely affected by financial constraints put emphasis on their role as social innovators, by extending continuing education and broadening access(25).

The reaction of one institution to stronger steering, formula funding and very rapid change is given in *Box 1* in order to illustrate how universities, though initially reluctant to change, can react positively when the situation is finally made clear to them.

Box 1.

> From 1981 to 1987 this university experienced severe cuts in funding. Despite the financial constraints, the programme coverage was maintained. At the end of 1986 a 'Radical Plan' was considered by the Senate but rejected and the university had to undergo staff losses.
>
> Under a second Plan in November 1987, every head of department was interviewed. Recommendations included the closure of seven departments, and cuts of 155 academic and 90 non-academic posts. An application for 'transitional funding' was made to the UGC but still there was resistance to any serious contraction in academic disciplines.
>
> A further financial squeeze had to be suffered in 1988 and at the request of the UGC, management consultants were appointed. The university's organizational structure was analysed: it was essentially collegiate in nature, with about 100 people reporting directly to the Vice-Chancellor. The lack of line management was felt to be a major impediment to decision-making in a contracting situation.
>
> From 1989, a new organizational structure came into being, with clear lines of management from head of department through dean of faculty, and relevant vice-principal to the Principal. In parallel to the new line management structure, a streamlined committee structure was implemented with the formation of new planning units and a powerful Joint Policy and Resource Committee. Within the new structure, deans were appointed, rather than elected as previously, and were charged with resource planning. Committees were reduced, and decisions were speeded up. Implementation was rapid, to ensure maintenance of momentum and to allow for flexibility in view of the further changes which were envisaged.
>
> The five major reforms were: budgetary devolution (the core of the new structure), a research initiative, the introduction of a summer school, a successful bid under Enterprise in Higher Education and modularization.
>
> The university's success in attracting national funding has greatly improved, with above-average increases in recurrent grant. Research levels continue to show improvement, student recruitment is buoyant, and modest but increasing financial surpluses are forecast.
>
> The conclusion is that though still in a learning process, the old institution appears to have been taught the value of management though it has some way to go yet in effecting structures and systems which will genuinely result in devolved management, improved communications, and better budgetary monitoring and control, with increased flexibility(26).

Two United Kingdom reports of implementation of TQM emphasized the need for sensitization and communication to overcome distrust of a business ethos, which seems to be a general feature of academic institutions. That from the South Bank University is particularly interesting, since it tackled not only delivery of services but the quality of teaching and learning. This institution had expanded its enrolments by 25 per cent in the last three years and was anxious to maintain standards. It had already streamlined its management structure in which 13 schools were grouped in four faculties with the back-up of 10 support departments.

A Dean of Quality Initiatives was nominated who also acted as Executive Assistant to the Vice-Chancellor. He organized a three-year programme of management training for heads of basic units, and all staff were involved in drawing up standards for their own units. For example, benchmarks were set for teaching such as:

- course to start within five minutes of time scheduled;
- well prepared handouts available;
- relevance of content and delivery.

It was recommended that such initiatives need commitment at the highest level, wide participation and a warning given that any process of improvement will be slow(27). Other experiences suggest the establishment of a Quality Council for discussion of the various administrative processes, as well as workshops for senior managers on taking responsibility for change(28). TQM is principally concerned with changing attitudes, showing the links between ends and means, and creating an awareness of the importance of service and cost effectiveness. It is therefore seen as an antidote to complacency in management, though it is too soon to say whether the time expended brings about commensurate returns.

(iii)   Netherlands

In the less strongly government regulated system in the *Netherlands*, a number of universities have decentralized management to faculties when introducing the cycle of planning and control activities described in *Part II*. The faculties were happy to have more freedom in resource allocation in return for more evaluation, and realised that cuts had to be made. A faculty management team is responsible for all the tasks involved and Annual Reports are the major instrument of accountability. For this purpose, the University Board sends a questionnaire to the faculties enquiring how they have executed the tasks delegated to them, including the production of specific Performance Indicators as well as peer review to establish quality(29). The executive level of the university has been strengthened by its role in allocating the lump sum budget and by the evaluation process but it has not in all cases been successful in taking a strong policy role, and the faculties still retain their power(30).

One small university, which had been threatened with closure during the period of government reform, designated itself an entrepreneurial university, and successfully expanded to overcome its financial problems. This was the University of Twente which in 1987 drafted a strategic plan to provide guidelines to its faculties on educational, research and service activities. Its mission objectives were set out as:

(a) A regional centre which should serve local needs.
(b) A target enrolment of 6,000.
(c) A core of technical, engineering and humanities programmes oriented to future professional activities.
(d) Research to be innovative and multidisciplinary.
(e) Less financial dependence on government.

University planning was designed to bring about changes and a consensus was established through rounds of discussions, each sector discussing strategies and ideas which then went on to the next sector. Faculties have become accustomed to planning and are encouraged to seek contract research assisted by an Industrial Liaison Officer. A Business Technical Centre offers space to graduates who want to start their own firms. Since universities cannot legally undertake entrepreneurial activities, a private 'technopolis' was set up to develop spin-offs from university research. There is also an International Conference Centre, a Biomass Technology Group and an Educational Computer Consortium. In the 1990s the university has 10 strong faculties giving multidisciplinary programmes and has embarked on R&D in technology for developing countries(31).

The move away from centralized management and low cost-consciousness has been significant in some institutions. The Central Netherlands Polytechnic decided to use contract management to transform itself into a task and market-oriented institution. First the structure was changed to reduce the number of faculties from seven to four, creating large enough units of between two and five departments, each headed by a Directorate of two or three staff. Management has been decentralized and is governed by two-year contracts. The new administrative system is laid down in a handbook which lists the information to be supplied for the annual accounts and reports. Quarterly meetings are held at which the Executive and Faculty Boards relate performance indicators and management information to the institution's objectives(32). The system has provided incentives for good performance, and faculties can receive as much as an extra 5 per cent on their budget from a Central Innovation Fund. Here again the emphasis is on streamlining structure and devolved management, as well as the drawing up of mission statements and the use of performance indicators.

(iv) Belgium

The Flemish Belgian experience seems to follow the general lines of that in the Netherlands. The case study at K.U. Leuven carried out for the IIEP research programme(33) shows that faculties have been grouped into three (Humanities, Exact Sciences, Biomedical Sciences) for the purposes of co-ordinating education, research and logistics(34). A General Manager for Administration, Finance and Personnel was appointed to serve under the Rector. However, faculties still have a considerable amount of autonomy. They retain ultimate responsibility for innovation, and small task groups have been set up within each department for this purpose. However, as the chapter on *Educational delivery systems* shows, basic units can take 'avoidance measures' if the policy set by the executive does not have their support.

(v) Australia

Reports from *Australia* on the results of the amalgamation reform show that in the first years net administrative costs are likely to remain higher than before, because of the distance between campuses, although economies of scale have been achieved in admissions and core curricula. Many institutions made changes to management structures, centralizing administration and computer units. They established new and smaller governing bodies and new regulations. Most have an executive and policy advisory group meeting weekly; there are fewer committees, and those that remain have a stronger planning and resource focus. Usually a central Planning Office provides statistical and strategic expertise. Some institutions have sophisticated financial management systems, and all have data on such indicators as staff-student ratios, average teaching loads, course costs and space utilization. Staff assessment has been introduced. These changes were in some cases assisted by external consultants who reviewed structure, functions, reporting lines and spans of control. Some multi-campus universities may not survive but many

75

seem to be operating smoothly with new communication technologies to link campuses for both committee work and teaching. It is felt that there is a new competitive and entrepreneurial approach, including an increase in industrial co-operative ventures and generation of revenue(35). A very recent report concludes that tension between collegial and managerial modes of decision making required definition of the domains in which the two operated, but that because of the need for stronger leadership and planning, the dominant mode is a consultative top-down style of decision-making(36). The lower echelons of the academic community have criticized the changes on the grounds that, in spite of their claim to reduce bureaucracy, there has in fact been an increase in detailed control and very costly information requirements. It is also alleged that, while purporting to aim at a more diversified and adaptive system, the reward structure will in fact encourage all universities to imitate elite institutions(37).

A description of the type of institutional changes which took place during this reform has been given by the University of Queensland. Economic restrictions were imposed when demand for courses was at its highest, though it was uneven across courses. In response to these shifts, the University restructured its organization to create five resource groups (health, biology, physics, social science, humanities) to deal with allocation of resources. These groups, headed by pro-vice-chancellors, compete for funds among themselves and with the computing centre and library(38).

(vi) Conclusion

Under systems of self-regulation and accountability, the noticeable major change has been towards stronger executive management, decentralization of budgets to the departments or faculties, and restructuring of basic units into larger groups. Strategic planning has been adopted, at least in form, but the extent of change it has brought about in university management has varied greatly or is yet to be evaluated. There has been a considerable amount of innovation in management, as will be more fully demonstrated in subsequent chapters.

b. Self-regulation in transition

(i) Sweden

In *Swedish* universities, as noted in *Chapter 2*, Vice Chancellors and Boards containing a majority of external members have been given responsibility for planning and the use of resources. There have also been efforts to rationalize and improve departmental management; department heads have been given increased management power and are now expected to determine (within given limits) the teaching loads and research time of staff. At the Swedish University of Agricultural Science in 1986, a three-year campaign was begun (called 'Care for your Department') to assist heads in identifying weak points. This consisted of drawing up (i) long-term goals and strategies (options for feasible courses of action), (ii) a planning structure for resources (staff, finance, buildings, equipment, library services), (iii) job planning and definition of responsibilities. However, as pointed out in a recent article, the changes have in most cases been steered from the top down and university staff tend to wait to hear from the central agencies how, for example, to evaluate and develop programmes(39). Years of experience under centralised management are not easily effaced, as can also be noted in Finland (described in *Box 2*).

(ii)   Norway

In Norway, all institutions were to introduce strategic planning in 1990. Much more weight is now given to departmental leadership, and at the University of Oslo, in line with directives, many of the departments have been amalgamated into larger units so that they may be assigned administrative staff to assist with the planning burden. At this university, changes have met with some resistance due to the increased administration and fear of competition for funding(40).

The co-operation of this small university with the request of government for pilot institutions echoes the Dutch experience. It is not the only pilot project; others are working on a comprehensive system of performance indicators or on creating new educational delivery methods and performance funds to encourage teaching and research excellence. Many departments use student evaluation of courses and follow-up of graduates' careers. In this respect, it has been noted that faculties of Medicine and Technology have taken more initiatives in the development and use of performance indicators and evaluation systems, while the reverse is the case for Humanities (42).

Box 2.

> The study carried out for the IIEP research programme at the Joensuu University, Finland, describes the changes implemented at a young regional university, which was designated as a pilot institution to put into effect *proactively* the changes necessary to survive in a much more competitive and financially constrained environment. This process, which began in 1986, is still continuing. Two main elements, which are characteristic of change in many universities in Western Europe today, i.e. decentralization and central management integration, can be seen at Joensuu. Decentralization has taken place in the decision-making structure and financial management, while the integrating elements have been lump sum budgeting, initiation of a dialogue between academic leaders, information systems, evaluation and a new role for central management of providing services and support to the departments, in particular information such as input and output figures, to form the basis for the dialogue.
>
> The Rector, conscious of the threat to his small university's survival in a much more competitive environment, was the major proponent and missionary of change in the university and at national level. Implementation was carried out by a Project Group of senior staff (Rector, the Director of Administration, and the Heads of Financial Management and Academic Affairs plus two externally recruited experts on economics and administration). Discussions were held in all departments to soften attitudes, concentrating on key individuals, specialists from the Ministry of Finance gave lectures so as to convince staff that the old administration was really changing and the Campus News kept all staff informed of events. Availability of information for decisions was the cornerstone of this change. Problems were the variable extent of managerial expertise among Department Heads, the long learning process and how to maintain the momentum of the process in coming years.
>
> The change from the former system of administration, where most decisions were made by civil servants and the main duty of Deans and Department Heads was to chair meetings, is quite profound. Department Heads have to take part in the dialogue on four-year planning and in the process of lump sum budget allocations, conduct self-evaluation and compete for a part of the Performance Fund. They are responsible for the use of their resources, including the various trade-offs that can be made in the use of staff, such as leaving a post vacant or recruiting part-timers. Internally, management consciousness has increased; the staff feel that they are no longer threatened by external events and that they are 'building up' their university. Externally, the experience has had an extensive impact on the development of the new management system in Finnish higher education.

c. Self-regulation in difficulty

(i) Central and Eastern Europe

According to Hufner, in Central and Eastern Europe the difficulties of transition are only now being understood. The speed and comprehensiveness with which former systems were abandoned and the market system adopted were not anticipated and it has become evident that 'market shock' does not work. Previous central planning which was all pervasive and regulated all aspects of life, has not yet been replaced by proper legal frameworks, etc. The group of countries classified as Eastern Europe is not a homogeneous one: for example, Poland, Hungary and the Czech and Slovak Republics (which are more attached historically to Europe) all intend to join the European Union and have begun to adhere to EEC requirements when drawing up new legislation. Other countries express a desire to return to their pre-centrally planned systems(43).

Recent reports from the Central European countries indicate that so far no significant structural transformation within institutions has taken place. Internal democracy has tended to block reform since too much power was transferred to collective bodies (Senates and Councils) and too little to the executive level. Rectors have no say in the hiring and firing of staff(44). The previous regime has left a legacy of suspicion of 'plans'; little is said about 'accountability' but on the other hand there is a great deal of conservatism. Curricula are overloaded but teachers do not want to implement change in case they lose students and their jobs. Differentiation is not easily accepted.

In Hungary, reform forces contributed to the creation of the Rectors' Conference but university rectors have little room for manoeuvre vis-à-vis the faculties(45). A report from the Czech Republic confirms that too much power was granted to the faculties where staff are often loyal to the old regime. It has been possible to replace only about 10-20 per cent of staff. The Academy of Science (and this is true for the other countries) still has a virtual monopoly of research and few researchers have transferred to universities despite their official new mission as research institutions. Nevertheless progress has been made in the opening of new schools, departments and programmes; external assistance from the EEC has contributed to staff development, private colleges for business administration, economics and languages have increased and students tend to be pro-reform.

(ii) Latin America

In Latin America the basic organization in public universities has changed little, retaining its independent faculty structure and chair system of tenured professors. Generally there is a lack of qualified management personnel, incentives and information systems. Some institutions, such as provincial universities in Colombia, Ecuador and Peru, operate with too low enrolment in certain faculties. There is evidence of excessive numbers of teaching and administrative staff in public universities; Brazil has a student-teacher ratio of 8:1, while private universities have ratios two or three times higher. There is also a low level of utilization of physical facilities due to the academic calendar in some countries. Management is conducted in a political environment with student and faculty participation and strong government regulation. Institutions do not compete for funding or students on grounds of merit or cost(46).

In the National University of *Costa Rica*, for example, the academic units are subject to four vice-rectors for academic, research, extension and administrative work from whom they must obtain approval of projects and budgets; these vice-rectors have serious problems in supervising 40 academic units with over 1,000 teachers and 12,000 students, and do not liaise with each other. The University Council seems to spend most of its time on administrative matters, rather than policy. Administration is divided into separate departments for staff, finance and services which have problems of co-ordination. The budget has become the main instrument of academic control and excessive centralization causes delay and inefficiency. Much administrative work is done by hand. Other problems are that there is no correspondence between plans and budgets, insufficient statistical and qualitative data, and lack of economic and financial analysis. The authoritarian conception of management and control discourages initiatives(47). This university is proposing both to centralize and to decentralize functions within the university; the tasks of setting mission and strategy, definition of objectives and policies are to be centralized, while administration of budgets, staff management, enrolment, supplies and general services are to be decentralized to the basic units.

A number of individual institutions are in the process of trying to improve management; universities in Chile, Argentina and Colombia have begun to develop strategic plans(48). UNAM, Mexico, is progressively deconcentrating services and great interest has been shown in computerizing administrative information systems. Thus, despite an environment so generally unfavourable to the concept of self-management, it is possible for initiatives to be taken at the institutional level. Two examples are given in *Box 3* and *Box 4*.

Box 3.

> The University of Concepcion, Chile, is private, but financed mainly by the state, with 12,500 students from all regions and 72 programmes). Sixty per cent of the academic staff are full time, which is high for Latin America. It is ranked third amongst 60 universities by number of research projects. In 1987 the university recognized it was heading for a financial crisis, and that its management structure was slow, out of date, bureaucratic, and over-staffed. An in-depth analysis was carried out and proposals made to decentralize management, create university enterprises and train staff. A series of internal seminars was held and a Commission for Administrative Modernization, composed of six academics, consulted staff and outside experts and formed ad hoc sub-committees for specific themes. It drew up a report in three months. The problems were to show the benefits of change, find extra resources for redundancies, etc. and establish channels of communication by which staff could participate.
>
> The motivation for implementation was 'democratization' of university decision-making. This involved decentralization of responsibilities to Faculties and Departments, which was begun in 1989. As from 1990, the Rector, Deans and Directors became subject to election and staff participated in a strategic planning exercise at all three levels of decision-making. Policy-making and evaluation are the special mandate of the Academic Council, while the Directing Committee (of ten elected professors plus the Rector and Vice-Rectors) is responsible for management. There are also Offices for Planning and Informatics and for Public Relations.
>
> Apart from this restructuring, there has also been an increase in research projects to obtain revenue, creation of a Division of University Enterprises and transfer of some physically distant units to the central campus to save staff time and space. The decentralized structure is slowly beginning to function with greater participation in Faculty Councils and Committees for Teaching. However, academics do not feel they have a real responsibility to manage; only 17 per cent knew anything about the budget and 25 per cent did some administrative work. Their salaries are relatively low and democratization may not provide sufficient motivation to give real momentum to the change (49).

This example from Chile illustrates the problems of building up management consciousness in academic staff, as well as the need to provide an incentive system, (as was seen in the Finnish case-study). The slow re-appearance of more collegial systems and greater activity by Governing Boards, for example in designating Rectors in Chile, has also been noted(50).

Box 4.

> The National Experimental University of Guayana, Venezuela. From 1982-1986, UNEG was a traditional style university, but in 1986 it adopted a mission to contribute to scientific and technological development in the region and establish a new management model. The university has the Venezuelan Corporation for Development on its Board, which also contributes financially. Courses were to be geared to regional needs and research to problems of development. Teaching is based on an introductory course emphasizing self-learning methods and project-oriented academic programmes with continuous evaluation by the individual student and teachers. Teachers had to undergo a training programme to implement the changes. Administration incorporates accountability and generation of alternative sources of funding. Five main areas of research were designated: food, social development, technological development, productivity and energy. This innovation was to have been the subject of evaluation but there have been problems of student unrest and lack of interest by academics in management(51).

The example from Venezuela reinforces the conclusions of the example from Chile. Where the base units are not sensitized, trained and rewarded for management tasks, they will be reluctant to change their usual working habits, particularly in environments where it is standard practice to take up additional outside employment.

d. Centralized planning and control

In these systems, the Ministry or State Department of Education may prescribe student admission numbers, size of staff, validate courses and set down the formal structure of university management. They may also carry out the necessary co-ordination, set specific standards or norms and be the main source of funds (often strictly delineated by type of expenditure).

(i) Continental Europe

Here the influence of executive level university management is generally limited. In both the French and German systems, units composed of subject groups (the object of a 1970s reform from the old chair system) tend to be powerful in distributing resources assigned to their programmes, in staff recruitment, in the academic sphere and in research. Such units (Unités de Formation et Recherche in the case of France) may even contact Ministries of Education directly concerning staff appointments. Administrative headship is often rotating and the incumbents are judged by their ability to represent and defend the unit efficiently. They are assisted by the administrative branch but resource allocations are usually routine. There are exceptional Directors who take initiatives (and crises assist them in bringing about change) but most are not expected to intervene(52). Initiatives at the institutional level have therefore been taken mainly in the academic rather than the managerial field. For example, in France there have been the setting up of special classes for entrance to the *Grandes Ecoles*; establishing courses competing with the *Grandes Ecoles* in chemistry and electronics; remedial courses; the expansion of distance learning centres; computer assisted instruction and continuing education in conjunction with economic sectors. In exceptional cases (Grenoble and Montpellier) where institutions undertook reorganization, changes had to be abandoned when new regulations were issued. In Germany, legislative decision-making processes have made the introduction of innovation difficult. For example, then the law on regrouping of institutions was implemented, some of them obtained derogations by writing direct to the Ministry.

A lot of information on governance and management in *French* universities is now being produced in the CNE reports. A recent publication (June 1993) on one university shows a continuation of the bottom-heavy style of management, and indicates that the institution is typical. Central management draws up the plan for submission to establish a four year contract, deals with administration connected with student admissions and certificates, collects and analyses information (since 1990 it has also produced forecasts), publishes key statistics and provides a management computer service. The units have a great degree of managerial autonomy: they define the content of courses, calculate the resources available to them (state credits for teachers plus supplementary assistance as set by official norms, plus funds from their own student fees, the *Taxe d'Apprentissage* and research/training services), select students and keep their records. So far each department has chosen its own software and there are no links to the centre or other departments. The Evaluation Committee recommended that services should be centralised, an information system developed, the various disciplines should be regrouped to provide a clearer distribution of teaching loads, and internal evaluation systems should be introduced for education, research and management. In brief, the university is being asked to regulate itself better. How far such recommendations can achieve a response without additional external pressure is open to question given past refusal to implement change.

The internal structure of *German* higher education institutions was reformed by legislation in 1976. This involved reorganisation of faculties and institutes into 'Fachbereiche' of manageable size, and the strengthening of central administration and representation of all groups of staff on university committees, with the professoriate having a majority on any that concerned teaching and research. In the event they still have a majority on all committees and the executive level is not noticeably stronger. There are complaints of bureaucracy and too many committees but despite this the Rectors' Conference (1988) advocated consolidation and only gradual change(53). There are no clear policies for rewarding success or sanctioning failure; for example, a department that attracts more students may not be given more staff for some years since all departments in a particular discipline are funded more or less equally(54).

In *Italy*, the situation is one of conservatism. The universities have been able to resist government demands for change, in particular in regard to diversification, vocationalisation and links with industry. Few institutions are willing to innovate. There are islands of efficiency and quality, mostly in technological areas.

From the above descriptions of Continental European universities under centralised planning and control, it is apparent that the legacy of the traditional powerful chair has impeded the growth of executive power and has in a number of cases during the 1980s caused the failure of proposed reforms. Evaluation as a strategy to bring about improvement is being tried in both France and Italy. It was also noted from a review of the literature that the subject of management as a research topic does not appear to attract the interest of academics from this group of continental European countries, whereas the opposite is the case for those under self-regulation. It is strange that the restructuring of departments and increased executive power which occurred in self-regulatory systems, particularly Australia and the United Kingdom and which was considered to be a prerequisite for successful management in the 1980s, was tried and largely failed in the 1970s in Continental Europe. Significantly, executive power is less in the Netherlands but the relative success there may be due to the earlier recognition of the realities of mass higher education and financial constraint were recognised. This is another instance of the importance of timing or pacing innovations, which has been noted at institutional as well as systems level.

(ii) Asia

In Asia, little change in university structures or management in the public sector has been reported, despite isolated innovations introduced to link universities with industry and increase external funding, an interest in using computers for management (Indonesia, Thailand) and an attempt to create a new university 'without bureaucracy' (Suranam Technology University, Thailand, 1991). Part II has already mentioned the general state of bureaucratic inertia. To give one example, in India, a country-wide pattern for university structure was adopted, with three tiers of senate, executive and academic councils plus a committee structure which may vary. Senate confers status on its members and is a body involving outsiders, but the Executive Council has the real power, and the vice-chancellor is almost at its mercy. It usually has a membership of some 300 staff and students, half of whom are elected. It is much too large and unwieldy for decision-making, and political interest groups flourish(55). Staff have an unspecified duty to assist in administration but take this lightly. In one state, Bihar, the government is taking over the administration of five universities because they had no suitable staff of their own to do the work(56). The plan for autonomous departments has been implemented only in two institutions and the University Grants Commission is still trying to develop appropriate models and management patterns, as well as a system of university accreditation(57).

Despite the unfavourable economic and cultural environment, however, there have been several reports from institutions where management has been dynamic and open to change; these have been private and often assisted by local industry and foreign aid agencies. One example is given in *Box 5* (others will be found in subsequent chapters).

Asia is a region of great contrasts from which relatively little information about innovations in institutional management, apart perhaps from India, percolates to the international community. However, from the short descriptions available, administrative systems appear to conform to those outlined previously for centrally planned countries; universities are basically government regulated with weak executive and faculty management(58). In China, for example, it is reported that administrations tend to make standard decisions, without regard to the wide variety of different institutional needs and situations.

Box 5.

The Birla Institute of Technology and Sciences (BITS), Pilani, India, is a wholly privately financed 'deemed' university. Few of this type of university exist in India and they must constantly innovate and modernize in order to compete. It was in a situation of stagnation and falling revenue in 1970 when a new leadership team began work and from then on instituted a series of cumulative reforms in academic structure, examinations, admissions and staff management, followed by changes in graduate programmes, research and consultancy, all subject to continual adjustment up to the present time. The new Director was an Indian having experience of institutional management in one of the best technological universities in the United States of America. He had the full support of a foreign funding agency during the process of change. One of his first steps was to obtain a greater contribution from fees. However, increases were made only for new admissions so that each batch of students could plan ahead. After each fee increase, the quality of intake was monitored. BITS also introduced an 'Earn while you learn' scheme in which 100 students work as assistants to faculty. The duration of courses is kept in line with state universities though intake is kept at the optimum since a modular programme allows admission in the second semester or at any point in four years' study. Students may work for two degrees at the same time and usually achieve them in 4+1 years. Weaker students are allowed to transfer into less demanding courses rather than drop out.

The department as an administrative unit was abolished. BITS acquired its first computer in 1969 and now has central computerized administration of students, staff, budgets, salaries, timetable, use of facilities and distance learning. The software was written by students and staff as part of projects. Central administration also has academic advantages where courses are interdisciplinary. All student welfare matters are dealt with in one unit.

Examinations are internal and continuous, with answers returned to students and marking discussed; this gives feedback to teachers and improves quality of teaching. The number of courses was reduced by, for example, constructing common courses in statistics, electronics and other subjects for students in different programmes. The Education Development Division plans and monitors curricula and textbooks. Classrooms and laboratories are continuously scheduled from 8 a.m. to 6 p.m. and the computer centre and library are open until midnight. A central inventory of equipment is kept with information on length of use, functioning and maintenance: purchasing is also done centrally. Construction and maintenance is done under the Civil Engineering Group, and electricity and instrumentation under two other groups. No outside consultants are used and courses include servicing and maintaining computers and other equipment by staff and students. The reduction in cost is found to be considerable. As to staffing, the ratio of academics:assistants:other staff is maintained at 1:1:1. BITS channels research activity into specified priority areas, and its links with industry enable projects to be conducted in industrial settings without incurring overheads. BITS also began distance learning programmes leading to BS and MS degrees on the recommendation of employers who provide physical facilities and manpower to supervise the students. The Technological Innovation Centre allows small-scale industries to use facilities and student manpower for projects(59).

A significant feature is the strong centralized management. Problems were experienced with the staff but were overcome by a mixture of incentives and pressure from the necessity for institutional survival.

The major conclusion of the study is that innovation unfolds a whole range of necessary changes, and strategy should determine how many can be tackled at one time. It is extremely rich in the number of lessons learned. Any developing country university constrained by an unfavourable environment may profit from and be given fresh hope by this experience.

In the Republic of Korea, higher education is centrally administered, leaving only details to be decided in the universities. In Indonesia also, public universities are given little autonomy in planning and budgetary decisions: they have to wait to hear what resources they have been allocated, use of student fees is highly regulated and other income is small. Rectors are regularly summoned to government offices for consultations. Data gathering and use is limited; little information exists about libraries, equipment and maintenance, and centralised accounting does not allow identification of the costs of university sub-units. Heads of Faculties and Departments (as in India) are elected in rotation so that the post is seen only as a temporary one. Philippine higher educational institutions are under state regulation: there are laws on governance, programmes, operations and educational policies. Control is exercised through the budget process and by Boards of Trustees appointed by the President.

There are cases where universities may exercise more management initiative. Singapore's universities have some latitude in deciding on admission numbers, course design, examination policy, staff selection and financial management, but this is being eroded as human resource development has become so critical for this island state. Malaysian universities, though largely dependent on public funds, have considerable autonomy in academic matters and internal administration, and may determine course contents and hire or fire staff. The Philippines' private universities, spurred on by financial constraints, provide some examples of dynamic management, as will be seen from the IIEP case-study in the chapter on Educational Delivery Methods.

In this region, Governments will have to provide the initial impetus for the improvement of institutional management. Several of them (e.g. India, Republic of Korea) are already looking into more remote output-based methods of steering.

(iii)   Africa

In Africa too, given the political and financial constraints, universities are often obliged to wait for official national policy changes. One author has pointed to increasing government encroachment on university governance and student intolerance as the reason for many of the closures and problems on campus(60). As noted in *Part II*, the AAU and donor agencies are now co-ordinating efforts with institutions in an attempt to improve the traditional, hierarchical, and often political university management prevailing in most countries.

A distinction must be made between those universities of French and those of British influence. The former tend to have a French 1968 authoritarian style management, with Rectors nominated by presidential decree. Lower down the hierarchy, deans may be nominated (Cameroon) or elected (Côte d'Ivoire and Senegal). Most universities have links with French or Belgian universities to exchange staff and students in order to maintain quality, but as yet little assistance in management is given apart from a series of meetings of vice-chancellors and some external consultant advice to the two universities who, as described in *Chapter 3*, regrouped their departments.

Universities which were begun under British influence, tend to have structures that conform to the collegial committee style of management, i.e. a Vice Chancellor, his deputy, Council, Senate, Faculty Boards, Deans and Heads of Departments. Administration is taken care of by the University Secretary (including finance) and by the Registrar (admissions plus some other tasks). However, here too the President of the country often appoints the Vice Chancellor (it was reported in one case that he was regarded as a conduit through which the government conveyed unpleasant messages) and the Ministry may appoint Deans and Professors. In theory, universities have administrative autonomy but erratic or low disbursement of funds has made the reality one of crisis management, in which the Government can at any time by-pass the university decision-making structure(61). The IIEP case study from Makerere University (see *Chapter 6* on Finance) reports that in this institution, the University Secretary's Office is powerful and conservative, and has marginalised academics in decision-making. In addition, student and staff unions may disrupt university activities for some months when any change is proposed. Visitation Committees have made some very useful proposals to improve efficiency but their reports may on occasions never be circulated or discussed.

Nevertheless, the first initiatives are being taken. The Universities of Botswana, Benin, Malawi, Senegal, Tanzania, Zambia and Eduardo Mondlane, Mozambique, have conducted strategic planning exercises. In Ghana the University Rationalization Committee in 1989 recommended that membership of university councils should be extended to two government nominees and to students as well as staff. The Council was to have direct responsibility for financial and staff administration. A post of Business Manager was to be created to co-ordinate income generation while each department would have an assistant registrar to deal with administrative matters. As regards facilities, it was suggested that standardization of classrooms, a central timetable for shared use (utilization rate could be increased by 35 per cent), and extension of daily sessions should be undertaken(62). A collegiate system has been instituted in Nigeria to reduce demands on vice-chancellors. Groups of departments and faculties are placed under provosts and the vice-chancellor then deals only with four or five provosts instead of 80 heads of departments(63). In Mozambique, a major reorganization of university governance and management is under way. A post of Deputy Rector for Resource Management has been created and the University Council is to include representatives of public and private bodies.

As far as computerisation to assist management is concerned, the Universities of Botswana, Lesotho, Nairobi and Moi in Kenya and Zimbabwe have systems for student records and staff salaries. Ghana, Madagascar and Nigeria are also investing in this field of management. However, there are problems of shortage of technical manpower, (since pay is higher in the private sector), of rapid obsolescence of hard and software, and high customs duties.

The most participative and dynamic review of activities and structure is that which has taken place at the University of Botswana, using seven Task Forces and external consultants. Management is being reinforced by two Deputy Vice-Chancellors (one for Finance and Administration and the other for Academic Affairs) who are being recruited on the open market. The new structure should be under way in 1994(64).

The *University of Dar es Salaam* has been the subject of numerous studies whose recommendations have for the most part never been implemented. It is currently well advanced in the preparation of its corporate strategic plan, entitled "Institutional Transformation Programme UDSM 2000", which emphasizes financing strategies, a modified legal status, improved governance, a different organizational culture, and greater management efficiency. Previously planning proved of little use since university budgets were cut in mid-year and it remains to be seen whether the latest efforts will bear fruit.

There is no doubt that recession, low salaries and uncertain university funding have militated against efficient management but it is also the case that management expertise, information systems, strong executive level university management and rational government steering have been for the most part lacking. At all levels, there has been little effective management.

(iv) Arab States

In this region also, it is acknowledged that universities are not well-managed(65). One researcher considers that most universities in the region suffer from lack of sufficient autonomy and a multitude of regulations and levels of reporting and control. Decisions are made at a high level, leaving lower levels with little or no discretion; this has resulted in a shortage of capable administrators and a crisis management approach. Most energy is spent on the daily routine. There is little managerial control of staff, and no knowledge of individual performance. Delaying tactics have been used to resist reform(66).

In Egypt, while the Supreme Council of Universities at the apex of the system is the body responsible for planning and coordination, administration is decentralized, each faculty being separate and managed by Councils. The Departments in these faculties are also independent in academic, administrative and financial matters. The activity of executive level university management is thus very limited. It is also stated that few administrators enforce the rules and since the effective academic year is only 20 weeks, the system can hardly be termed efficient(67).

Other countries of the region also show relatively inactive executive levels. In Morocco, the University and Faculty Councils meet only two or three times a year to ratify the decisions taken by the Ministry, while day-to-day administration is carried out in the departments. Saudi Arabia's universities are supervised by the Ministry and senior level administrative staff are appointed by Ministerial decree; changes may, however, take place soon, since the recent Fourth National Plan expresses a concern for productivity, quality and operational efficiency.

The University of Qatar is at present under the direction of the Ministry for day to day financial administration, and has become aware of the inefficiencies caused by delays in obtaining expenditure approvals. It has proposed a reorganisation to equip itself for greater autonomy. The President is to be supported by three Vice Presidents (Academic Affairs, Administration, and Research/Community Services), and administrative capacity is to be reinforced by giving each Faculty a Vice-Dean and each Department a secretariat(68). Tunisia, where the government wishes to give universities more autonomy, has strengthened managerial capacity by regrouping faculties around administrative units, and intends to tackle the problem of poor administration at the middle levels by establishing a two-year course for university administrators, as well as giving four-week in-service training to those in post. It is also trying to motivate teaching staff by giving a special budget for overtime payments(69).

However, for the most part in this region, the traditional hierarchical government centralized management, with departmental administration confined to day to day affairs, gives little margin for executive or even faculty initiative in management. The two exceptions, as far as government intentions are concerned, are Tunisia and Algeria, as noted in *Chapter 2*.

4. Conclusions

There has been less change in university management in those countries under centralized planning and control than in those where self-regulation and accountability is the norm. In developing countries, this has mostly been because governments themselves have taken little action, and the institutions can take no initiatives until they do so. In some cases, like India, central government may not have the power or the political will to enforce change. Nevertheless, a certain interest and support for change can be discerned in a number of countries which are inclined to decentralise responsibilities other than finance, to implement strategic planning exercises, to establish norms for resource allocation and to improve administrative expertise.

Within universities in self-regulated systems, the most radical changes have been reported from new institutions, anxious about their survival. Recognition of the urgency of adopting a more managerial and cost-effective approach was initially resisted by academics in many older universities, who considered it inappropriately commercial. They did not want to spend their time and energy on matters which they felt to be the responsibility of administration and the Vice-Chancellor. However, under this type of system, it soon became apparent to staff that they would be obliged to participate in management if they were not to suffer in the competitive allocation of resources. What this participation entails will become clearer in subsequent chapters.

Such an approach has attracted the attention of many governments in developing regions but has not generally been adopted. There are many obstacles to be overcome, such as centralized government bureaucracy and distrust of the local level; lack of management know-how at the middle staffing levels; unwillingness to assume management responsibilities when energy has to go into earning from outside jobs. Evaluation is ineffectual because of the lack of trained management staff to supervise it, either in the institutions or in the government. The effect of this on university management in specific domains such as staff or space will be examined in subsequent chapters.

However, this chapter was primarily designed to present experiences of change within certain policy contexts. A more in-depth discussion of steering policies, strategies and changes will be given in the following chapter which will bring together the information in *Chapters 2, 3* and *4* in order to show more clearly and succinctly:

- what changes have been commonly adopted under particular steering policies;
- how change has been brought about;
- what lessons can be learnt at this stage of the analysis from these trends in steering policies and organizational structure.

References

(1) Clark, Burton R. *The higher education system*. Academic organization in cross-national perspective. Berkeley: University of California Press, 1983.
(2) Mintzberg, Henry. *Structures in five*. Designing effective organizations. Prentice-Hall, 1983.
(3) Weick, K. "Educational organizations as loosely couled systems"; *Administrative Science Quarterly*, Vol.21, March 1976.
(4) Nordvall, R. "The process of change in higher educational institutions". ASHE ERIC, Report 1982.
(5) Rutherford et al. "Strategies for change in higher education". In *Higher Education*, 14, 433-445, 1985.
(6) Wurzberg, G. "Reconstruction of higher education". In *Meek, V. and Harrold, R. (eds.) TAFE and the reconstruction of higher education*, Arnudale: University of New England 1989.
(7) Becher, T.; Kogan, M. *Process and structure in higher education*, Routledge, London 1992.
(8) Allen, Michael. "The goals of the universities". The Open University Press: The Society for Research into Higher Education, 1988.
(9) Norris, Graeme. *The effective university: a management by objective approach*. Westmead: Saxon House, 1978.
(10) Fincher, Cameron. "The lust for efficiency: a down-home story of the implications of zero-based budgeting". In Fenske, Robert H. and Staskey, Paul (ed.), *Research and planning for higher education*. Montreal: The Association for Institutional Research, 1978.
(11) ASHE-ERIC "Higher education reports 1987". No. 8 Strategic planning.
(12) Tabatoni, T. "Introduction to strategic management of universities". Summary report of symposium on innovation policies in universities. European Centre for Strategic Management of Universities, Brussels, May 1989.
(13) Middlehurst, R. and Elton, L. "Leadership and management in higher education". In *Studies in Higher Education*, Vol.17, No.3, 1992.
(14) Taylor, A. and Hill, F. "Implementing TQM in higher education". In *International Journal of Educational Management*, Vol.6, No.4, 1992.
(15) Arguin G. and Caron A. "Strategic planning or TQM: what model to improve university education?" IGLU No. 4 April 1993
(16) Clark, B. and Neave, G. "Encyclopaedia of Higher Education". Pergamon Press, Oxford, 1992. See Academic Administration.
(17) Johnstone, Bruce D. "Central administrations of public multi-campus college and university systems". Studies in *Public Higher Education*, No. 1. SUNY, USA.
(18) Schmidtlein, F., Milton, T. mimeo, University of Maryland, 1988.
(19) Massy, W. "A strategy for improvement in college and university academic departments". Paper for Forum on Post Secondary Governance, Sante Fe, October 1989.

(20) Cowles, D. and Gilbreath, G. "TQM at Virginia Commonwealth University". In *Higher Education*, No. 3, April 1993.
(21) Coate, E. "Introduction of TQM at Oregon State University", USA. In *Higher Education*, No. 3, April 1993.
(22) Cowen, R. "Management and evaluation of the entrepreneurial university – the case of England". Paper for CEPES meeting, Plovdiv, November 1990.
(23) Toyne, P. "Higher educational institutions: an appropriate structure?" In *EAIR 13th Forum Papers*, September 1991.
(24) Times Higher Education Supplement, 29 March 1991.
(25) Buchert, L. "Practice of strategic management in Summary report of symposium of European Centre for Strategic Management", Brussels, May 1989.
(26) Clarke, K. "Managing change: a case-study". Paper for the 18th Annual Meeting of the Conference of University Administrators, Belfast, 20-22 March 1991.
(27) Geddes, T. "Total quality initiative at South Bank University". In *Higher Education*, Vol.25, No.3, April 1993.
(28) Clayton, M. "Towards TQM in higher education: Aston University". In *Higher Education*, Vol.25, No.3, April 1993.
(29) Agenent, M. "Performance and control: the use of indicators". Paper, EAIR 13th Forum, September 1991.
(30) Van Vught F. "Governmental strategies and innovation in higher education". Jessica Kingsley, London 1989.
(31) Maagen, P. et al. "Turning problems into opportunities: the University of Twente from Schmidtle" In FA (ed.). Adapting strategic planning to campus realities. Jossey Bass Inc., San Francisco, 1990.
(32) Shuter, H. "The introduction of contract management". Paper for EAIR 13th Forum, September 1991.
(33) Vandenberghe R. *Rationalization of curricula at K.U. Leuven*, IIEP Paris, 1993
(34) Harman, G. "Institutional amalgamations of the binary system in Australia". In *Higher Education Quarterly*, Vol.45, No.2, Spring 1991.
(35) DEET "National Report on Australia's Higher Education sector", Canberra 1993.
(36) Lynn Meek V. "The transformation of Australian higher education from binary to unitary". In *Higher Education*, Vol.21, No.4, June 1991.
(37) University of Queensland, "Strategies for institutional resource allocation", *Higher Education Policy*, Vol. 2, No. 2, 1989.
(38) Brandstrom D. (op.cit. *Chapter 2*)
(39) Aaamodt P. et al. "Norway: towards a more indirect model of governance?" In Neave G. (ed) Prometheus Bound Pergamon Press, Oxford, 1991.
(40) Holtta, S. and Pulliainen, K. *Improving managerial effectiveness at the University of Joensuu, Finland*, IIEP, Paris, 1992.

(41) Jappinen, A. "Current situation of the development and use of personal indicators in Finland". In *International Journal of Institutional Management in Higher Education*, Vol. 11, No. 2, July 1987.
(42) Hufner K. Presentation to the IIEP Current Issues Seminar, 25 February 1994.
(43) Amsterdamski S. et al. "Perceptions of dilemmas of reform". In *European Journal of Education*, Vol 28 No. 4 1993.
(44) Lajos T. "Perspectives, Hopes and Disappointments". In *European Journal of Education* Vol. 28, No. 4 1993.
(45) Drysdale, R. *Higher education in Latin America*, mimeo, World Bank, March 1987.
(46) Vargas, Lora W. et al. *Propuesta de Modificacion de la Estructura Organica de la Universidad Nacional, Hweredia*, September 1990.
(47) Hecquet, I. *Projet Columbus. Visites auprès de huit institutions*, 6 August 1991.
(48) Merino Brito, C. et. al. Modernización administrativa de la Universidad de Concepción, Chile. IIEP, 1994.
(49) Cox C. (ed) "Forms of governance in higher education, new prospects". FLACSO Santiago de Chile November 1990.
(50) Lampe, A. *National Experimental University of Guayana, Venezuela*. IIEP research proposal 1990.
(51) Musselin C.; Friedberg E. "Weakness of government system in universities". Conference on the Financing of higher education. *Revue française de Finances Publiques* No. 27, 1989.
(52) Peisert H. et al. *Higher education in the Federal Republic of Germany*, CEPES Bucharest 1990.
(53) Teichler U. Germany in Neave G. (ed.) op.cit.
(54) Moscati R. Italy in Neave G. (ed.) op cit.
(55) Ghanam, A. *Indian study for ACU*, New Delhi Conference of Executive Heads, January 1991.
(56) Rao, K.V. "Financial deficits in universities". In *University News*, 19 July 1993.
(57) Saxena, R. *Governance of Indian universities in higher education*, Vol. 20, No. 1, July 1990.
(58) Clark, B. and Neave, G. *Encyclopaedia of Higher Education*, Pergamon Press, Oxford, 1992.
(59) Mitra, C.R. *Management of innovation: a case-study of the Birla Institute of Technology and Sciences*, IIEP, Paris, 1994.
(60) Gaidzanwa R.B. *Governance Issues in African universities*. Paper for DAE, University of Zimbabwe, January 1994.
(61) Maliyamkono T. "Higher Education in Eastern and Southern Africa". *Prospects* Vol. XXI No. 3 1991.
(62) Ghana University Rationalization Committee Report 1989.
(63) Information Bulletin, Universities of Nigeria No. 304, 1990.
(64) Mokoena, M. Visit November 1993.
(65) Clark, B. and Neave, G. idem.

(66) Moustafa M. "Faculty Development Plan for Arab Universities". In *Higher Education Policy*, Vol. 5, No. 4, 1992.
(67) Richards, A. "Higher education in Egypt". *World Bank Working Paper* February 1992.
(68) UNESCO, University of Qatar Evaluation Report, Paris 1993
(69) Nachi, M. Ministry of Education and Science, Tunisia. Visit September 1992.

Chapter 5

Strategies adopted at national and institutional levels to improve overall university management

Chapters 2 and *3* have shown the critical role of government agencies in initiating change in the management of higher educational institutions, while *Chapter 4* noted the trends in overall institutional management and gave some specific examples of change. It is the purpose of this chapter to bring together government strategies and the institutional changes and to explore in particular the implications for developing countries.

1. Self-regulation and accountability implemented

The countries in this group for the most part differ in the extent of government pressure, the detailed guidance given, the extent and rapidity of change and the way it was designed and implemented. The previous type of management structure and the main locus of decision-making influenced the way universities responded to government or market requirements.

Analysis will start where government pressure has been strongest, i.e. the United Kingdom and Australia. Both formerly had similar collegial styles of decision-making and the governments adopted strategies with much the same objectives. They have therefore been grouped together (see *Chart 1*).

More details of the strategies and changes as they affected specific management domains will be given in subsequent chapters.

The two governments have fairly comprehensively covered both system and institutional management. Strategies were designed to cover all domains. They were introduced progressively and those concerned with quality of teaching and educational delivery are still under review. Such an overall approach to implementation of change corresponds to the thesis put forward in the BITS case study at the institutional level: *change in any domain of higher education is likely to affected all others.*

Chart 1. Changes in institutional management resulting from Government strategies in Australia and the United Kingdom

Major Government Strategies	Changes in Institutional Management
Australia/United Kingdom Strong, direct pressure, detailed guidance, rapid change.	
1988 Policy Statement: unified national system. Rationalization according to target student numbers (Australia). 1988 Educational Reform Act (United Kingdom), rationalization by funding pressure.	Multi-campus amalgamations Mergers. Regional networks and other linkages.
Commission reports outlining ways of improving university management.	Centralization of administration and services. Consultative top-down management. Management teams, e.g. Vice Chancellor supported by Pro Vice Chancellors for Finance, Administration, Research. Flatter hierarchy, fewer committees. Grouping of departments into fewer Schools or Faculties.
Policy of value for money. 1988 Formula funding, and incentive schemes. 1991 Relative funding adjustment mechanism (Australia). Separation of funding for teaching and research. Financial audit with stronger influence on financial management in institutions (United Kingdom).	Applications for funding supported by profiles and performance data. Basic units as cost centres. Use of similar formulae or adjustment mechanisms for allocations to basic units.
Clarification of role and objectives. Educational profiles, Conceptual framework for quality management (Australia).	Mission statements, strategic plans. Attempts to implement TQM. Special units or posts for planning, quality, evaluation, research, etc.
Investment in computer networks and software Investment in staff development.	Computerization, MIS production of statistics and performance indicators, training programmes.
Accountability mechanisms. Higher Education Committee to monitor profiles (Australia). 1993 HEFC Quality Assessment of teaching affects funding (United Kingdom) Use of performance indicators and comparisons.	Annual reports oriented to accountability and marketing. Self-evaluation according to set guidelines. 1990 United Kingdom University Higher Education Quality Council peer review.

Implementation was preceded by studies, pilot projects, commissions, green papers, and widespread discussion in the universities and the press. There was a stream of articles and studies from the academic community, many of them anxious about quality, and some of them latterly pleading for some respite from continual change. Problems were experienced. Some institutions procrastinated; some lacked the necessary managerial skills – in one or two cases in the United Kingdom, the university lost its financial autonomy until its affairs were put in order. The changes proved very expensive in time and money. In the United Kingdom a debate is still going on about just how much evaluation is necessary, whereas in Australia, accountability mechanisms are simpler.

Descriptions of change at the institutional level in the United Kingdom showed greater resistance at older universities with traditional collegial multiple committee decision-making structures than in former polytechnics where the executive level had always been more powerful. Strategies to implement change within institutions followed those adopted at national level: sensitization and communication, task forces and committees. The more radical the change, the more emphasis had to be given to sensitization and the more the staff had to be involved. It was important to keep the momentum going, and for all concerned to realize that the process was a long-term one.

In Australia, decisions to amalgamate were left to the institutions, the target numbers and deadlines being set by the government. They resulted from senior level consultations between, the most critical discussions taking place in the junior partners (colleges) who felt they were to lose their independence. Some of these did withdraw from preliminary negotiations to seek more equal relationships elsewhere. Amalgamations have in some cases resulted in the type of federated multi-campus institutions or systems common in the United States, where the parent institution has the role of negotiation for funding, overall planning, collection of data, reporting and monitoring its system.

The Netherlands is a formerly highly centralized system, in which the Ministry still decides on admission numbers and standards of entry for each institution. Faculty power predominates in the institutions. As might be expected, some differences in the implementation of self-regulation are therefore apparent (see *Chart 2*).

Chart 2. Changes in institutional management resulting from Government strategies in the Netherlands

Major Government Strategies	Changes in Institutional Management
Netherlands Strong pressure but implementation by universities association.	
1985 Law on Higher Education Autonomy and Quality to permit greater autonomy. 1987 Plan for Higher Education and Research covering publication of Government plan in year 1 and university plan in year 2. Three-year policy/budget/evaluation cycle. Formula output funding. Separation of teaching and research funds. Mission budget for innovations.	Strategic plans as basis of funding. Mission statements. Devolvement of policy/budget/ evaluation cycle to faculties. Faculty management teams. Annual reporting system.
1987-91 selective contraction and expansion according to priority sectors.	Mergers of polytechnics.
Six-yearly quality assessment by discipline. Inspectorate to ensure that assessment carried out.	1989 Universities Association to take responsibility for self-assessment, peer visit and report.
Ministry Information Statute (list of basic data to be supplied).	Information systems and use of performance indicators.

There are fewer government mechanisms, and less change in the decision-making structure in the universities; faculties have taken on the new tasks and have to a large extent retained their decision-making powers. The executive level has not always been successful in imposing strong policies to counterbalance the faculties, and the structure may still be composed of separate 'fiefdoms'(1); in other words, there has been less change in the location of decision-making power in this type of continental bottom-heavy university structure. A more radical approach to institutional management was taken by a polytechnic which regrouped its faculties and then negotiated contracts with them which incorporated incentives. Here the executive level is stronger and more corporate in nature.

The last country to be examined in this group, the *United States*, is the one where the least government intervention has been experienced (see *Chart 3*).

Chart 3. Changes in institutional management resulting from Government strategies in the United States

Major Government Strategies	Changes in Institutional Management
United States Diversified, market-oriented, periodic state evaluation.	
Increased establishment of State Boards for Education. Commissions and reports, e.g. 1986 Governors' Task Force on college quality. Federal and state audits. Periodic state evaluation. Rankings by educational agencies.	Multi-campus state systems headed by system-wide administration for policy, information base, reporting and business management. Professionalization of executive-level posts. Strategic planning, mission statements. Implementation of TQM. Reinforcement of management at faculty and department levels. Performance incentives for management and research. Extensive use of MIS and performance indicators. Annual self-evaluation by each basic unit.

The improvement of managerial capacity at all levels seems to have been a major feature in United States universities, due, it is said, to the demands made by expansion(2). The additional level of system-wide administration evidently assists state governments in obtaining the information needed for state planning and in theory should assist control. On the other hand, the universities are widely criticized for the amount they spend on administration. This style of management requires extra specialized staff (for the production of data, information systems, and plans) whose cost may to some extent be offset by the eventual elimination of manual processes and by improved decision-making. A study conducted in the USA(3) attempted to establish whether management was more cost effective under conditions of de-regulation, since there are institutions with degrees of autonomy ranging from state agency to complete independence. The study found no evidence of lower or higher administrative costs in the different classifications. Better quality of students, staff and research was associated with large universities located in high income areas or with a high level of state support. The degree of autonomy made no significant contribution to any of the limited number of variables considered. However, these findings have to be supplemented by further research on, for example, the costs of centralized control. There are also other benefits of flexibility which are harder to measure, such as value added in the learning process, administrative performance and adaptation to environmental needs; these may be precisely those which governments implementing self-regulatory measures are seeking to maximize.

Change in USA institutions was accomplished by extensive discussions, presentation of information, monthly forums, pilot projects and academic participation. These strategies were also used in other self-regulatory systems although professionalization of top executive posts, especially in finance and business management, by recruitment of non-academics has not been common in Europe outside the United Kingdom. However, training academics for management has been a feature in all countries of this group. University structures now also contain a number of specialized posts or units, such as Planning, Industrial Liaison, Computing and Information Systems, etc. Indeed, it has been suggested that one advantage of the Australian amalgamations was the acquisition by institutions of expertise which they could not have afforded previously(4).

Lack of time for team-work was found to be one obstacle to change in United States universities. Another was resistance by any group which perceived a threat to diminish their sphere of responsibility. Avoiding such threats provides a good reason for the Dutch universities' implementation of their planning/budget/evaluation cycle through faculty management, though it remains to be seen whether in the long run this weakens the effect of the change. The location of power in the United Kingdom and Australian collegial committee systems was always much more fluid, and the government pressure for management change was greater, so the strengthening of the executive level in these two countries was less difficult.

a. Improvements in efficiency and effectiveness?

What has been achieved by all this investment in management changes between 1985 and 1993? The OECD IMHE programme and the governments concerned are endeavouring to supply an answer. The former has just established a revised set of indicators for higher education which, while not allowing direct comparison between countries, will nevertheless give a better idea of performance. Each system, of course, is still very much marked by traditional characteristics from its past; for example, the United Kingdom was a low entry system with high completion rates and emphasis on quality. However, the present general objective for all these countries is the establishment of a system of mass, lower cost higher education which maintains quality and is capable of adapting appropriately to rapid socio-economic and technological change.

Statistical yearbooks and journals give some information about progress towards these goals up to 1990 or 1991.

(i) Student numbers

The pace of expansion towards mass higher education has quickened:

Table 1. Number of students per 100, 000 inhabitants

	1985	1989	1990
Australia	2 348	2 622	2 839
Netherlands	2 795	2 948	3 205
United Kingdom	1 824	2 057	2 192
USA	5 136	5 469	5 591

Source: UNESCO Statistical Yearbook 1993.

(ii) Cost

Governments and researchers have issued a number of reports on trends in expenditure. For example, the Netherlands increased student numbers by 40 per cent between 1975 and 1990, but the unit cost decreased by 27 per cent, leaving the total budget unchanged (5). In the United Kingdom, the unit of resource per student granted by the HEFC in the United Kingdom fell 22 per cent from 1989 to 1993 (Times Higher, 3 December 1993). These trends are confirmed by the UNESCO World Education Report (1993):

Table 2. Current expenditure per student at tertiary level as a multiple of GNP per capita

	1980	1990
Australia	0.51	0.56
Netherlands	0.74	0.62
United Kingdom	0.80	0.42
USA	n.a.	0.21

Source: idem.

The USA, of course, relies more on private funding mechanisms and university programmes are relatively costly. Both the United Kingdom and Australia are proceeding to greater cost recovery with the introduction of student loans, and fees-only grants, etc. (see *Chapter 6*)

(iii) Quality

Indicators from the OECD publication "Education at a Glance" 1992 and 1993 shed some light as regards quality:

Table 3. Indicators for the years 1988 and 1991 for certain self-regulatory countries

| | Graduation rate as per cent national age group || Per cent with Science or Engineering degree ||
	1988	1991	1988	1991
Australia	20	24	22	19
Netherlands	11	8 (dr.)	23	22
United Kingdom	16	18	-	26
USA	26	30 (colleges also)	14	15

Source: OECD: Education at a Glance, 1992-1993.

Three of the four countries increased their graduation rates, while maintaining roughly similar proportions of Science and Engineering graduates.

A considerable number of performance indicators have been established, towards which institutions contribute information annually. Apart from the more usual ones of graduation rates, drop-outs, staff/student ratios by discipline, etc., national governments (in this case Australia) are looking at:

- ratio of applications to places offered;
- percentage of minority groups enrolled;
- graduate employment immediately following graduation, by field of study;
- starting salaries of graduates;
- employer satisfaction;
- tertiary education attainment in the 25 to 64 year old age group.

For specific assessment of the effectiveness of institutional management, the following factors have been listed for use as indicators in external review (Williams Committee, Australia 1976):

- objectives set for the institution, their clarity and relevance;
- selection procedures for staff and students and design of courses consistent with objectives;
- provision for staff induction, development and performance assessment;
- codes of professional conduct for teaching and research;
- dropout rates; their level in the light of admission policies;
- review of exam results by course and type of students;
- review of teaching and exam methods in the light of exam results;
- relation of academic and financial plans;
- comparative cost studies and performance indicators in resource management;
- structure of decision making that allows redeployment of resources according to changing needs;
- provision for external and internal appraisals that do not rely directly on interested parties.

Most of these are used in peer evaluations in self-regulatory systems, examples of which will be given in subsequent chapters in *Part III*. It may be concluded that a good beginning has been made in converting what were high cost systems into much leaner and more accountable ones by a means (self-regulation) which is in keeping with the traditional autonomy of the universities and with the free market economic context. Decision making is based on hard data, priorities and accountability: institutions are in principle better equipped to face a period of rapid social and technological change, though improvement is still needed; the respective governments are not entirely happy with university performance or accountability and envisage further legislation in the near future.

2. Self-regulation in transition

Governmental pressure to improve the effectiveness of universities has increased more gradually in the Nordic countries. However, it began to be felt more strongly in the 1990s, particularly in Finland, where the financial situation had become much more difficult (see *Chart 4*).

Chart 4. Changes in institutional management resulting from Government strategies in Finland.

Major Government Strategies	Changes in Institutional Management
Finland Gradual change steered by forward mapping and pilot projects.	
1987 Act on Development of HE for 1987-96 including decentralization of decision making.	
1988 Act to increase authority of executive level and Deans. Relaxation of bureaucratic controls.	
Planning dialogue between Ministry of Education and universities. Five-year plans, profiles, objectives and resources needed.	Pilot project model for system: Executive-level role of integration by dialogue, information systems, plan and mission statement.
Funding of pilot projects on institutional management, budgeting and educational delivery. Lump sum budgets according to output formula.	Devolved budgeting to departments and decision-making on use of staff and physical resources.
Council of Higher Education Departments: evaluation of teaching and research.	Self-evaluation annually.
National computerized data base, 13 performance indicators selected.	Central support services, including computerization and performance indicators

The changes in Finland are particularly interesting, since until recently the system had been highly centralized, even in institutional administrative matters. The executive level, departments and support services have all been given attention. The strategies used to bring about change may provide useful pointers for other centralized systems. In this case, apart from discussions and dissemination of information in campus newsletters, government officials came to lecture in order to persuade staff of the reality of the change. Certain key individuals in each university were identified as crucial actors to be won over. Obstacles were similar to those found elsewhere: wide variation in the managerial ability of department heads and the time needed for the change, during which momentum has to be maintained. The use of a 'model' in the Finnish case appears to have been necessary because of the reluctance of universities in the system to make radical moves(6).

Elsewhere in the Nordic countries, similar action was taken to hand over more managerial authority to institutions. The situations of Sweden and Norway differ markedly, however (see *Chart 5*). In Norway from 1970 to 1987 there were few government initiatives, and a continuous modest increase in resources, so there was little to disturb the administration. The 1990 Act was therefore greeted with greater scepticism, and there was both resistance to increased departmental management and fear of competition for funding.

Sweden, on the other hand, had experienced reform on a grand scale ever since the 1977 amalgamations. Over 100 institutions were then merged into 34, and responsibilities were decentralized to the regions. More reforms came in the 1980s, giving greater managerial discretion to universities. Complete self-regulatory management came only in 1993, as part of a process which is apparently intended to culminate in fully autonomous chartered universities. This gradual transition to self-regulation has been steered from the top down, and thus may also provide useful input for a model of change for centralized systems. The effects in the base units have varied; for example, some awaited instructions on evaluation from the centre, while others went ahead with course evaluation by students(7).

All three countries have strengthened institutional management at both executive and departmental levels, and have given management training in the basic units. Changes were all initiated from the top down, after pilot projects and studies. Parts of the centralized system remain, and there is some hesitation in the institutions to entirely believe in the change and a tendency to wait for further orders.

Expansion of higher education, as can be seen from the figures below, has taken place at a fairly regular pace in Finland and Norway, leaving behind Sweden, which remained stable up to 1990. It will be noted that the figures for Finland and Norway are somewhat higher in 1990 than in European countries in the first group examined. These

Innovations in university management

countries also spent relatively less in 1980, but in Norway and Sweden, expenditure had risen by 1990 to reach the same proportion as in the United Kingdom. in 1990:

Table 4.   Number of students per 100,000 inhabitants

	1985	1989	1990	1991
Finland	2 611	3 126	3 326	3 478
Norway	2 279	3 061	3 357	3 613
Sweden	2 200	2 169	2 248	2 407

Source: Idem.

Chart 5.   Changes in institutional management resulting from Government strategies in Sweden and Norway.

Major Government Strategies	Changes in Institutional Management
Sweden	National Association for Higher Education established by institutions.
1980s Informatics: regional centres and national network.	Information systems.
1986 Reform of structure of academic profession.	Universities may appoint non-tenured staff.
1987 Broad programme budgeting. Boards of Governors (six out of eleven to be external)	Greater discretion in resource allocation Greater external influence.
National Board projects on self-analysis and self-evaluation. 1990 Council for Renewal of Undergraduate Education: projects.	Vice Chancellors and Governing Boards responsible for internal structure, planning, finance and staff appointments.
1993 Ministry of Education Evaluation Agency and national audit unit. Three-year funding system with quality incentives.	Self-evaluation part of annual budget process. Department heads given training and more management responsibility in setting goals, planning and use of resources.
Debate on adoption of university charters for full autonomy.	

Norway	
1990 Act giving greater self-government to universities (plus guidance on role of Senate, etc.).	Senates (of nine to thirteen members) to act as steering committees.
Five-year strategic planning. Government office to oversee strategic planning. Lump sum funding.	Strategic planning and mission statements Grouping of departments and assignment of administrative staff Training in departmental leadership.
Reporting: universities to demonstrate results.	Each department to plan, manage its own funds and report each year.

Table 5. Current expenditure per student at tertiary level as a multiple of GNP per capita

	1980	1990
Finland	0.37	0.41
Norway	0.42	0.31
Sweden	0.35	0.42

Source: Idem

Table 6. Other Indicators

	Graduation rate as per cent national age group		per cent with Science or Engineering degree	
	1988	1991	1988	1991
Finland	17	17	32	33
Norway	24	31	15	17
Sweden	13	12	24	26

Source: idem.

As to output achieved, Norway's graduation rate at 31 per cent much increased in only 3 years, while Finland is stable at a much lower figure of 17 per cent. Sweden at 12 per cent is also low, especially when compared with the United Kingdom, which has proportionately fewer students. Proportions with Science and Engineering degrees increased in all three countries and are high in Finland (33 per cent) and Sweden (26 per cent) but relatively low in Norway (17 per cent).

These countries did not suffer so much from the problem of relatively high cost when compared with the first group, where the need for radical action was consequently greater. However, Finland and Sweden are obviously interested in attaining greater efficiency in the educational process.

The above completes the analysis of the two classifications where self-regulation and accountability have actually been introduced. There are some common trends in changes to institutional structures and decision-making though the way these were brought about differs. Some were the result of detailed government policy (e.g. Norway); some derived from general guidelines (e.g. United Kingdom), while others derived from management theory or analysis of business experience (Finland, United States), which was a basis for policies in all countries. Implementation was led by the government from above in most countries, an exception being the Netherlands. However, universities in all these countries made major inputs to policy through pilot projects, studies and discussion.

The experiences described show that the greatest decision-making power may lie at the bottom (the Netherlands), at the apex (Government, Norway) or at the university executive level (United States), but that the trend is towards more balance between all levels. Where the executive had little power, it has been increased, and where academics had the most power, this has been decreased. Should this continue, efficient management in universities may reflect real partnerships between those at all levels of responsibility, each contributing its own expertise and being accountable to the others. Universities have attempted by collective action to strengthen themselves in dealing with government. An example is the United Kingdom Committee of Vice Chancellors and Principals, which has become an important pressure group, proactive on policy and ready to deal with hard economic issues.

Another change that is highlighted is the much greater support for the improvement of management performance at all levels by the provision of additional equipment, expertise, staff and guidelines.

3. Self-regulation in difficulty

For those countries where "self-regulation and accountability" has not already been implemented, a summary can be made of legislation or proposals for change in government higher education steering policies (see *Chart 6*). Where there is information on actual recent changes in university management, this will be included. However, many of these

Chart 6. Changes in institutional management resulting from Government strategies in Eastern and Central Europe

Changes in Government Steering Strategies	Changes in University Management
Eastern and *Central Europe* Strong pressure for change.	
Policies support university autonomy and need for modern management. Privatization. Revenue generation.	Joint ventures.
Russia/Bulgaria: contract funding with state/ enterprises. *Ukraine/Poland:* system reform.	University Boards: participation of enterprises and banks. Control of land, buildings, budgets and programmes.
Hungary: Rationalization. 1993 Bill on Higher Education: accreditation. *Poland*: September 1990 Law academic career structure, more autonomy on structure and curricula. Election of Rectors and deans. *Slovak Republic*: May 1990 Law on Higher Education. Full autonomy to universities. Elected Senates. Accreditation Committee to evaluate quality of teaching and research. *Czech Republic*: May 1990 Law as above. 1993 New Act on Higher Education to clarify mission of research university. 5 Year Plan 1992-97: target 20 per cent revenue from private sources.	Rectors Conference established. Regional higher education centres created by grouping institutions around universities and organizing common facilities. Self-assessment of course content. No change in structures Growth of private colleges for languages, business, economics Growth of teacher training in languages. Council of Higher Education of elected university representatives established. Universities to formulate their own statutes, structure, programmes and number of students. Opening of branch institutes in towns supported by municipalities. Rectors and Deans elected.
Latin America: General desire for reform More autonomy, evaluation, closer links with industry. Long-standing privatization but still increasing.	Strategic plans. Computerization, information systems.
Mexico: National Commission for the Evaluation of Higher Education. Incentive bonuses to staff.	Some institutional self-analysis and decentralization of management functions.
Chile: National Council on Higher Education to accredit and supervise institutions. Fund for Institutional Development to improve quality.	Some institutional self-analysis and decentralization of management functions.

universities are not able to take management initiatives until the government has agreed. The universities of two groups of countries suffer from this difficulty. Those belonging to Central and Eastern Europe on the one hand and a large number of those belonging to Latin America on the other.

Of these two groups of countries, those in Eastern and Central Europe seem to have taken a more direct approach to management reform, but without 'accountability' measures. Change has been impeded by the poor economic situation, creating fear of unemployment among academics. The general situation is reflected in student ratios which are for the most part decreasing. In consequence, relative unit expenditures have increased in Poland and the Czech and Slovak Republics, while in the former USSR expenditure has been contained by measures such as payments by employers.

Table 7   Number of students per 100,000 inhabitants

	1985	1989	1990	1991
Former USSR	2 060	1 930	1 900	
Poland	1 221	1 330	1 427	1 398
Hungary	933	954	970	1 017
Czech/Slovak Reps.	1 093	1 191	1 216	1 128

Source: Idem.

Table 8   Current expenditure per student at tertiary level as a multiple of GNP per capita

	1980	1990
Former USSR	0.42	0.42
Poland	0.47	0.76
Hungary	0.88	0.79
Czech/Slovak Reps.	0.47	0.58

Source: idem.

As noted in *Chapter 4*, in the Central and Eastern European countries, too much power has been granted to faculties and their Councils. The executive level has little, and Rectors therefore have difficulty in establishing leadership in order to initiate organizational change. However, there has been some development of new curricula and special institutes for business management, economics and languages; a number have benefitted from donor assisted staff development programmes.

Latin American countries have tended to adopt the more indirect strategy of evaluation in an attempt to change attitudes gradually and to avoid the confrontation which has previously caused reforms to be shelved. However, this may take rather a long time (as suggested by the French experience) unless it is backed up by stringent follow-up action. Only Mexico and Chile have introduced incentive measures, the other general strategy which is useful where salaries are relatively low. Some individual institutions have undertaken strategic planning, computerization, information systems and self-analysis.

Of those countries which have made specific attempts to improve management, the student ratio in Brazil has remained stable, Mexico's is declining while Chile (due to greater emphasis on privatization) and Venezuela (where funding was maintained) have steadily expanded student numbers in recent years.

Table 9   Latin America: Number of students per 100,000 inhabitants

	1985	1989	1990	1991
Brazil	n.a.	1 065	1 074	1 075
Chile	1629	1 843	1 938	2 144
Colombia	1328	1 496		
Mexico	1598	1 589	1 552	
Venezuela	2581	2 798	2 847	

Source: UNESCO: Statistical Year Book, 1993.

About expenditure, less information is available. The effects of privatization measures can be seen in Chile and Colombia, with a heavy impact from student loans and tuition fees in Chile.

Table 10. Current expenditure per student at tertiary level as a multiple of GNP per capita

	1980	1990
Brazil	0.59	1.10
Chile	1.11	0.29
Colombia	0.41	0.36

Source: idem.

4. Centralized planning and control

a. Continental Europe

The desire to improve university management has been clearly expressed by governments in France, Portugal and Italy, less so in Germany and Austria (see Chart 7). Italian, French and German universities underwent internal restructuring in the 1970s when the chair system was changed to departments, *Unités d'Enseignement, later Unités de Formation et Recherche* (UFR) and *Fachbereiche*. However, as noted in the CNE report cited in *Chapter 4*, these may now need further regrouping.

In Belgium, the central government authorities have not given much attention to the structure, management or autonomy of universities, being concerned with holding the political-ideological balance. Following federalization, change is expected in the Flemish universities(8), (see *Chapter 7*).

In Italy, the political parties have agreed on reforms but have been opposed by the universities, whose structures have been described as 'balkanized'(9). In Germany, the Federal Ministry wanted to take over stronger powers in education but the States refused, by default leaving the universities able to continue as before.

Chart 7. Changes in institutional management resulting from Government strategies in France, Germany, Belgium and Italy.

Changes in Government Steering Strategies	Changes in University Management
France 1984 CNE (evaluation). 1988 Information Systems for accounts, students etc. 1989 Four-year contracts and partnerships with regional authorities. 1992 Group for Computerized Management. 1993 Statement on Higher Education Costs. 1994 Pilot project for 7 new universities to opt out of national framework.	UFR information systems. Four year plans. Some additional funding from local authorities. Cable networks.
Germany HIS to assist with software. State funding of pilot projects to teach more efficiently.	Information systems. 1988 West German Rectors' Conference defined performance indicators.
Belgium 1986 Saint Ann Plan. 9 per cent budget to research, universities to increase revenue generation. Fixed cost price per student reduced. 1989 Federalization. Flemish to follow Netherlands model.	University programmes free to respond to market. Little government intervention except for funding. Some regrouping and additional posts in Flemish universities.
Italy 1989 Law: universities control staff appointments and teaching methods. National Committee for Evaluation.	

The Friedberg and Musselin study(10) of management in French and German universities concludes that the management model is a bureaucratic and collegial one of cohabitation without conflict, with most decisions being made in the basic units, except for the budget. The importance of the university structure is seen to lie more in what it impedes than in what it enables. University executive management is weak, being directed by elected and rotating representatives who are not expected to intervene in their colleagues' work. The experience of regrouping departments was similar in the two countries, occurring only after long resistance and having only small impact or none at all. The major difference found between the two systems was that the German universities were more organized and better maintained, and had more respect for the regulations. The reasons for the negligible impact of this major restructuring will be discussed later in this chapter. It is particularly interesting, since regrouping departments, in self-regulatory systems, been considered critical in achieving more effective management.

The number of students has steadily grown in this group of countries, ratios being similar to those in the European self-regulatory countries. Current expenditure per student as a percentage of GNP per capita is much lower than in the European countries of the first group, but this efficiency indicator is offset by the lower graduation rate as a percentage of the total age group; France is the only country to have increased its ratio over the period. This is a function of public policy. Admission to universities is open to all those with the requisite secondary school leaving certificate, and selection is by drop-out during the first years of university. In these countries, therefore, as with the Nordic ones, the preoccupation is to improve efficiency in the educational process; particular problems are the long duration of study in Germany and the high drop-out rates in Belgium and France. It is not yet clear whether the new French contract system will have an effect.

Table 11. Number of students per 100,000 inhabitants

	1985	1989	1990	1991
France	2 318	2 812	2 995	3 245
Germany	2 540	2 810		
Italy	2 074	2 359	2 519	2 656
Belgium	2 511	2 725		

Source: Idem.

Table 12. Current expenditure per student at tertiary level as a multiple of GNP per capita

	1980	1990
France	0.29	0.23
Germany	0.31	0.29
Italy	0.18	0.28
Belgium	0.49	0.30

Source: Idem.

Table 13. Other Indicators

| | Graduation rate as per cent national age group || Percentage with Science or Engineering degree ||
	1988	1991	1988	1991
France	12	16	30	n.a.
Germany	13	13	29	32
Italy	8	9	15	17
Belgium	12	13	33	n.a.

Source: Idem.

In *Asia*, changes have been mostly those designed to allow universities to acquire some additional funding from students or industry. These have had only a marginal impact on management practice and structures have remained unchanged, bureaucracy and politicization in some cases constituting major obstacles (see *Chart 8*).

It is difficult for heavily populated countries to raise the proportion of students. India had 583 per 100,000 inhabitants in 1985, Pakistan 266, and China 180 and decreasing in 1991. Malaysia and Indonesia are slightly higher at 700-800, while Thailand (1763) and the Philippines (2596) approach European levels. The Republic of Korea, which in 1991 had 4023, is rapidly catching up with the USA.

Chart 8. Changes in institutional management resulting from Government strategies in Asia.

Changes in Government Strategies	Changes in University Management
Privatization.	Private initiatives.
Some new technology.	Links to industry.
India: 1985 National policy (including autonomous departments). 1993 incentives for income generation. Control of quality tightened.	Implemented in only a few departments.
China Economic-administrative changes with reference to funding students, fees, a few mergers, broader curricula.	Widely implemented but did not affect management - see chapters on finance and research.
Pakistan Decentralization to provinces. Universities may acquire industrial assets.	
Hong Kong Accreditation system.	
Philippines Accreditation system.	Internal self-assessment.

Current expenditures per student are in most cases declining, the effect of privatization and the introduction of fees being very evident in China, the Philippines and the Republic of Korea. The problems of management at government and institutional levels in Pakistan and India may account for the relative rises in cost in those countries.

Table 14. Current expenditure per student at tertiary level as a multiple of GNP per capita

	1980	1990
India	0.72	0.83
China	3.62	1.93
Pakistan	1.34	1.57
Malaysia	1.49	1.24
Philippines	0.14	0.11
Korea Rep.	0.16	0.06

Source: Idem.

The variety of contexts for higher education in Asia would require implementation of different strategies and styles of management. It is evident that centralized planning and control has served the Republic of Korea well; the government ministries involved have made use of copious data and analyses and forecasts in their orientation of higher education(11). In other countries, centralized planning has not been managed so well, and a mix of free market and self-regulation might function better. Despite the unfavourable environment, there are examples of good practice in Asian countries which show that given the necessity to survive private institutions can prosper and innovate in ways which have not succeeded in public institutions (see case study of BITS, India). The managerial practices of some private institutions in developing countries offer useful examples to state institutions; they base their decisions on hard data, give incentives to staff and generally display many of the features shown in self-regulatory systems. While such private institutions may rely largely on serving the wealthier sections of society, this has also been a feature of many public systems.

The situation in Africa as regards higher education is less varied (see *Chart 9*).

Innovations in university management

Chart 9. Changes in institutional management resulting from Government strategies in Africa.

Changes in Government Strategies	Changes in University Management
Off-campus students. Cuts in student allowances, self-financing bookshops and cafes. Privatization.	Computerization. Strategic plans.
Ghana Rationalization. Computers.	University Council to be responsible for finance and staff allocation. New posts of Business Manager and Department Administrator.
Nigeria Consolidation and rehabilitation. Formula funding on course balance, number enrolled, staff quality and norms. Evaluation by Visitation Panels (including administration and finance).	Grouping of faculties under four or five Provosts.
Zambia Stipulation of types of expenditure to be met by fees. Staffing norms. 1993 decline in enrolments.	
Kenya Staffing norms. Double intakes.	
Mozambique	Reorganization of university management. New posts, e.g. Rector for Resource Management.
Botswana	Self-analysis. New posts of two Deputy Vice Chancellors for Finance and Administration.

Student participation ranged from 21 per 100,000 inhabitants in Tanzania to 572 in Zimbabwe (1989 figures).

Table 15. Number of students per 100,000 inhabitants

	1985	1989	1990
Ghana	132	127	126
Botswana	181	266	299
Kenya	109	137	187
Senegal	209	253	
Uganda	67	87	100
Tanzania	22	21	
Zambia	128	184	189
Zimbabwe	368	572	496

Source: Idem.

Current expenditures per student have declined relatively to GNP, except in Tanzania where the number of students has remained extremely low.

Table 16 Current expenditure per student at tertiary level as a multiple of GNP per capita

	1980	1990
Botswana	7.04	2.84
Kenya	9.82	6.80
Senegal	4.87	3.44
Uganda	9.16	4.65
Tanzania	19.15	28.43
Zambia	5.85	2.07
Zimbabwe	4.13	1.37

Source: Idem.

The extent of the effort to improve institutional management widely from countries where governments have taken few initiatives, such as Senegal, to Nigeria, where a number of self-regulatory mechanisms have been implemented. The variability might be explained to some extent by donor assistance, which funded the two major reorganizations in Ghana and Mozambique, and differing economic circumstances, such as the relatively prosperous Botswana, where changes are largely a university initiative. There are as yet no reports on the outcomes of major management change. Studies undertaken for the IIEP research programme tend to point to lack of managerial expertise at government level as being a major obstacle to making improvements (see *Part III*).

In most Arab countries, governments have retained strong centralized control over what are generally mass systems, the exceptions being Tunisia and Algeria, which have recently attempted some managerial reforms (see *Chart 10*). The details and experience have not been reported in the non-Arabic world.

Chart 10. Changes in institutional management resulting from Government strategies in Arab countries.

Changes in Government Strategies	Changes in University Management
Kuwait, Egypt: Privatization.	
Tunisia 1988 Grouping of faculties around basic administrative units. 1989 Law on more diversified and autonomous system.	
Algeria 1990 Decentralization of all responsibilities except for budgetary allocation.	

Student numbers are relatively high, though Egypt, Syria and Morocco have recently experienced a slight decrease.

Table 17. Number of students per 100,000 inhabitants

	1985	1989	1990	1991
Egypt	1 837	1 737	1 717	
Algeria	801	1 066	1 146	
Tunisia	573	794	851	925
Qatar	1 493	1 559		
Syria	1 734	1 762	1 740	1 718
Morocco	822	982	952	

Source: Idem.

Tunisia, Morocco and Syria have managed to bring about a relative decrease in current expenditure per student, while that for Egypt has risen.

Table 18. Current expenditure per student at tertiary level as a multiple of GNP per capita

	1980	1990
Egypt	0.58	0.82
Morocco	1.55	0.84
Tunisia	1.94	1.16
Jordan	0.95	1.04
Syria	0.75	0.52

Source: Idem.

Two strategies are common to these developing regions: privatization and the encouragement of income generation. The internal management of institutions has not been a major concern. and the role assigned to many universities in developing countries is often described as merely "day-to-day administration". This situation is, however, becoming less and less acceptable in the face of the demands being made on institutions, such as strategic planning exercises, frequent adjustment of staffing levels, and the mass expansion of student numbers, including double intakes. All these require a management capacity which is often not to be found, as shown by some of the case-studies in subsequent chapters. Such demands are certain to increase in the future as countries develop new policies, such as priority for vocational education, student loans, or creating a market amongst higher educational institutions.

5. **Lessons drawn from the experience of implementing management change: what may be useful for the developing countries?**

Whatever the system at present existing in a country, therefore, institutional management needs to be strengthened. Most systems are at present centralized, the experience of similar systems which are changing may therefore provide the most relevant guidance. For example, the Netherlands bottom-heavy institutional structures may be relevant to Latin

America, though there is a large difference in capacity to fund change. In some developing regions, executive, faculty, and even government management, levels are weak, and the experience of Sweden and Finland may be more pertinent. The purposes of change will depend on the different objectives of national policy, but the processes may have much in common.

Van Vught(12) in 1989 made examined in some detail the theory and experience of change in higher education. Research in the 1980s had shown that most government-initiated reforms had failed, particularly in the curriculum and in governance. It was considered that change could be achieved only when the specific characteristics of individual higher educational institutions, and their departments, were accommodated. On the other hand, it was also seen that departmental innovations in bottom-heavy institutions were for the most part incremental, and often not disseminated because of the fragmented organizational structure of institutions.

However, by 1989 it had become apparent that new ways of steering had brought about some relocation of power. In addition, the greater influence of the market, where this had been allowed to operate, had led to the adoption of managerial styles of management commonly found outside higher education. In Van Vught's opinion, self-regulation appeared to fit the characteristics of higher education better than planning and control since it offered flexibility, responsibility and self-determination. A mix of mildly restrictive instruments was thought likely to be the most successful. This conclusion, is, of course, set within the culture and framework of Western European countries; he does not consider other systems.

A great deal more information has come to light from self-regulatory systems since 1989; this study concentrates on the period from 1987 to 1993. The conjunction of external pressures (economic recession and mass social demand for higher education) and government action in certain countries compelled the universities to acknowledge, some more slowly than others, that changes had to be introduced. Management was to be the main vehicle of change, and had effects throughout the institutions. In these countries, the institutions were assisted with funding and expert advice to make the changes. Consultancies, commissions, pilot projects and surveys have guided universities who possessed little management expertise in specific directions. Each country, though perhaps influenced by experience elsewhere and by current trends in economic thought, adopted the type of steering and institutional management that suited it best; for instance, Australian accountability mechanisms are lighter and simpler than those in the United Kingdom.

Somewhat paradoxically, the governments of the centrally planned systems of Continental Europe, which appeared to have more power over their systems of higher education, were rebuffed in the 1970s and 1980s when they tried to implement major reforms similar to those introduced later in self-regulatory systems. This has since left them more hesitant, and their base units if anything rather stronger. More indirect methods, such as the French strategies of contracts and evaluation, have been used. The significant differences seem to lie in the use of 'evaluation' in the centrally planned countries, as opposed to 'accountability' measures in self-regulatory systems. The general model of 'evaluation' consists of:

- a government or independent agency to oversee the evaluation system;
- self-evaluation prior to regular peer evaluation;
- periodic peer review and site visits by the agency;
- post-evaluation visits by the agency;
- annual reports compiled by the institution from departmental evaluations.

The differences lie in the follow-up: only in the United Kingdom do evaluations or assessments affect funding decisions. Most rely for their effect on publication and the veiled threat that if institutions have not acted to improve matters, the government will do so. This has not so far been shown to be strong enough. The problems of this approach were shown by the analysis of present governance and management systems in French and German universities by Friedberg and Musselin (op.cit.). It was found that the upper decision-making levels played merely a negative role; they might veto proposals emanating from base units but they did not initiate. Staff were more loyal to their units than to the institution as a whole and any change was likely to be resisted by the unit. In the opinion of these authors, changing structures alone would not change the functioning of the institution, which they described as an 'evolving confederation', in which the *leadership* style of management was inappropriate. However, the authors went on to observe that the executive or top level management could only have a real impact if it served the university as a whole, by detecting opportunities and constructing visions for future development. They proposed that the structure be based on a network of intermediate university entrepreneurs capable of managing and animating teaching and research activities. These key staff should be selected by appropriate mechanisms and their capacities and loyalty to the university reinforced.

These suggestions have much in common with self-regulatory systems, but emphasize the location of considerable power in the base units, which presents a risk of continual disequilibrium. Kogan(13) has pointed out that the stronger the base unit, the greater the need for a sound framework for equitable resource allocation and for executive power which can apply rules and criteria across the institution. Moreover, though academics may initiate some kinds of innovation, its diffusion through the institution can only be ensured by the executive. He does not therefore support the view that change can only be achieved "when the specific characteristics of individual higher educational institutions are accommodated", but considers it necessary to develop certain characteristics and erode those which have been demonstrated to be obstacles to improvement. Kogan agrees with Musselin and Friedberg that the values of entrepreneurial management are not intrinsically hostile to academic values. Within universities there have always been market pressures such as those based on research reputation, graduation results, and the award of chairs and grants. Strategies in Continental Europe might build on these characteristics more than they have done, at the same time increasing the responsibilities of the executive and base levels in accountability, and ensuring that follow-up action is taken after evaluation.

One of the major lessons learnt from the experiences of developed countries is that governments cannot afford to neglect the importance of management capacity in institutions. Without it, necessary reforms and economies may fail because of incompetence, inertia or outright resistance.

Another major lesson is the need for university management expertise at government level. Most developing country institutions must wait for government direction or approval; Ministries should therefore ensure their own capacity to give adequate support, facilitating as well as intervening. In some developed countries, the extent of support for successful management reform in the form of expertise and funding has been extremely high. In this respect, groups of developing countries could profit from the setting up of regional forums, on the OECD IMHE model, to pool their expertise and experience. Associations of Universities, such as the A.A.U. in Africa, have such an objective and impetus needs to be given to their work.

Proposed changes must be seen by the public to be necessary and appropriate. They should also be introduced in a comprehensive and phased package, which takes account of the integrated nature of university activities, and ensures that funding and structural change work in the same direction.

Institutional management is the means by which reforms are extended throughout university departments. Reforms should ideally be preceded by analysis of institutional management structures and procedures to ensure that they are adequate. A sufficiently powerful executive level is needed to ensure overall institutional planning, coordination, evaluation and accountability; much of which is lacking in centrally planned systems. Governing Boards with a majority of external can be used to reinforce the executive level, as the Nordic countries have shown.

It has been realised in many countries that not enough emphasis has been put on 'accountability' measures. Evaluation on its own without follow-up exerts insufficient pressure. Government agencies and good executive level management can ensure 'accountability', by providing the necessary. Data, available in a reliable and timely form, have been the basis for successful development in both self-regulatory and centrally planned systems. Developing countries can benefit from the considerable work done to devise meaningful indicators of effectiveness and efficiency.

It is essential to ensure that the momentum of reform is maintained. Deadlines and targets should be set, and mechanisms for feedback established. Pauses for consolidation may prove to be a resistance manoeuvre, and should themselves be resisted.

Similarly, governments, acting as clients and supervisors, should try to establish a policy of continual search for improvement. Systems left to their own devices for long periods come to resent demands for reform as disruptive, rather than seeing them as part of the normal pattern of governance to keep the system up to date. Adaptation and acceptance of change will be an increasingly critical factor in institutional efficiency in the coming years.

The bottom-heavy nature of the centrally planned and controlled Continental European universities may make their experience useful to the Latin American and East European countries. It may be less so in many developing countries, where institutions at both executive and faculty levels are generally weak in decision-making. Here, the Swedish and Finnish experiences may be of some help since they have had a tradition of waiting for the results of pilot projects, surveys and commissions and after discussion, following the government guidelines. Their strategies of change, given below, may thus suggest a useful approach to the improvement of management in institutions in developing countries which already possess relatively efficient government bureaucratic systems.

1. Projects to analyze existing institutional management, budgeting, educational delivery, and particular problem areas defined.
2. Dialogue between Ministries and universities about their respective profiles, objectives, development plans, and projected innovations or solutions.
3. Agencies to support institutional management offering advice and training on structure of decision-making, financial management, computerization, evaluation and accountability mechanisms and organising pilot projects on the innovations or solutions suggested.
4. Setting of timetable for change, and issue of guidelines including accountability procedures (usually annual report and periodic evaluation of institutional activities and programmes).
5. Continuation of reforms in phases to introduce greater discretion in decision-making to universities according to their managerial capacity and national aims and priorities.

The above represents a top-down progressive approach to the improvement of institutional management, consistent with centralized control and weak decision-making capacity in institutions. It emphasizes preliminary analysis, dialogue, support and continued control, with responsibilities only being devolved as capacities improve and trust increases.

Other countries, like India and Pakistan, suffer from the politicization and bureaucratization of the higher education system, which subvert rational management processes. Here strong accountability measures may be the best strategy. Another is the analysis of good practice in successful institutions as a means of changing attitudes and disseminating experience.

In *Part IV*, other lessons will be drawn for specific domains of university management, to be brought together in the final chapter.

References

1. Van Vught, F. *Government strategies and innovation in higher education* Jessica Kingsley, London, (1989).

2. Seagren, A. et al. "The Department Chair", ASHE-ERIC. In *Higher Education Reports* No. 1, 1993.

3. Volkwein J. "State regulation and campus autonomy". In *Higher Education: Handbook of Theory and Research* Agathon Press New York 1987.

4. Sharma, R. Swinburne University of Technology. Briefing, 5 August 1993.

5. De Groot H. *New financial models in higher education: the Dutch case.* IMHE Xth General Conference, Paris September 1990.

6. Kivinen, O.; Rinne, R. *How to steer student flows in higher education.* In Neave, G. and Van Vught F. (eds.), Prometheus Bound, Pergamon, Oxford, 1991.

7. Brandstom, D.; Franke Wieleberg, S. "Steering higher education systems in Europe: the case of Sweden". In *Higher Education in Europe*, Vol. XVII, No. 3, 1992.

8. Wielermans, W. and Vanderhoeven, A., "Market impact and policy". In Neave, G. & Van Vught F. (eds.), Prometheus Bound, Pergamon, Oxford, 1991.

9. Moscati, R., Italy, in Neave, G. (ed.), op. cit.

10. Friedberg, E. and Musselin, C. *En quête d'universités*, L'Harmattan, Paris, 1989.

11. Sanyal B.; Yu Hyun Sook: "Technological development in the micro electronics industry and its implications for educational planning in the Republic of Korea", IIEP Research Report No. 72, IIEP Paris 1989.

12. Van Vught, F. Idem.

13. Kogan, M. "Models of governance and developments in the United Kingdom". In *Higher Education in Europe*, Vol. XVII, No. 3 (1992).

Part IV

Improving selected areas of university management

Chapter 6

Financial management

1. Different types of funding mechanisms

Governments and institutions have rather different requirements as regards funding mechanisms. The State requires a mechanism that can steer and control the higher educational system and provide a means both to ensure value for money and give protection against bad management. Institutions, on the other hand, would like a system that provided stability, predictability, equity (between programmes and institutions), simplicity and practicality. However, stability and predictability have not been characteristics of funding in the past decade in the majority of countries(1), and for some systems funding has become very much less simple.

According to one study(2), until the 1960s funding was mainly incremental; in the 1970s guidelines or formulae tied to enrolment, programme budgeting and evaluation appeared on the scene, while in the 1980s some governments began to provide institutions with incentives for meeting specified priorities. In the 1990s, mechanisms were further developed to empower institutional leadership. The search for an appropriate level of intrusion of the state has led to a great deal of development work(3) on techniques for measuring productivity, programme validity, costs and student outcomes.

In the 1990s, therefore, there exists a much greater variety of funding mechanisms, particularly in developed countries, and research has already begun on their classification. Kaiser *et al*(4), in their study of the OECD countries, suggested three factors in analysing funding mechanisms for their usefulness as instruments of control:

(1) Basis of the grant: Input (staff, operating costs, investment); throughput (educational process; activities performed); output (achievements).

(2) Methods by which allocations are determined: types of criteria and norms set.

(3) Conditions laid down for spending: These may range from wide discretion in spending a lump-sum grant, with the retention of any savings made at the end of the year, to very restricted freedom under earmarked allocations, with savings reverting to the Government at the end of the year.

Incorporating these factors into the four broad categories of university funding prevalent today (as described by Williams(5)), we have the following four types, though in practice elements of more than one category are usually adopted.

Type 1. The university receives a single block grant based on the grant received in the previous period plus an increment and is free to spend this money as it wishes within very broad legal limits. In many countries, this type of funding extends only to expenditure other than salaries and investment, so the freedom is in practice limited.

Type 2. The university submits a periodic (usually annual) budget based on its estimate of the costs of its commitments, and bargains with the government over the proportion of this budget which is to be met. The grants are then 'earmarked' in a line-item budget, and tied to the items specified by the government, with reimbursement only of their actual cost.

The above two funding types have the advantage of being predictable and simple. Planning and control is achieved by prior determination of the funding to be provided, according to certain norms and criteria. Their weakness is the limited extent to which an institution is required to justify existing programmes or to eliminate those that are no longer in demand. Line-item budgets also imply more bureaucratic procedures. In a period of decline in funding per student (as opposed to the usual past increments), universities have found it difficult to make the necessary hard internal choices. Some, as will be shown below, began to operate with mounting deficits under *Type 1* or began to suffer from overcrowding and poor conditions under *Type 2*. There are no incentives to improve output and quality in these types of funding mechanism. Hence the increasing introduction of contracts and formulae.

Type 3. Funds are based on a formula reflecting past performance, but the university is free to spend the funds as it wishes once they are received, though the way it does so may affect future funding. The basis of most formulae is full time equivalent student numbers. These are weighted for factors such as subject mix and level of study, and increasingly governments are trying to extend the elements of weighting to reflect such factors as academic performance and research quality. Formulae have the advantage of making the funding process more transparent, and can be used to steer the activities of institutions. They are becoming more sophisticated. The simplest were based on average cost per full time equivalent student according to field of study and level. However, this offered no incentive for timely completion of degrees and some countries stipulate that funding for any one student may allow only one year's repetition, while others give special bonuses for each student completing a degree on time(6).

Type 4. The university sells its teaching, research and consultancy services under various types of contracts to a wide variety of different customers: students, employers and public authorities (i.e. the market model). As in *Type 3*, this type provides incentives for efficiency but also improves responsiveness to needs as well as encouraging the private sector to take over some of the cost burden. Its operation, for example in the United States, is easier in a modular credit system where students are defined as aggregates of credit according to individual learning programmes, which dissolves distinctions between on- and off-campus students. Students can then purchase specific courses with their grants or vouchers – or from their own resources – and institutions can contract to supply a quantum of credit by category and level. The academic world is somewhat wary of this type of funding mechanism in its pure form, fearing that basic teaching and research could suffer in the long run since the market fluctuates, signalling only short-term changes. It would create greater disparities between institutions, and no agency would be responsible for taking account of the wellbeing of the institution as a whole.

Types 3 and *4* both require information systems, cost analyses, production of indicators and expertise in the preparation of proposals, accounts and reports. Tendering to carry out specific services or research is already quite common, but it is now also seen to be of value for teaching (Denmark, Netherlands, United Kingdom).

It is therefore increasingly the practice to divide up funding into a number of different areas of teaching and research, or to relate it to priority objectives which the government wishes to achieve. Earmarked funds are allocated for such purposes as the establishment of a new programme or research unit at one or several institutions, financing an early retirement or 'new blood' policy, funding investment, information technology, or compensation for teaching overload. Such special purpose funds may take the form of contracts: money is provided on condition that certain objectives are accomplished within the resources available. The same aim can be achieved by incentive budgeting.

Looking to the future, it seems likely that institutions will receive the funds they need in the form of multiple budgets, drawn up according to different criteria: this will give them more autonomy and flexibility with respect to the management of the institution as a whole, and at the same time reduce state appropriations and encourage institutions to attract additional non-state money.

The type of funding mechanism in operation has a strong and often intended impact on institutional practices. Research carried out by the OECD in developed countries(7) showed that even in countries at a similar level of economic development, institutional financial management is quite different under self-regulation, whether in a market or government-steered framework, than in bureaucratic centrally-planned systems. The administration of a university in which the main financial decisions are concerned with allocating a predetermined sum according to academic priorities is very different from one in which most of the important decisions concerned with, for example, the employment of staff, are taken outside the institution. Neither of these has much in common with the market-oriented university in which income is earned directly by the activities of the basic operating units and the individual members of staff within them. In the last case, one of the main preoccupations of the managers is to establish a system of incentives that will encourage all members of the operating units to respond to changing market opportunities in a manner that simultaneously contributes to the income of the university and maintains its academic integrity.

For most countries, it is usually possible to identify a dominant model corresponding to one of the four types in the case of most countries. Though external funding mechanisms may not exactly determine the procedures for internal resource allocation, experience in many countries suggests that *Type 2*, and to some extent *Type 3*, require a substantial measure of bureaucratic regulation to ensure that resources are spent as required by the central funding agency. *Type 1*, and some aspects of *Type 3*, usually permit some degree of collegial management in which academic priorities are very influential, while *Type 4* requires varying degrees of market-orientated management in which entrepreneurialism and the satisfaction of market demands are rewarded.

All institutions must undertake at least the short-term annual budgeting process in order to acquire resources. However, their systems of internal financial management, including allocation of those resources and control of their use, production of accounts and reports, and audit, may be very different according to the type and extent of government funding and policy, the type of institution and its decision-making structure. These differences have in recent years begun to widen considerably as between the self-regulatory and centrally-planned groups of countries.

2. Institutional financial management

The preparation of financial plans and budgets for the institution as a whole and for its different units has always been an important management tool for the co-ordination, control and evaluation of a university. It was the general practice for a special committee to give guidelines to each department for the construction of their budgets. An iterative process then took place in which the plans were submitted, reviewed and revised. This was a centrally managed bargaining process in which individual goals were traded off to the benefit of the organization. Nowadays, however, financial management procedures may take various forms in different institutions. Examples are:

(1) all resources are received, allocated and administered from the centre;
(2) strategic financial decisions are taken at the centre but routine decisions and expenditures are made in departments;
(3) income is top sliced for central administration and services, and the remainder allocated to departments to use in accordance with institutional priorities;
(4) most income is passed on to departments which buy services from the centre.

Systematic attempts to improve institutional budgetary procedures have also been taking place over the last two decades. Examples of these are:

1. *Zero-based budgeting* (ZBB): While an incremental budget may not scrutinize the baseline, ZBB aims at eliminating low-yielding programmes from an institution's activities. It requires periodical defence of all the system's programmes to identify and eliminate those activities that are not necessary. This approach requires four steps:
    (a) each budget unit has to develop a series of packages which describe an activity or function of the unit, and outline alternative levels of provision;
    (b) budget requests are accordingly presented in increments from minimum to maximum levels;
    (c) the results of funding at different incremental levels are shown; and
    (d) incremental packages have to be ranked in priority order by the budget unit.

   The core of the zero-base budgeting model lies in formalized comparison of alternative expenditures. Final budgets are prepared on the basis of the decisions taken between alternatives.
   The complexity of this procedure has deterred most institutions from attempting to adopt it. Where it was tried, it was found that ZBB resulted in *considerable workload, but did not demonstrate a convincing ability to facilitate resource redistribution.* On the other hand, it did assist the process of institution-wide constraint and reduction, ensured that decision-makers were better informed about the programmes of each department, and led to greater involvement of base units in budget preparation. It has been successfully implemented at the University of Amsterdam and in at least one United Kingdom university, and much interest in it is still being shown in India, where the Government is encouraging its introduction(8).

2. *Programme budgeting*: This has been taken up by a large number of universities in the United Kingdom, United States and other self-regulatory countries. It consists of:

    (a) breaking down the university's activities into programmes, with the understanding that each programme is to generate well-identified results;
    (b) budget presentation clearly showing the estimated costs of each programme and their breakdown;
    (c) indicators of *means* (number of teachers, non-teaching staff, unit costs consumable, space, etc.), of *products* and of *results*.

This form of budgetary presentation provides a management framework that allows monitoring of a programme in terms of its resources, its products and its results. Differences between estimates and out turn, and comparisons between programmes, can be analyzed and appropriate corrective measures designed. It has many features in common with ZBB, but does not require prioritizing as a part of the budgetary process. It places emphasis on showing the *actual* resources used and results to be achieved.

Efforts to ensure more rational internal allocation have run into many difficulties, particularly in larger universities. In smaller institutions, allocation is often still done centrally by the administration, but in bigger ones it is more usually negotiated by powerful deans, who have a monopoly of information about the operation of their faculties which is difficult for others to dispute. Scarce resources exacerbate competition, and the relative strength of power relationships between deans, senate, board of governors, governing council and administration influences the outcome(9). Where power is dispersed, conditions favour budgetary approaches which repress conflict; the incremental budget was the classic way of achieving this, since baseline allocations naturally tended to reflect existing power structures. Thus it may be expected that any change in budgeting procedures will meet opposition(10). In addition, decisions as the allocation of resources are in the short run highly determined by the resources the institution has already acquired, in particular its staff and buildings. It is only over time that more options for switching real resources become available. The section below will show how various institutions, under different conditions, have adapted their practices of financial management to meet changing situations.

a. Self-regulation and accountability implemented

In the more market-oriented higher education system in the USA, most of the 3,400 colleges and universities have had to struggle to balance income and spending over the last two decades. A survey by the American Council on Education showed that two-thirds of public four-year institutions have suffered mid-year cuts in their operating budgets since 1990-91. Funds are received from a number of sources, the most important being the federal and state governments and non-government organizations. Most of this income is subject to norms (input and output) and earmarked for particular purposes; it has been calculated that only 10 per cent is unrestricted. However, institutions generate sometimes substantial additional income from short courses, conferences, etc. and thus have quite a degree of freedom for innovation in financial management.

For much of the last decade, the method chosen by many universities to balance budgets was to raise tuition fees, which led to criticism from their clients. It was found that administrative and support costs amounted to 30 per cent of expenditure in public and 40 per cent in private institutions and that these were increasing faster than direct costs of instruction and research. The explanations normally given by university administrators to account for their high costs are labour intensiveness, introduction of the use of technology, salary increases to meet competition and the need to spend more on student aid in order to support special talent. A survey(11) found that elements of a cost-management strategy had been adopted by most universities, i.e.:

- clarification of mission and priorities;
- data base on revenues and costs adequate to determine which programmes are self-supporting and which need subsidy;
- improvement of budgetary procedures and their link with planning;
- accountability mechanisms.

One case in the USA in which such strategies were adopted is described in *Box 6*.

Some institutions have gone further in devolving financial management, using a system of "responsibility centre budgeting". Indiana University is one. The new President, on taking up office in 1987, found that the University's budget "seemed designed to conceal rather than reveal what was going on"(13). He introduce a system which was open and rational and could be simply described. Its three basic principles were: that all costs and income attributable to each school and other academic unit should be assigned to that unit; that appropriate incentives should exist for each unit to increase income and reduce costs to further a clear set of academic priorities; and that all costs of other units, such as library or student counselling, should be allocated between the academic units. A number of factors are important for the successful implementation of such a system: strong and committed leadership, clear institutional objectives and a good working relationship with the state funding body. While many universities have succeeded by such strategies in bringing their expenditures under control, others (Yale and Columbia for example)(14) have suffered setbacks, because powerful, high-income-generating departments wish to go their own way.

Financial management

Box 6.

> To try to cut administrative costs, Stanford University adopted block budgeting with each department taking responsibility for its own finance so as to impose clear resource constraints and empower local decision-making.
>
> The procedures were:
> - central administration developed a long-range financial forecast and decided on the allocations to each unit;
> - units prepared multiple-year plans;
> - central administration reviewed and approved block budgets;
> - units prepared a detailed budget by which they control expenditure. The academic database needed for each unit contained:
> - expenditure by function (instruction, research, administration etc.);
> - expenditure by object (types of staff, equipment, etc.);
> - courses and student enrolment;
> - teaching loads by level, technology used, etc.;
> - research
>
> Previously voluminous data had been collected, but never used. Now each unit's plan includes a situational analysis, including such performance indicators as normal teaching load, research, use of technology and support services. Incentives have been built in: units that maintain good records are treated more sympathetically when new funding is available, faculty whose publications receive favourable reviews are allocated more time for research, excellent teaching is given awards, and salary increments are extended to give a wider range. In particular, higher pay is given to Chairs to emphasize the importance of good management. In practice, half to two thirds of staff were judged as performing well and given increments, which are paid only so long as performance remains good. The change was carried out after open discussion and presentation of information, with each unit defending its record as regards teaching loads and other factors(12).

Reports from *Canada* describe increasing financial constraint, closure of departments and job losses. Formula funding was introduced in the 1960s, but since the mid-1970s provinces have tended to revert to incrementalism. Ontario retains a formula but the historical element outweighs enrolment factors. The Quebec formula allows for slight modification in historical distribution ratios and in 1992 added an element for the number of diplomas awarded. The reasons for this were the broad access policy adopted and the need to control expenditure and educate more students at a lower cost. Universities have suffered a 3 to 5 per cent decline in funding per student in recent years. Formulae can assist policy implementation, but need sophisticated adjustment mechanisms when funds for higher education are declining. The province of Alberta, for example, in 1993 decided simply to impose of a 5 per cent cut from the previous year's funding. Most universities have introduced quotas for the expensive professional courses, used colleges to teach the first year of degree courses and reduced non-teaching staff(15). Increasing revenue from fees is difficult, since these are regulated by the government(16). Programme budgeting has been widely adopted in institutions, with the departments providing the data and keeping accounts, and the faculties producing the necessary reports and indicators.

In the *United Kingdom*, government policy has been dominated since the early 1980s by (i) the concern to reduce public expenditure and (ii) to increase efficiency by encouraging universities to earn income and to be more strictly accountable for grants received. The accountability requirement has become much more important in the 1990s. The first round of cuts in the early 1980s ranged from 6 to 30 per cent according to the institution. No university was forced to close, though several London colleges merged. Some special arrangements mitigated the worst effects; for example early retirement compensation and protection for priority Engineering programmes. Subsequently, strategies focused on separating resources for teaching and research and making funding conditional on delivery. The 1988 Education Reform Act provided greater autonomy in resource management, but also laid down stricter accountability measures. The argument was that resources were likely to be used more effectively if those responsible for educational services were given maximum discretion in deploying them. The Universities Funding Council (now Higher Education Funding Council) introduced a system of formula funding based on numbers of students by level and broad band of discipline plus an allowance for special institutional factors. The unit of resource has fallen over time. The UFC attempted to introduce greater market competition by setting up a bidding system but in practice universities were reluctant to bid too low and so force down the unit of funding even more. As a result, in 1991 the UFC abandoned the system and set only provisional targets. For the next two years universities were guaranteed only the number of funded places allocated for 1991-1992. Any decisions on increases would be based on the proportion of students at a university above the funded number, i.e. those for whom the university received only fees and no government grant. In short, a way was found to secure expansion at low marginal costs and institutions were obliged to accept this in order to obtain their funds. Public spending per graduate in Britain is now lower than in most other European countries, the exception being countries with open admission systems like France, where there are high drop-out rates.

This restructuring of financial sources imposed great strains on the management of institutions: many of them devolved budgets to the departmental level, either including or excluding staff salaries (the latter make up 72 to 90 per cent of department expenditure). Most institutions also appointed or increased the number of senior officers concerned with fund-raising, industrial liaison and overseas students. A great deal more information has to be made available for accountability and decision-making purposes and its quantity and quality increased and improved, particularly with the annual publication of "University Management Statistics and Performance Indicators". This obliges institutions to seek reasons for variance, and it is now possible to compare expenditure on central administration, libraries, computers and premises. Programme budgeting has been generally adopted and the cost per student per annum by discipline is now compared between universities.

Most universities have adopted some type of formula funding (often reflecting that set by the HEFC)(17) in allocating resources internally, e.g. such weightings as 1 Ph.D = 3 undergraduates for staff, library and laboratory allocations. Some maintain central control over staff establishments, while others allocate all funds – after top-slicing, usually 40 per cent, for central administration – to faculties to be shared among the departments(18).

Several universities have taken steps to assess more accurately the cost of central services used by each basic unit. Examples are use of the library according to staff and student numbers; the Registrar's Office and student facilities by student numbers; buildings by square metres occupied and staff facilities by staff numbers. This has had drastic effects on faculties with a high number of students, but has impelled them to scrutinize their costs more closely and in some cases to seek alternative suppliers for some services, such as computing and accounting(19).

There is a new emphasis on the department as a performer under the pressure of competition. In line with this, most universities have incentive systems for staff who generate income (perhaps a percentage of the total earned) and the proportion of staff not wholly financed from university funds has increased from 22 per cent in 1980 to 36 per cent in 1989(20).

British universities have had to adapt quickly to a new system and a lower level of funding. For some, this proved difficult. In 1990, 31 universities were told by HEFC to take action to avoid continuing in deficit. One experience of the adjustment process is summarized in *Box 7*.

The experience of the United Kingdom shows that the ways in which higher education institutions receive their funds has a powerful influence on internal resource allocation and management and thus affects organizational behaviour and the academic services provided. Management of finance is considered to be one of the critical tasks for the next decade. As Cowen has observed, the arena for action of Finance Officers in the United Kingdom universities is increasing(22). The skills needed to find ways round a rapidly changing higher education funding system, with new structures and new penalties, has meant a rise in the need for very alert, skilled professional administrators. This needs to be taken into account by other countries wishing to implement formula or contract funding.

Box 7.

> The University of Edinburgh(21), a large and old institution possessing substantial reserves and endowments and having a tradition of collegiality and faculty autonomy, during the period 1985-89 adapted to increasing financial constraint by a gradual and phased programme of staff reductions. However, in 1989 the government agreed pay rises and a 1 million pounds deficit arose, which by 1991 grew to be 6 million pounds. The first small task force in 1990 proposed emergency measures to allow time for a fuller investigation, i.e. freeze on recruitment, building and departmental balances and reduction in non-teaching staff. The UFC visited the University six times and require it to submit quarterly reports on its finances.
>
> A Recovery Plan was drawn up to increase income from students, reduce expenditure on administrative services and on staff (voluntary redundancies of 10 per cent in each Faculty). Throughout all these changes, staff were kept informed by newsletters and meetings.
>
> The crisis was seen primarily as a result of inadequate management, particularly as regards financial and staff information systems. There were too many committees and unclear lines of responsibility. The future wellbeing of the university is now safeguarded by a more streamlined structure of central management group (see *Figure 1* page 145) and devolved planning and budget process whereby Faculty managers prioritize and cost their activities before passing them to the central group. The latter takes its decisions in accordance with he strategic aims of the university. The change from general lack of financial control to a more managerial approach and cost consciousness, within two or three years has been quite radical.
>
> The lessons learned by the university were that they had taken insufficient account of the fact that all academic decisions have resource implications and had placed over-reliance on forecasts of income and expenditure instead of monitoring actual figures. The process of change by the use of small task forces, open communication and wide consultation, adopting a strategic view within a tough but achievable time-scale and setting aside sufficient funds to implement the change from economies achieved, was felt to be appropriate within a university context.

Financial management

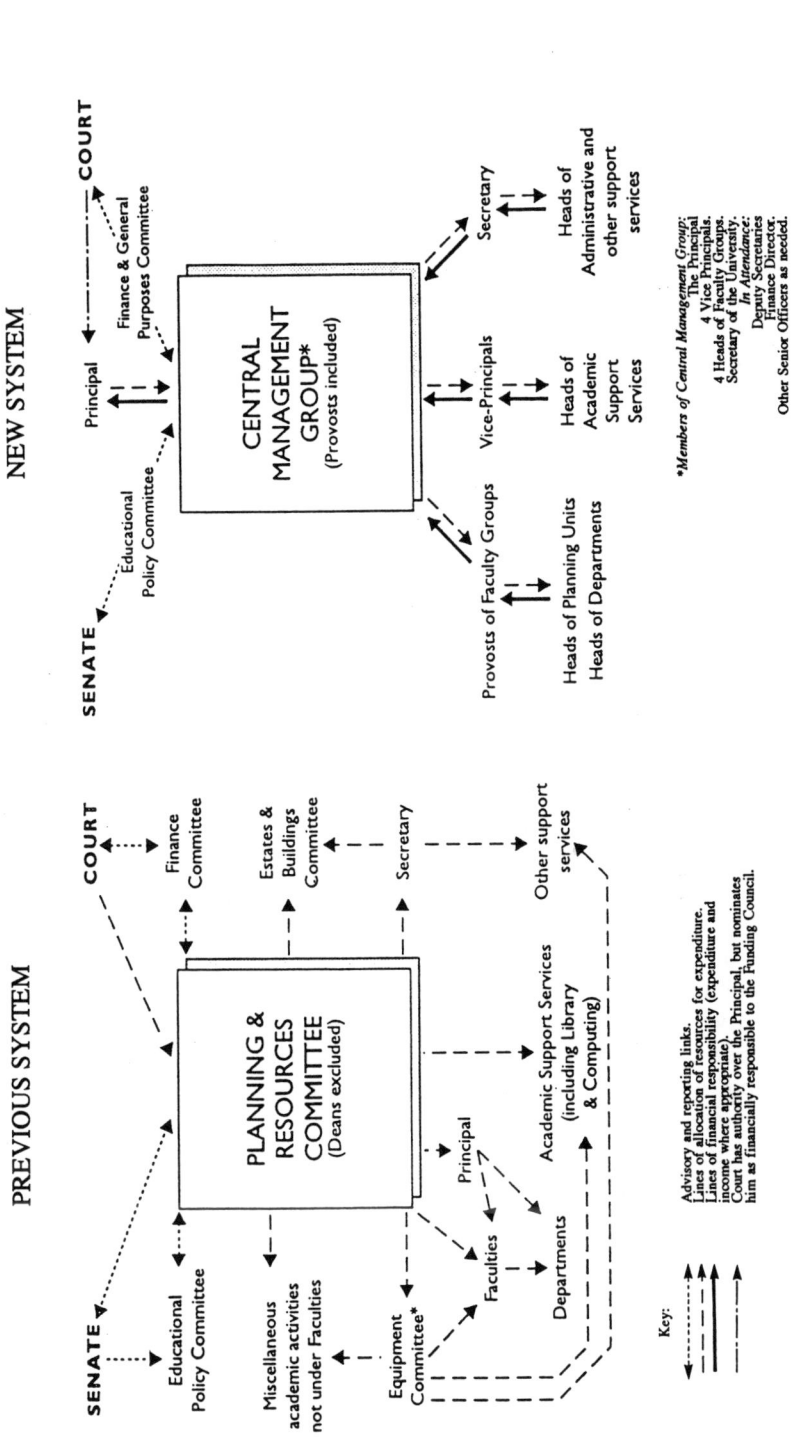

Figure 1. Lines of financial responsibility at *University X*

In 1988, the *Australian* Government introduced block funding of operating grants to institutions on a rolling triennial basis(23). Funding was based on an agreed total student load, with weights assigned to undergraduate/graduate/research programmes by cluster of disciplines, e.g. the lowest weight is 1.0 for accounting, economics, law, and humanities, as against 4.7 for a research degree in medicine or agriculture. Each institution also had to prepare an educational profile that is examined each year by the Higher Education Council and monitored by a Task Force conducting institutional visits. The profile consists of:

- broad mission statement;
- teaching load (number of students by level and discipline);
- research work and research management plan;
- measures taken to achieve national priorities;
- other significant activities.

Variations from previous grants of as much as 35 per cent in funding under the formula occurred. The move away from incremental funding based on historical precedent had to be phased in over a period of some years, and a mechanism, the Relative Funding Mechanism, was established for this purpose. It takes account of size, location, regional role, number of campuses and leasing costs. In the 1992 exercise some institutions' funding declined by 22 per cent while others increased by as much as 20 per cent.

A further major change in funding was the Higher Education Contribution Scheme (1989). Under this, a student repays his grant through the tax system when he begins work, unless he chooses to pay a lump sum in advance and get a 25 per cent discount.

Universities on average obtain 30 per cent of their income from other than government grants and therefore have some latitude in spending. As they develop greater ability to undertake contracts, and to secure private funding, they will enjoy greater autonomy(24). Most, after top-slicing, have devolved financial management to faculty deans by lump-sum funding, usually incremental with small variations. However, some universities have tried to implement a type of relative funding model to achieve re-allocation as between growing/declining disciplines.

The Swinburne University of Technology, for example, reserves 32.5 per cent for central management, maintenance and services, plus a further 1 per cent for strategic initiatives. From the remainder, departments are allocated lump sums according to student numbers. From this, they pay for staff, materials, printing and, soon, for space.

It is felt that the government has acted boldly in exerting leverage on higher educational institutions but is now becoming more aware of the possibilities of using softer discretionary financial instruments related to performance, in preference to the hard conditions of grants(25).

Since 1986 *the Netherlands* has adopted a selective retrenchment and growth policy. A cut of 20 non-academic posts for each university was requested and certain departments and institutions were closed by government decree(26). Ninety per cent of the government lump-sum funding to institutions is calculated according to a formula based on student numbers. This is modified by the drop-out rate, and is calculated by nine fields of study, enabling the government to influence output by discipline. Unit costs in the different fields are based on normative student:staff ratios, for instance 34.5 in arts and law, 28.5 in social science and 20 in engineering and medicine. The resulting total is then adjusted to take account of percentages graduating and number of dissertations produced. An additional mission budget is given to fund innovative projects and centres of excellence.

A further incentive for timely completion of study programmes is given by the student voucher system. Programmes are modular and each student is given, once in a lifetime, vouchers to cover fees for a certain number of modules. For families whose incomes are below a set level, the vouchers also cover 60 per cent of maintenance. This is conditional upon passing examinations each year(27).

Within limits, universities are free to spend their lump sums according to their own preferences. The limits are that salaries are fixed by legislation, government approval is required for the highest posts, and most importantly, only 1 per cent of the total sum is allowed to be carried over at the end of the budget year.

Reactions to this funding system depended on how secure institutions felt. Most used allocation models different to the national one. The University of Amsterdam experimented with zero-based budgeting, while the small and new University of Twenty decided it would have to make some very radical changes if it was to survive. It divided its annual government funding into 85 per cent for distribution to the faculties and 15 per cent for incentives and new strategic areas. Faculties were pressured to seek income and rationalize their programmes by designating them as cost centres, to which all costs including overheads are charged. A new accounting system was introduced and a separate business organization established. By these methods, the university overcame its financial problems, and rapidly increased private income and student numbers. However, this entrepreneurial style of financial management brought other problems: an intensive training programme was needed for the staff of the faculties, and was not completely successful. In order to be able to establish output-related costs, an efficient management information system had to be set up, able to give precise and reliable data(28).

b. Self-regulation in transition

The *Nordic* countries were perhaps farther sighted in the funding of their higher educational institutions. Though the financial situation was not yet critical, they realized that within a few years they would need to make economies. Finland, in particular, embarked on a policy of experimentation in improving financial management, designating two institutions (Joensuu and Helsinki School of Economics) as pilot projects for change. After 20 years of government control, with all staff civil servants and the budgets set by line-item, these two institutions were given lump sums and the task of devising an efficient financial management system which, after approval, would be used by all institutions in 1994. Joensuu, as a small institution, felt it needed to be in the vanguard as regards efficiency. It has decentralized financial management to departments, organized departmental self-evaluation, a management information system and a means of dialogue both between academic heads and with the government in order to negotiate the outcomes to be achieved. The process has been gradual. In 1991 lump sums were allocated to departments with no set obligations except for salaries. As from 1992, departments can decide on how to use their staff; until then teaching responsibilities prescribed. Benefits are already seen in rising cost consciousness, and the possibility of trade-offs is influencing decisions; not all vacant posts are being filled, there is more use of part-time staff and sharing staff with other departments(29). It was hoped that by 1994, when the Finnish Government announced that it intended to make economies by imposing a 5 per cent staff cut, the system as a whole would be able to benefit from the experience of the pilot institutions to make a smooth transition to lump-sum budgeting and departmental management.

In 1987, *Sweden* changed from line item budgeting to a formula based on teaching by broad bands of disciplines, plus research and special projects. It allowed greater discretion in spending. This system was revised in 1993 to allow for institutional development planning by granting funds on a three-year contract basis, but also including criteria for rewarding high quality(30). As noted in *Chapter 5*, department heads have been given more responsibility in planning and use of resources but the extent of devolution has not been clearly reported.

In 1980, *Norway* adopted five-year strategic planning and lump-sum funding. Institutional budgetary proposals have to contain a description of the results to be achieved by the budget and those achieved last year, and be accompanied by planning documents. At institutional level, each department has to manage its own funds and report at the end of the year. A carry-over of 5 per cent from one year to the next is permitted(31). This has reduced panic at the year end, but there are still fears that if the carry-over is too great, the budget will be cut. Some innovation has occurred in financial management but most institutions tend to operate in much the same way as they did before.

In most of these self-regulatory countries, allocations to institutions are increasingly based upon formula funding. There is a tendency to reduce the link between funds for teaching and research, and to create separate funds for priority projects or innovations. Governments are beginning to see such funds as effective in influencing academic activities. The bulk of funding is based on set criteria and norms, and is given in a lump sum that permits substantial flexibility in spending, and a carry-over of a small percentage (1 to 5 per cent) to the next year. Outputs, performance and institutional development plans have recently been incorporated into the formulae, for example in Australia, Netherlands, Norway, and Sweden.

A number of these countries (Netherlands in particular) have incorporated methods of student funding into their mechanisms(32). Another common strategy is to encourage study at local institutions. In Australia and the United Kingdom, overseas students pay much higher fees, and in the United States, this extends to American students from out-of-state(33).

Formula funding has given greater managerial flexibility to those countries which were formerly under centralized line-item budgets (the Nordic countries and the Netherlands) but on the other hand requires much more accountability where universities had already been functioning with lump-sum budgets (United Kingdom and Australia). There has in this way been a convergence of policy thinking.

Debate about the appropriate type of departmental financial management and the extent of devolution is now taking place. One study argues that the pursuit of profits is a highly effective motivator when some benefits can be retained: central management is freed from operational matters to concentrate on strategy, and less information needs to be circulated. However, more resources have to be devoted to auditing and more staff are required for the profit centre data base, implying that such centres need to be of sufficient size if they are to be cost-effective(34).

c. Self-regulation in difficulty

In the *Eastern and Central European* countries, public expenditure on higher education has fallen quite substantially. For example, in *Hungary*, the decrease was calculated at 26 per cent between 1978 and 1988. States have tried to reduce student numbers in accordance with projected manpower needs, but this has tended to result in institutions hiding their unused capacities and maximizing additional demands(35).

Poland still bases its allocations on the historical base and according to student numbers, by a process of bargaining. In Hungary the annual block grant is distributed by the Ministry of Education via the Student Fund, Tuition Fund (grants to institutions according to enrolments), Research, Facilities and Development Funds. Universities have reacted to declining income by introducing less expensive programmes and eliminating outdated ones, as well as hard currency courses for foreign students. There has also been a rapid expansion of private business schools.

As noted in *Chapter 2*, the trend to privatization has been strongest in Romania, but that government has also introduced two categories of study place in public universities – those with and those without government-funded tuition fees. The latter applies to students whose examination results were not good enough for a grant, but whose families may pay the relevant fees for entry(36).

The only report(37) of the introduction of formula funding comes from the *Czech Republic*, which in 1992 began to move from its previous historically based budget system, under which requests were constantly inflated to take account of expected cuts. A more transparent process was needed, which would allow government policy to steer the system. Formula funding now covers 65 per cent of institutions' income, the remainder being for student welfare services and buildings. A standard rate was set based on historical data for students in each discipline but it was found that strict application of the formula would have led to extreme fluctuations, ranging from an increase of 59 per cent for one institution to a decrease of 23 per cent for another. Therefore the transition had to be phased, with no institution suffering a change of more than 10 per cent either way in any one year. This temporary measure will continue for four or five years, during which more realistic costing will be carried out. At present the most expensive institutions cost four times as much per student as the cheapest, so there are some benefits to be achieved from more rational allocation mechanisms. However, there is no national planning of enrolments by institution or programme. Universities may generate private income but so far this only amounts to 2 or 3 per cent of total revenue.

The *Czech Republic* has also taken cost-cutting measures in the domain of research staff: regular budget decreases for the Academy of Science have brought about a decline in staffing from 13,000 in 1989 to 8,000 in 1993. Most of the cuts were achieved by natural wastage as younger staff found better employment in the private sector(38).

Institutions of higher education in the Russian Federation have been under great financial pressure. All the Russian universities are suffering from the present galloping inflation, which has necessitated funds being received monthly instead of annually(39). Increases have to be paid to students and teachers two to three times a year and the number of students has fallen by about a third over the last five years. Enterprises or parents may fund students but this is only feasible in high-wage areas. Institutions have reacted by changing their courses to take into account the demands of enterprises, sometimes in return for equipment that is needed, and organizing commercial lunchtime and evening courses, mainly in business and computer studies, and English.

Funding mechanisms in Eastern and Central Europe therefore remain for the most part historically based, though there are elements of a market emerging. There are no reports of the introduction of accountability procedures as regards performance and mission.

In *Latin America*, increases in enrolments in public universities have been rapid and government funding has not kept pace, so that the quality of education has declined. Costs per student are only a fraction of those in Europe. For example, in 1985 Argentina's were 20 per cent of those in Belgium, and Uruguay's 15 per cent(40).

Public universities generally are not free to establish their own budgets or pay scales; their financial management deals only with minor current expenditures. The basic organization has remained the same for decades, consisting of a centralized budget with an independent faculty structure, in a system of open admissions with free tuition. Though universities have acquired broader social and educational functions, there has been limited organizational response, which has been a factor in increasing the spread of private higher education(41). A substantial number of students is enrolled in private institutions; according to Levy, Latin America leads the developing world in the scope of its privatization(42).

In *Brazil*, self-governance was given to the universities under the 1988 Constitution, but it is subject to a series of administrative and financial restrictions. Universities still cannot manage their budget and redistribute it internally, but must respect the criteria set for budget items, and adhere to national salary scales(43). Collegial and political models of decision-making predominate within institutions and decisions are usually based on compromises between competing groups. There is strong resistance to the cancellation of courses with low attendance and to curricular change. On the other hand, there has been an excessive increase in the number of commissions and electoral colleges(44). Teaching staff are preoccupied with negotiations about pay; real income has fallen and many staff take additional part-time jobs or leave to take better paying positions in newly-established private universities. The scope for improvements in financial management is obviously very limited(45). However, the State of Sao Paulo has granted 9 per cent of tax revenue to state universities, with the right to make their own internal allocations, while the government has announced its intention to phase in a new formula and performance indicator-based budget system over the next ten years. The problem is that the universities are opposed to this move(46).

A rather similar situation exists in *Argentina* where, inflation having been got under control, it was possible to institute an annual budget as from 1992. The government wishes to change from its present line-item budgeting to lump-sum grants, and to deregulate salaries, but the universities disagree. Public universities are also resisting the introduction of fees(47).

Reports from *Venezuela* refer to budgets being absorbed by salary increases; unit costs in public universities being triple those in private; excessive non-academic staff; and cuts in equipment and books. Many institutions have accumulated debts and the central government has had to rescue them. Despite this, pressure groups of staff and students oppose the introduction of reforms(48).

In *Mexico* also, SEP (the main co-ordinator of state universities) has denounced institutional non-co-operation, while the National Association of Universities has requested more time and information for discussions. SEP allocations are lump sums for teaching research, based on annual university budget requests divided into broad categories. Funding per student has fallen and universities have increased tuition fees and cost of services to students and the public. However, it is generally recognized that financial procedures are inadequate: there is a lack of cost analysis, reporting and managerial supervision. Many institutions are in a state of chronic deficit(49).

Chile acted as long ago as 1981 to rein in the state's responsibility for funding higher education, allowing the growth of private institutions and technical training centres and implementing a system of student loans. Four types of funding exist: (i) a lump sum calculated on a historical basis; (ii) a proportion given according to number of students in the first year; (iii) credits for students who meet set criteria; and (iv) a small percentage linked to the best 20,000 academic results. Civil service status for staff has been abolished and salary differentials permitted. From 1981 to 1991 state funding to universities fell from 4 per cent of GNP to 2.5 per cent. Approximately 16 per cent of university income is obtained from services (staff have to give much more time to this activity now), with 10 per cent derived from investment(50). However, according to another source,(51) while external efficiency has improved with more students consuming less public resources, input-output ratios in the old universities have deteriorated and unit costs per graduate are still high.

Interest in cost analysis is growing in the region. In *Peru* it has been found that one institution may be allocated eight to nine times as much per student as another, and recurrent crises lead to considerable volatility(52).

A study in *Colombia* has compared financial management in public and private institutions. Here the state institutions are 90 per cent financed by the government, despite rises in tuition fees and sale of services. The average cost per student in private institutions is less than half that in public but this is explained to some extent by lower spending on equipment and the fact that, in private institutions, the majority of staff are part-time and there is only one support staff for every 12 students compared to one per seven in public. But the private institutions maintain a tighter control over employee productivity, and financial management is facilitated by the fact that they receive tuition fees at the beginning of the semester, while state universities receive their grants irregularly and have to pay employment benefits and subsidize cafeterias, residences and extension courses. In addition, some prestigious private universities earn high levels of income from short courses and receive donations, while this is not the case for the state universities(53).

Financial management in Latin American universities may be typified by the analysis carried out at the National University of Costa Rica(54). The budget is the main instrument of academic control, but the process is over-centralized, causing delay. On the other hand, there is little correspondence between plans and budgets, insufficient statistical and qualitative data, and lack of economic and financial analysis. An authoritarian concept of management and control has tended to stifle any latent interest in cost efficiency that might exist.

Exercises such as that carried out at the University of Monterrey, Mexico(55) could be useful to governments wishing to support their case for change to lump-sum budgeting and institutional accountability. In this institution, the direct and indirect instructional costs were calculated in order that staff should better understand their origin, better judge their operational efficiency, and make optimal use of various sources of funding. It was found, as is the case for most institutions, that the low direct instructional costs of business studies, humanities and law were associated with high student:staff ratios, large class size, low faculty salaries and longer hours of instruction. In contrast, the higher costs incurred in the arts and education programmes did not seem to be justified, thus indicating where greater efficiency might be achieved.

In both these groups of countries, institutions are acting defensively and lack adequate systems of financial management to enable them to produce cost data. The first group, Eastern Europe, has utilized opportunities provided by the market by taking in more fee-paying students, and eliminating or changing courses. In the second group, Latin America, government policies have been much more openly pro lump-sum formula funding and reform, with Chile and Mexico introducing some incentive mechanisms, but so far university reaction has been to oppose or delay though there are some signs of preparatory activities, such as research on financial management and cost analysis.

d. Centralized planning and control

In developed countries under centralized systems, university funding is usually by means of a variant of the line-item budget. The institution receives state funding subdivided into expenditure categories, to which certain amounts are attached which must be spent only within these categories. Basically the categories are determined by the input factors of higher education, i.e. 'production functions' (personnel, investments, teaching and research material, travel expenses, building maintenance etc.) and the organizational sub-units of an institution. In a line-item budget, the institution does not receive funds for personnel expenditure, but for each of the posts authorized. Within this framework, the relations between state and higher education institutions might be characterized as 'input-steering'. Planning and control functions are integrated into the budget with the main emphasis on tight advance determination of the proportions to be spent on each input factor. The model offers no incentives for output, quality, or outcomes improvement; the funds are allocated on the basis of increments which correspond to inflation and staff expansion. Such systems still prevail in most developing countries and this was the method used generally in Europe prior to reform and the financial constraints imposed by mass expansion of higher education at the beginning of the 1980s.

In *France*, three quarters of the funds are not in institutional budgets at all. Their purpose is only to provide for complementary expenditures other than salaries, student welfare and capital investment, and there are three basic provisions: costs of materials, etc. (by teaching hours by discipline); maintenance and cleaning costs (by surface area); overtime and part-time staff (since 1989 paid in a lump sum). Universities also generate their own income from fees, local authorities, apprenticeship tax and services(56). The latter can differ quite markedly by area, e.g. the Universities of Strasbourg and Valenciennes earn an additional 50 per cent of their total budget while others may earn only 35 per cent(57).

The first steps to change financial management began in 1989 when the Ministry of Education started a system of four-year contracts, which now cover most universities. The purpose of the contracts was not to increase competition (as in the United Kingdom) but to transfer more planning responsibility to the institutions. They cover the above types of funding but by ensuring provision for four years it was hoped to strengthen the executive level and encourage universities to analyze present activities, propose projects, fix objectives and carry out self-evaluation. The first report on the experience(58) found that the partners in the contract were unequal since the universities, though they had analyzed past and existing situations, had not presented future plans in any detail. Contracts tended to be handed out by the state rather than negotiated. The information systems on student flows and achievements were not yet functioning so as to be able to evaluate performance, and responsibility for verifying that the objectives of the contract had been achieved had not been officially assigned. The Ministry and universities are now experimenting with new procedures and tools, including computer software. Funds for basic running costs will be calculated on standard criteria while a complementary funding system (5-10 per cent of total funds) will finance new projects and take care of specific local costs. In order to establish the criteria for basic running costs, studies are being undertaken in seven universities. Institutions will soon have to accept some real autonomy, and the executive level will have more power as it becomes a negotiator. It will require better administrators, while department heads will also have the responsibility for working within the set allocations. This is considered to be a revolutionary move(59), given the long years of centralized management. The experience shows the need for preparatory work and for subsequent evaluation and adjustment.

Funding for higher education in *Belgium* fell by 29 per cent between 1975 and 1987. Cuts were made in resources per student and some students became no longer eligible for grants. The universities had some degree of flexibility in managing the decline in unit cost since student numbers continued to grow and budgets were divided into four broad categories, between which limited virement was possible: general administration, teaching and research staff, administrative and technical staff, and materials. Grants are made according to an input formula for teaching, i.e. the number of students enrolled on 1 February of the preceding academic year classified by field of study. The university also receives grants for social services and investment. In Belgium, as opposed to France, greater managerial discretion has always been exercised in institutions since payments for staff are their responsibility and the categories are broad enough to allow flexibility.

Germany, as a whole, has made little change to its line-item incremental system of budgeting. The basic state (*länder*) subsidies account for 84 per cent of institutional expenditure, with the remaining 16 per cent for research coming from external sources (75 per cent from public funds and 25 per cent from private sources). Staff positions take up 80 per cent of the budget and institutions are allocated a certain number of posts at particular levels. However, two of the *länder* have recently allowed institutions to make limited use of savings from any unfilled posts(60). Students pay no tuition fees. The pattern is thus one of input steering and earmarked funds which do not incorporate incentives for output or quality. Nevertheless, some change in policy thinking is occurring; one state (Lower Saxony), has now begun a pilot project on lump-sum budgeting in three universities. Each will draw up its own budget, and development plan and negotiate it with the state(61).

Italy also has a system of input, earmarked and normative budgeting where funds are allocated to staff salaries, general administration according to weighted student load, and capital costs. The 1992 Act giving more autonomy to institutions is still being debated, in particular the implications for financial management. *Greece's* system of input, earmarked line-item budgeting, in which expenditures are reimbursed at cost, remains unchanged.

To summarise, the possibilities of using budgeting as a tool to increase university responsibility and accountability, particularly as regards development plans, have now been recognized in France and in one German state. Belgium, by means of a more flexible input budgeting system, has encouraged improvement of institutional management in order to cope with financial constraints. In these three countries, work has been carried out on data collection, cost analysis, information systems and specific software which will enable institutions to act more as 'partners' in the financial management of higher education. The precise form and balance of power of these partnerships has still to evolve but such a trend is in line with the developments that have taken place in the Nordic countries, as opposed to the competitive market model adopted by the United Kingdom.

In the *developing countries*, most governments have been unable to keep pace with inflation or to fund expansion of higher education, and have tended to keep an ever tighter control of resource allocation. They have sought solutions in privatization, increases in tuition fees and student loans, but this varies according to region.

Robert Blair has observed that "*African* universities tend to be expensive, inefficient and inadequately financed" leading to "poor maintenance of buildings and equipment, deteriorating library resources, totally insufficient access to hard currency, inflexible management of financial and staffing resources, and ineffective relations with their governments, particularly in respect of financial matters"(62). Universities have been closely regulated by the state and have suffered to the extent that the state itself has proved limited and inadequate(63). According to Blair, the current state of the financial relationship between universities and their governments in most countries is chaotic. The way governments chop university budgets quite arbitrarily by up to 70 per cent, whilst not allowing the university to reduce its staff, and requiring it to continue to take in increasing numbers of students, is a recipe for disaster as far as the university is concerned. A system of negotiated funding prevails, which is not usually based on specific criteria but rather on last year's budget.

Almost all universities are public and receive 90-100 per cent of their funding from the government, which in many cases appoints the key staff for administration and academic affairs. They may have some control over the internal allocation of resources for the relatively small amount not devoted to salaries. The extent of flexibility depends on the prevailing system: former French-West African universities have little room for manoeuvre whereas in about half the Anglophone countries, institutions have some room to reallocate(64). Internal management, as might be expected, suffers from uncertainties of funding; central administration, takes an average of 18 per cent of the overall recurrent budget compared to the United Kingdom average of 5 per cent.

The conclusions of the IIEP Workshop for East African universities held in Mauritius in 1993 (65) noted:

- Absence of costing norms and other standards (teaching loads, student-staff ratios, teaching space required per student, standard unit costs for teaching, research and consultancy) so as to establish budgetary needs in a detailed manner.
- Lack of proper cost classification and codification leading to improper cost recording and attribution.

- Absence of well-defined cost centres for the effective assignment of all costs attributable to each centre or unit.
- Lack of adequately trained financial managers and brain drain due to low salaries and position in the administrative hierarchy.
- Lack of control over donor funding leading to institutional fragmentation and weakening of internal financial management capacity.
- Lack of modern data processing techniques for accounting and records, which are in most cases manually processed.

Capacity to manage finance within institutions varies greatly. The example of the University of Makerere, Uganda (*Box 8*) may be said to be the lowest extreme of the spectrum as regards freedom to spend. The University of Dar-es-Salaam has recently acquired a little more flexibility in that budgeting has been partially decentralized to faculty level under strong administrative control(67). The Ministry sets the ceiling and the Bursar top-slices for salaries, administration and student welfare. The remainder is allocated to departments and services on a quarterly basis; expenditures are controlled by the Bursar's Office in accordance with the limits voted. The university recognizes that this is only a beginning: there are no norms set for workloads, student:staff ratios, materials etc. Unit costs have not been analyzed and except for the payroll, all financial procedures are still conducted manually(68).

The University of Zimbabwe's budgeting process is still the traditional collegial incremental line-item process and auditing is conducted by a private firm, but here too Departmental Heads are responsible for controlling and certifying expenditures against their cost centres and they may re-allocate funds, generate income for departmental use and carry forward underspending to the next year(69).

One case which is particularly interesting is that of the University of Botswana which has begun using task forces and workshops to implement extensive structural changes. These will enhance cost effectiveness, including accountability and the development of more effective and efficient delivery systems, based upon forecasts of rapid growth in student numbers for the remainder of the 1990s, as well as rapidly rising costs. The university has taken budget estimates out of the hands of the Bursar's office and these are now under a specially established estimates committee composed of deans of faculties, the vice-chancellor, the deputy vice-chancellor, the registrar and the bursar. It is still a centralized process but one which aims to match resource allocation with strategic plans. The cost figures are available for all to see and allocations may be challenged. A computerized information system is being introduced, particularly for student records since allocations will be based on numbers enrolled and performance(70).

Box 8.

> In Uganda, the University of Makerere draws up its budget according to the Ministry's target ceiling, a practice begun in 1990, prior to which budget requests were always inflated. The Bursar gives instructions to departments who submit requests for non-staff needs: many of them do not bother to submit such requests and are given the same as last year; this is probably due to the smallness of the sums, since 40 per cent of the operating budget is spent on salaries and a further 30 per cent on student boarding costs. The university may not itself issue cheques. Its quarterly income is received by the Bank of Uganda and the Treasury issues cheques for university expenditures after authorization. Any revenue generated accrues to the Treasury. The system has intricate checks and cross-checks which make it almost impossible to get funds quickly. These are designed to enable the Treasury to control expenditure and satisfy itself that public funds are utilized properly and sparingly. All requests for funds must be made through the head of department, who will pass on the claim to the Finance Department with appropriate comments. The request will first go to internal audit where it is either cleared or rejected outright, or the claimant is invited to clarify certain aspects of it. If it is cleared, it is passed on for authorization by the chief accountant if the sum concerned is less than Shs.15,000, or by the university Bursar. When finally authorized, a voucher will be raised, signed by the person preparing it, and authorized by the chief accountant or university bursar, as appropriate. After passing through all these steps, a cheque will be prepared.
>
> The steps outlined already take between two to ten working days and sometimes even longer. Cheques are now printed in the Treasury's computer department and drawn on Makerere's account with the Bank of Uganda. Therefore, what the Finance Department at Makerere does as the first step in requisitioning a cheque is to fill in computer input sheets and send them to the Computer Department in the Treasury. Depending on the volume of work at the university a cheque will take several days before it is ready.
>
> The next stage is that the signed cheques together with the copy of a signed voucher will be returned to the Treasury for clearing, after which they are returned to Makerere and only then will a claimant be able to go to the Bank of Uganda to draw the cash. This also depends on whether the cheque is an open one. If for one reason or another, it is a closed one that will mean losing more time before getting the money or before the funds are transferred to one's account.
>
> *On average it takes Makerere University a minimum of four weeks and sometimes up to two months*, to make payments. The consequences of this have been that fuel stations refuse to supply petrol and deliveries of food and other materials are delayed. The university has requested more responsibility for financial matters but the Treasury remains to be convinced that the proper financial controls can be exercised by the university(66).

Certain governments have taken a stronger role in guiding financial management in institutions. Ghana has set norms by discipline for student:staff ratios; ratios for support staff; and materials as a proportion of teaching costs. However, the government grant is still historically based and the institutions are trying to adhere to the set norms by, for example, expanding student intake in overstaffed disciplines(71).

Nigerian universities are undergoing a similar process under new input-based formula funding. Efficiency is being monitored by the National University Commission, and the government has directed that the universities should generate 5 per cent more of their current expenditure each year so as eventually to earn 50 per cent of the budget. However, so far commercial ventures have not been successful, mainly due to university bureaucracy, and the fact that staff are not motivated to take consultancies, preferring to take such work on a private basis(72).

African universities are generally becoming more cost-conscious, stimulated by their own financial problems and the work of different agencies, like the Association of African Universities (AAU) and the Association for the Development of African Education (DAE). For example, in order to reduce uncertainty and financial overdependence on government grants, the Universities of Lagos and Sierra Leone (Fourth Bay College) devised a policy of budgeting to build up financial reserves. The University of Lagos has reserves amounting to 22.29 per cent of its annual income, while the University of Sierra Leone has 38.21 per cent. Universities have implemented government policies for cost-sharing by students, and revenue earning. To give a few examples: Kenyan universities in 1991 introduced a registration charge of KSh.6,000 annually, while Ghanaian students in October 1993 were asked to pay for hostels, for which they might take out a loan to be repaid when employed. In Chad, students no longer have the right to a grant in the first year, and many never get past this level. Overall, the trend is for universities to withdraw from the provision of canteens and staff quarters and to charge for student accommodation. However, the hostel fees which universities are allowed to charge are pegged at very low rates by the government, and an unduly high percentage of university finance has to be spent on administration, since the university is often a self-contained community with its own services.

Universities are now aware of what needs to be done, as is illustrated by the Windhoek Declaration(73) of August 1992, which was adopted by high-level policy-makers and vice-chancellors from Angola, Botswana, Lesotho, Mozambique, Swaziland, and Zimbabwe. The 16 points of the Declaration stressed:

- maintenance of information systems and their analysis, i.e. ratios, unit costs;

- devolution of financial responsibilities to cost centres;
- diversification of funding sources;
- rational budgeting and allocation;
- clear criteria for cost reduction;
- incentives so that cost centres benefit from savings made;
- regional co-operation to reduce costs of some programmes;
- establishment of an appropriate unit to promote fund-raising activities.

In *Asia*, as elsewhere in the world, government funding per student in real terms generally decreased substantially in the 1980s; for example, in Indonesia it declined 22 per cent per student from 1980 to 1985. In Pakistan and India, universities regularly have to resort to overdrafts. Quality becomes hard to maintain while at the same time there is pressure to expand, to give short courses and professional upgrading, and to carry out applied research.

The proportion of revenue earned from tuition fees, which are controlled by the government, is usually small and has declined in public universities; in Nepal fees have remained unchanged for 13 years and in Pakistan for 40 years prior to 1989. In Thailand, universities obtain 5 per cent of their funds from fees, the Philippines 10 per cent, India 12 per cent, Singapore 20 per cent, Indonesia 25 per cent, but in Korea it is 50 per cent. Private institutions in Korea and the Philippines derive 80 per cent of their revenue from fees but unit costs are much less; for example average costs in Philippine public universities were US $572, compared to $55 in private ones.

Funding is allocated according to line-item budgets on a historical incremental basis. Even in those countries previously noted in *Chapter 4* to have taken some steps towards self-regulation, there is little freedom of manoeuvre in financial management. The University of Singapore, for instance, negotiates its budget on a line-item basis. Its administration is highly centralized and hierarchical, though faculties manage themselves within the limits of their allocations and the regulations and may make *virements* between sub-heads(74).

The situation is similar in the Philippines, where budgets are negotiated on the basis of staff posts plus operating expenditures, on the basis of enrolments. Cash allotments are released monthly but these are sometimes delayed, as are capital expenditures, though salaries are paid regularly. Some analyses of university costs have been made which showed a reduction in administrative expenditure, the proportion falling from 17 per cent in 1987 to 15 per cent in 1990(75).

In *China*, power is still concentrated in central government, which allocates resources, controls teaching plans, appoints staff and assigns students with grants(76). Funding by a lump sum based on a formula related to the number of government-financed f.t.e. students; universities may keep any savings at the end of the year. 1986 Regulations laid down basic standards for the size and quality of staff, classroom space and books per student. However, the universities are acquiring more flexibility in financial management. The State Education Commission is implementing a plan to reorganize the country's network of universities and colleges to 'rationalize small departments, broaden specialties, eliminate duplications of programmes, and make more effective use of staff and physical resources'. Universities can enrol students funded by employers and fee-payers, and the proportion may be as high as 40 per cent in some institutions. Ways are being sought to reduce the heavy welfare costs, and a scheme whereby staff will pay 10-20 per cent of their medical costs is being tested in three provinces(77). These changes plus some rather successful income-generation activities (see *Chapter 8*) allow more freedom to exercise initiative.

This is not the case yet for *India*, where the system is dispersed according to whether universities are federally funded by the UGC ('central' or 'deemed') or by the State. Governments met 80 per cent of expenditure in 1992 (only 40 per cent in 1947) while fees account for just 12 per cent (46 per cent in 1947). Universities have had to give up considerable autonomy in return for increased state funding but have not questioned this, and seem reconciled to perpetual shortages. In 1989 an Association of Indian Universities survey of 80 universities found that 45 had financial deficits, 10 of them amounting to more than 10 per cent of recurrent expenditure. Higher education no longer figures high on the states' list of priorities – it is considered that it has already had more than its fair share(78).

The lack of proper rules on staff ratios, infrastructure and admissions, together with cuts in funds for books, laboratories and equipment, have resulted in some undesirable patterns of expenditure, where the proportion spent on non-teaching staff is too high and those for materials and libraries are too low (see *Table 19* below).

Table 19. India: Percentages of expenditure in universities (1982-1985)

Type of institutions	Teaching staff	Non-teaching staff	Materials	Library	Other (Scholarships, Sports, Examinations)
Central	21	30	5	25	41.5
Deemed	35	18	13	4	30
State	31	25	7	2	35

Source: Sharma, M.M. *Financial management of universities in India*. Concept Publication Company, New Delhi.

All central and deemed universities conform to UGC budget lines, as well as 80 per cent of state universities, though only 54 per cent of state agricultural universities. The internal budgeting procedure is based on departmental budget proposals and the previous year's level of funding; the total is therefore usually incremental, but is declining in real terms and in relation to student numbers. Allocations are decided by a Finance Committee on which Deans, Directors and a few teaching staff sit, the Finance Officer being the Member Secretary. This pivotal staff member is often deputed from the Finance Department of the State Government. Though he may be proficient in financial procedures, his expertise in university management is limited and queries cause considerable delay. The system of payments and accounting is centralized and Heads of Department may make only petty expenditures. Many state agricultural universities operate differently, with a decentralized system, because of the dispersal of teaching units. Salaries and other bills are processed by Heads of Departments and sent to the Financial Officer to issue cheques and prepare the accounts. The success of these institutions in agricultural development is remarked upon in *Chapter 8*.

Researchers tend to agree that the present system is neither realistic nor motivating. An effort to break out of the mould was made by the Maharashtra Government in 1987 when it requested all departments to prepare their budgets assuming 80 per cent of the previous year's revenue. Zero Base Budgeting (ZBB) was introduced, with each unit preparing proposals based on a decision package, the minimum, current and expected future expenditure. The goals of the package, their relevance to the university's overall objectives, performance indicators, alternative methods of achieving goals and the likely consequences of each were set out. Appraisal of the proposed budgets is designed to eliminate programmes of low relevance and to increase funds for priority activities. However, the system requires clearly defined university goals, measurement criteria, commitment, trained staff, and preparation of a ZBB manual and calendar, and all this caused considerable work and difficulties for the institutions; no evaluation of the experience is yet available.

At central level, the UGC is also devoting considerable attention to financial management and intends to propose some flexible norms, particularly as regards non-teaching staff. Meanwhile (1993), as reported in *Chapter 2*, tax concessions have been made to assist universities in income generation.

In Pakistan, the Government in 1989 instituted some measures to improve the financial position of universities by wiping out deficits, and raising tuition fees. Institutions will henceforth be allowed to create endowment funds, acquire industrial and agricultural assets and negotiate foreign assistance(79).

In the Arab countries, line-item budgeting for universities, with reimbursement of actual costs, remains the standard procedure. Ministries pay salaries and decide on investment for building. Reduction of student intakes, privatization and tuition fees financed from taxation have been some of the measures adopted(80). A recent improvement in flexibility for Tunisian institutions has been that any credits not spent at the end of the year may now go into a fund at the disposal of the institution which has then to obtain approval for their expenditure in the following year.

To summarize, government funding mechanisms and institutional financial management have not changed to any great extent in the developing countries, irrespective of their levels of economic and educational development. Here, as elsewhere, financial constraint has tended to result in tight control to be expected where innovation and risk cannot be afforded. However, some governments, particularly where economic development has already taken place, such as Thailand and Korea, are investigating the possibility of implementing some form of formula lump-sum funding, and the experiences recounted here, placed within their particular steering contexts, may provide a significant input to policy-making in this sphere.

3. Lessons learned

However insufficient may be the financial resources allocated to higher education, in both developing and developed countries, significant improvements could be achieved if they were used more efficiently.

Globally, very few universities operate with modern financial management practices.

In most developed countries, it is now accepted that the introduction of flexible budgeting and disbursement procedures is a prerequisite for institutions seeking to increase the cost-effectiveness of their programmes. The modern view of organizations sees individuals as having different goals and only by harnessing these can the organization increase commitment. Slack exists within most well-run institutions, in order to give room to manoeuvre within budgetary constraints. Research has shown that better performance can be obtained if employees have a say in the budget which will subsequently be used to evaluate their performance (81). This is the first major line of current thinking in financial management for universities under self-regulation and accountability policies.

To balance this decentralization, however, there is a need to co-ordinate and centralize financial planning in line with the university's aims and objectives. This implies:

1. A strategic plan to provide a framework and an information system designed on programme budgeting lines to relate results to costs.
2. Consideration of alternative patterns of expenditure (including some zero basing which gives the possibility for cutbacks or growth).
3. A budget that represents the optimal allocation for achieving objectives, expressed in terms of performance indicators. Emphasis on the relationship between resources and desired objectives provides a clear framework for systematic thinking on resource management(82).

According to OECD(83), one of the key management issues of the 1990s will be the extent of financial devolution to institutions, departments and other basic operating units. Centralized hierarchical control is more and more being replaced by an arm's-length relationship. For example, the search for additional sources of financing is of little use to institutions which have no control over the number of new students. Similarly, if income diversification is to be effectively promoted, institutions which are successful in raising additional resources must be allowed to keep them rather than being compelled to surrender them to the Treasury, as is standard practice in some countries.

The arguments in favour of more departmental autonomy are:

1. It will encourage a greater sense of responsibility in the use of resources, since opportunity costs are more easily appreciated in small decision-making units.
2. Departmental loyalty is more likely to encourage individual members to seek outside funds for the benefit of the unit as a whole.
3. Comparisons of performance indicators between independently managed departments can help central administrators judge the relative efficiency with which different activities are being carried out.

The arguments against department financial autonomy are:

1. The smaller the cost centre, the less likely it is there will be staff with the necessary expertise to take meaningful resource allocation decisions. (The siting of cost centres is at present either at departmental, faculty or central level, depending on the size of the institution and its managerial ethos).
2. If too much time in academic departments is spent on management issues, this will conflict with the performance of their central academic tasks.
3. Decisions on academic staff salaries cannot be fully delegated to small departments because they constitute such a large proportion of total costs that relatively minor variations in individual salaries can have a major effect on the finance of a relatively small cost centre. In many countries, the main decisions on academic staff establishments are still taken outside otherwise autonomous universities for similar reasons.
4. It requires an up-to-date computerized management information system to provide the necessary continuous monitoring and control system.
5. Most developing country universities have not embarked yet on strategic planning. A rational approach is problematic where goals are ambiguous and the relation between means and ends is unclear; this is the situation in many educational institutions, with incremental budgets and short time horizons.
6. Many higher educational institutions function as political organizations, where budgeting is perceived as a bargaining process, with the departments making bids for resources and the centre attempting to make a balanced distribution. Objective evaluation is not possible where information is not available; emphasis therefore has to be put on control and accountability.

As we have seen, in the developing countries and in centrally-planned systems, publicly-funded higher education institutions suffer from very tight control which prevents them from redeploying resources more efficiently. In some countries, it is impossible to reallocate funds from one budget category to another; even when there are savings at the end of the fiscal year, the universities cannot use them to purchase items from a different budget category. Governments have no confidence in the universities' capacity to deploy funds in the most rational and efficient way.

One of the first steps, therefore, is to ensure that the university can demonstrate efficiency with the necessary accounting and financial expertise *at the centre,* backed up by an adequate information system. It should also have established good and harmonious working relations with the government, enabling decisions on funding to be negotiated and adhered to. Preferably, government funding should be based on objective criteria in order to ensure a fair distribution and promote cost consciousness within institutions. As soon as possible, some performance and quality elements should be incorporated. Any change should be negotiated within *set time limits.*

Other steps which may be taken in order to give confidence to all concerned that the financial management of the university is functioning well include these:

A. The *acquisition, or mobilization of resources.* These are normally allocated by the governmental authorities, or raised by tuition fees, plus additions from a variety of other sources, such as the community, parents, charities, etc. As we have seen in the foregoing sections, public universities in developing countries may receive 95 per cent of their funds from the government, whereas some universities in self-regulatory countries may now receive only 60 per cent. While public subsidies are likely to remain the major source of funding in most countries, they are becoming increasingly insufficient to ensure the financial viability of systems which are rapidly expanding under the pressure of rising social demand. Even when government funding is forthcoming, it is disadvantageous for the institution to rely on a single financial source. With less state support and limited opportunities to impose or increase fees, many universities have had to become involved in a wide spectrum of income-generating activities. In this regard Blair (idem) recommends broadening the membership of university councils to reflect the partnership of interest groups, to strengthen links with industry and commerce and to develop marketing methods.

The UNESCO *Principal Regional Office for Asia and the Pacific* (PROAP) compiled a list of possible sources of funding(84):

- private students;
- variations of tuition fees: these depend on level of economic development and may provide from 3 per cent (Egypt) to 15 per cent (Malaysia in public universities);
- examination fees;
- residence fees;
- contracts for research, courses and consulting (usually a percentage of the revenue earned goes to the Department concerned);
- intellectual property rights (patents and books);
- commercial activities (printing, software);
- investments in productive areas;
- endowments (this is a tradition in the USA and in certain prestige universities in the United Kingdom and Japan);
- foreign aid.

A variety of routes have been followed to diversify funding sources. Traditionally income is generated by undertaking research and service contracts on behalf of public and private companies. The returns on such services as consultancies and developmental work are expected to cover all costs and indeed to provide the institution with a net income. This source of funding is becoming increasingly important and is viewed, according to Taylor(85), a significant new funding mechanism in developed countries. In western Germany, external earnings of institutions increased by 50 per cent during the period 1975-90, the industrial component having risen rapidly by 130 per cent between 1980 and 1985. In the United States, public and private institutions receive about the same proportion of their incomes from the sale of services (20 and 24 per cent respectively). Other regions are beginning to follow suit: some technological institutions seem to have benefited greatly even in the developing countries, e.g. in China the Guandong Light Industrial Research Institute has increased its research income nine-fold(86).

In many countries public institutions are free to make use of these earnings; in Japan, Germany and Denmark, special provisions have been made to enable them to do so. However, the scope for service contracts is obviously limited where countries are predominantly agrarian or have a small modern industrial sector.

Another traditional way of raising financial support from industrial and commercial firms is in the form of grants or scholarships for specific academic or professional programmes. As far as developing countries are concerned, Salmi(87) found that direct donations have been most common in Asia, where the establishment of foundations offering financial support for students has been common. Private foundations, for instance, have developed in Indonesia, Thailand and South Korea. He notes, however, that even under the most favourable circumstances, such additional resources are not likely to represent a high proportion of university budgets.

Any income-generating activities should be in accord with the modalities of the particular higher education institution, and be demand-oriented. If not tested in an experimental phase, they can fail and bring losses. Special legislation is sometimes required to permit engagement in commercial enterprises, as in France.

B. The second stage in the financial management cycle is the *allocation of resources*, which involves setting priorities among all the activities of the university. In the short run, these decisions are highly determined by the resources the institution has already acquired, but over time more options for changing allocations become available. These real resource constraints and decisions are reflected in the budget plans drawn up for the coming financial year. A basic budget plan shows the amount of funds to be raised and the shares that are expected to be spent on each of the individual budget heads. As we have seen, some universities are now keeping a certain proportion (5-10 per cent) at the centre for strategic use, such as incentives, innovations, and information system development. They are also separating teaching and research funds.

Other principles commonly adopted have been:
- development of an internal resource allocation authority (often a planning and resources committee) serving as an investor, to whom proposers of activities must make commercial and financial, as well as academic, sense;
- structuring the university's activities and financial accounting records round cost/profit centres so that the entire university community is made aware of the cost of each activity and the sources of income which fund it;
- devolving financial responsibility and accountability closer to the operating units, as far as expertise and the information system permit. This should not involve abdication of all central control.
- adopting formula funding, often based on enrolments, output of graduates and other performance indicators. Where governments use formulae for funding purposes, institutions often

follow the same procedure for internal allocation. It may be necessary, when instituting formulae funding, to put aside some resources to assist certain faculties in the transition phase.

C. The third stage is *utilization,* or putting the budget plan into operation. Broadly interpreted, this task encompasses all the management activities of staffing, timetabling, running the premises, ordering supplies and so on, which incur expenditure. Other activities, such as running a university bookshop, hiring school premises or selling courses for a fee, which bring in additional income, may also be included. The specific task for financial managers is to monitor the budget regularly throughout the year in order to compare actual income and expenditure under various budget heads with those planned. If divergences persist and imbalances occur, as is likely, the job of management is to correct them. This may involve adjusting certain expenditure plans or implementing better financial control over internal budget holders, such as the heads of departments, in order to curtail or stimulate spending as required. It is here that an efficient management information system is important in keeping administrators up to date on the academic and financial performance of the various parts of the institution.

Some special training in budgetary competence for all administrators and heads of units can prove useful. Most higher education staff have very little background in fiscal management, but consistent budgetary incompetence should not be tolerated. Some indicators of the latter are: patterns of tardiness in meeting deadlines, mistakes in completing forms, mistakes in computation, failure to prioritize the uses of discretionary funds, and failure to communicate appropriate budgetary information to those concerned. It has been found that a series of short workshops or courses held internally can much increase cost consciousness and financial competence generally.

D. The fourth stage of the resource management cycle is *evaluation and auditing,* currently the most underdeveloped aspect. With increased autonomy, higher education institutions have to be accountable for their academic and financial performance. While considerable educational evaluation is undertaken, very little of it relates the value of resources used to the resulting educational outcomes. Though educational outcomes are not easily measured, nevertheless decisions have to be made, so there is certainly merit in quantifying wherever possible. Fielden (88) stresses that there is no one absolute and correct way of costing, but if there are several alternative ways to achieve an objective, then their relative costs can be measured. Cost analysis should aim at summarizing the net resource implications of an educational activity over a period of time, particularly if a change is involved. Cost per student year or hour are measures commonly used.

At present educational evaluation is usually undertaken by government advisers and inspectors while, quite separately, auditing is restricted to checking the financial probity of transactions undertaken by administrators. The auditors ideally should also assess the efficiency and effectiveness of resource utilization by relating service outcomes to policy objectives (effectiveness) and resource utilization (efficiency). Since in education the major operating cost is teaching staff, cost effectiveness is usually related to staff hours used and number of students benefiting(89). It is becoming more general for institutions to conduct their own self-evaluation, i.e. comparing performances both within the university and with strategic targets set. Procedures should be established to involve many of the staff in setting targets and measuring actual performance. Accountability exercises may be carried out by staff assessing work in other parts of the university to their own, so as to engender a sense of corporate responsibility. The objectives, optimum numbers and teaching hours for each course should be clearly defined, with the expected success rate and the educational techniques to be used. Once this has been done, the information provides a stable data base for the future which may be reviewed each year.

In the framework of accountability procedures, it is becoming common practice for universities to publish an annual report, which includes comparative data to show present and past results and budgets. Such reports are circulated not only to government departments but also to local authorities, industry and students.

Institutional financial management is evidently very much influenced by government policies and regulations, and this is likely to increase. Funding mechanisms are not only for resource allocation, but are *also a system of control and two-way communication between providers and users*. Funding policy reflects priorities and involves issues of equity, efficiency, quality, and responsiveness; it increasingly regards public institutions as purchasers of academic services of good quality on behalf of the community to meet national requirements.

It has always been recognized that the success of a university depended on academic expertise in the various disciplines. There is now no question that the availability of financial expertise will also be crucial. The staff development plan should therefore provide for the development of a body of staff with that expertise.

References

1. Ackerman, J. and Brons, R. *Changing financial relations between government and higher education*. Lemma, The Hague, 1989.
2. Aper, J. "Higher education and the State: accountability and the roots of student outcomes assessment". In *Higher Education Management*, Vol. 5, No. 3, November 1993.
3. For example: Kells, H.R. (ed.). *The development of performance indicators for higher education*, OECD, Paris, June 1993.
4. Kaiser, F. et al. *Public expenditure on higher education*, Jessica Kingsley, London 1992.
5. Williams G. " Financial management". Paper for IIEP Workshop on Institutional Management in Higher Education, Mauritius, September 1993.
6. Williams G.; Furth D. *Financing higher education, current patterns*, OECD. 1990.
7. OECD. 1990, idem.
8. Hartley, H. " Zero-based budgeting for schools". In *Financial management in education*, Open University, Milton Keynes 1989.
9. Hardy, C. "Hard decisions and tough choices" in *Higher Education*, Vol. 20, No. 3, October 1990.
10. Simkins, T. "Budgeting as a political and organizational process in educational institutions". In *Financial management in education*, Open University, Milton Keynes 1989.
11. ASHE-ERIC *Higher Education Report No. 8*, 1991.
12. Massy, W. "A strategy for improvement in college and university academic departments". Paper for Forum for Post-Secondary Governance. Santa Fe, October 1989.
13. Whalen, E. *Responsibility Center Budgeting*. Indiana University Press 1993.
14. Times Higher Educational Supplement, 29 October 1993.
15. Visit of Professor R. Pannu, University of Alberta, 27 July 1994.
16. Jameson, D. *Resource reallocation to meet quality concerns*. Paper for EAIR 13th Forum, September 1991.
17. Mace, J. "University funding changes and university efficiency". In *Higher Education Review*, Vol. 25, No. 2. 1993.
18. Lockwood, G. and Davies, G. *University: the management challenge*. Windsor, NFER 1985.
19. Bourn, M. "Some aspects of cost analysis in universities". In *Higher Education Policy*, Vol. 6, No. 3, September 1993.
20. Williams, G. "An evaluation of new funding mechanisms in British higher education". In *Higher Education in Europe*, Vol. XVII, No. 1, 1992. Also, *Changing Patterns of Finance in Higher Education*. OU Press, Buckingham, 1992.

21. Cornish, M.D. *Managing budget deficits in higher education: the experience of the University of Edinburgh*, IIEP, Paris 1994.
22. Cowen, R. "The management and evaluation of the entrepreneurial university: the case of England". In *Higher Education Policy*, Vol. 4, No. 3, September 1991.
23. Department of Employment, Education and Training. National Report on Australia's higher education sector. Canberra 1993.
24. Ferris, J. "A contractual approach to higher education performance". In *Higher Education Supplement*, Vol. 24, No. 4, December 1992.
25. Harrold, R. "Evolution of higher education finance in Australia". In *Higher Education Quarterly*, Vol. 46, No. 4, 1992.
26. Brons, R. "Changing the national funding system for higher education in the Netherlands". In Ackerman & Brons (eds.), *Changing financial relations between government and higher education*, Lemma, The Hague 1989.
27. NUFFIC. *Higher education in the Netherlands*, The Hague 1989.
28. De Leur, A. *Transformation into an entrepreneurial university*. Paper for the 10th European Air Forum. An explanation of the financial model is given in Boskar, D. University of Twente: its budgetary system, University of Twente internal working document 29, 1989.
29. Further details of the financial management system may be found in Holtta, S.; Pullainen, K. *Improving managerial effectiveness at the University of Joensuu*, Paris, IIEP 1994.
30. Brandstrom, D. and Franke Wiberg, S. "Steering higher education systems in Europe: the case of Sweden". In *Higher Education in Europe*, Vol. XVII, No. 3, 1992.
31. Furnes, F. and Matland, R. "Budgetary reforms in Norway". In Ackerman, J. (ed.), idem, 1989.
32. For a fuller discussion of this aspect, please see Woodhall, M. *Student loans in higher education* Nos. 1 to 3, IIEP, Paris, 1990 and 1991.
33. Times Higher Educational Supplement, 9 April 1993.
34. Old, J. and Morris, D. "Profit centers, cost centers". In *International Journal of Educational Management*, Vol. 6, No. 2, 1992.
35. Kozma, T. and Seteny, J. "Changing policies and dilemmas in higher education finance". In *Higher Education in Europe*, Vol. XVII, No. 1, 1992.
36. Sadlak, J. "The emergence of a diversified system". In *European Journal of Education*, Vol. 29, No. 1, 1994.
37. Turner, D. "Formula funding of higher education in the Czech Republic: creating an open system". In *Studies in Higher Education*, Vol. 19, No. 2, 1994.
38. Times Higher Educational Supplement, 29 January 1993.
39. Ovodenko, A. *Concept of development of Russian higher education: Advanced Technical Higher School, St. Petersburg*, Paper, IIEP, Paris, June 1992.

40. Brunner, J. *Educacion Superior en America Latina: Cambios y Desafios,* S. Fondo de Cultura Economica, Santiago, 1990.
41. Drysdale, R. "Higher education in Latin America". In the *World Bank*, March 1987.
42. Levy, D. "Problems of privatization". Paper prepared for the World Bank Seminar on Innovation and Improvement of Higher Education in Developing Countries. Kuala Lumpur, 30 June - 4 July 1991.
43. Schwartzman, S. "Policies for higher education in Latin America: the context". In *Higher Education*, Vol. 25, No. 1, 1993.
44. Vahl, F. "The decision making and management process in federal universities in Brazil". In *Interamerican Journal University Management*, April 1991.
45. Esteves Garcia, W. *Crisis in the management of education: the case of Brazil.* OEA/Cinterplan 1987, Caracas.
46. Champagne, R. *et al.* "University management in different socio-economic contexts". Report of Round Table of UNESCO, Geneva, 1992.
47. Marquis, C. *Argentina: Federal government and universities.* In Neave, G. and van Vught, F., idem.
48. Navarro, J. "Venezuelan higher education in perspective". In *Higher Education Supplement*, Vol. 21, No. 2, March 1991.
49. Levy, D. *Mexico: towards state supervision?* In Neave, G. and van Vught, F., idem.
50. Merino Brito, C. and Zemelman, R. *Modernización administrative de la Universidad de Concepción, Chile, (Improving the managerial effectiveness of higher education institutions),* IIEP, Paris, 1994.
51. Brunner, J. *Chile: Government and higher education.* In Neave, G. and van Vught, F., idem.
52. McLauchlan, P. and Melgar Salmon, E. "Public university financing in Peru". In *Higher Education Policy*, Vol. 5, No. 2, 1992.
53. Franco, A. "Financing higher education in Colombia". In *Higher Education*, Vol. 21, No. 2, March 1991.
54. Vargas, Lora W. *et al. Propuesta de Modificacion de la Estructura Organica de la Universidad Nacional,* Hweredia, September 1990.
55. Ahumata, M. "US methods for costing in higher education: taking the technology abroad". In *Higher Education*, Vol. 24, No. 3, October 1992.
56. Kaiser, F. *et al. Public expenditure on higher education.* Jessica Kingsley, London, 1992.
57. Darvogne, C. "Resources and allocations in higher educational institutions". In *Revue Française de Finances Publiques*, No. 27, 1989.
58. *Inspection generale de l'administration de l'education nationale. Rapport La Documentation Française,* Paris, 1993.
59. Courtois, G. "La gestion des établissements à l'heure de l'informatique". In *Le Monde*, 12 May 1992.
60. Taylor, M.G. " New financial models". In *Higher Education Management*, Vol. 3, No. 3, November 1991.

61. Daxner, M. "Flexibility in management by global budgets: the case of Lower Saxony". In *Higher Education Policy*, Vol. 7, No. 2 1994.
62. Blair, R. *An assessment of progress and the potential for financial diversification and income generation at selected African universities.* A report to the World Bank, Harare, December 1991.
63. Court, D. *Issues in higher education: a note from East Africa.* Norag News No. 11, December 1991.
64. Saint, W. *Universities in Africa.* World Bank Technical Paper No. 194, Washington, 1991.
65. Sanyal, B.C.; Martin M. *Institutional management in higher education* Report of a sub-regional workshop, IIEP, Paris, 1994.
66. Passi, F. 1994. *Implementing change to improve financial management in Makerere University*, Occasional Paper, IIEP, Paris, 1994.
67. Wield, D. *Beyond the fragments: donor reporting systems at the University of Dar-es-Salaam*, SAREC, January 1994.
68. Mahanga, M. *Management of finance at the University of Dar-es- Salaam.* Paper presented at IIEP Workshop, Mauritius, September 1993.
69. Mageza, R. *Mobilization and management of financial resources, In higher education.* IIEP Workshop, Mauritius, September 1993.
70. Harvard, Williams P. *Strategic planning: a five-year process.* Mimeo, 1992.
71. Adu, K. *Recurrent programme linked budget at the University of Science and Technology, Kumasi.* IIEP Workshop, Accra, June 1994.
72. Adesola, A. "Nigerian university system: challenges of growth in a depressed economy". In *Higher Education*, Vol. 21, No. 1, January 1991.
73. AAU/British Council Roundtable on *Cost reduction and recovery and alternative funding of universities*, Windhoek, August 1992.
74. Selvaratnam, V. *University autonomy versus state control: the Singapore experience.* In Neave, G. and van Vught, F., idem 1994.
75. Arcelo, A. *Governance and management issues in Philippine higher education.* Paper, June 1992.
76. Weifang, Min. "Higher education finance in China: current constraints and strategies for the 1990s". In *Higher Education*, No. 21 1991.
77. Times Higher Educational Supplement, 13 December 1991.
78. Balachander, K. *Financing higher education in India.* University News, 26 October 1992.
79. Siddiqui, M. "Programme for reform of university education". Academy of Educational Planning and Management, Islamabad, August 1990.
80. Bubtana, A. "Financing Arab higher education: a search for new alternatives". In *Higher Education Policy*, Vol. 5, No. 4, 1992.
81. Arnold, J. and Hope, T. *The budgeting process in financial management in education.* Open University, Milton Keynes, 1989.
82. Simkins, T. "Budgeting as a political and organizational process in educational institutions". In *Financial Management in Education*, Open University, Milton Keynes, 1989.

83. OECD. "Changing patterns in finance of higher education". *Innovation in Education* No. 55, February 1990.
84. PROAP, UNESCO, *Mobilization of additional funding for higher education*. Bangkok, 1989.
85. Taylor, M.G. "New financial models – summary report". In *Higher Education Management*, Vol. 3, No. 3, November 1991.
86. Cleverley, J. "The concept of enterprise and the Chinese universities". In *Comparative Education*, Vol. 23, No. 3, 1987.
87. Salmi, J. *Perspectives on the financing of higher education*, World Bank, December 1991.
88. Fielden, J. "Costing educational practice". In *Financial Management in Education*. Open University, Milton Keynes, 1989.
89. Jones, D. "A practical unit cost approach to budgeting and accountability in colleges". In *Financial Management in Education*, Open University, Milton Keynes, 1989.

Chapter 7

Academic staff management

The effectiveness of a university essentially depends on the efficiency and quality of its staff, and especially its academic staff. In a period of declining resources and expanding enrolments, staff costs have become by far the largest element in institutional budgets, generally taking 80 per cent, and in some developing countries as much as 95 per cent. Most academics have also suffered a decline in the real value of their salaries with consequent problems of recruitment and retention.

Human resource management embraces staff planning, recruitment, selection, retention, appraisal, control, and development, together with the negotiation of agreements about conditions of employment with an association or with the individual. It is in this domain of university management (together with finance) that the greatest differences amongst universities can be seen. Some may have complete autonomy (certain United States and private institutions) or a high degree of autonomy (as in the United Kingdom), while others may have little autonomy at all, with centralized staff management carried out by the Government, which may not only fix salary scales and staff levels, which is quite usual, but also decide on the number of posts and the proportions at each level. The Government may also incorporate the staff into the civil service, which involves control of recruitment, promotion, dismissal and retirement.

Once recruitment has been made, however, the management of academic staff in their university functions is usually devolved to deans and heads of academic departments. How this very valuable resource is to be used is therefore a matter for the lower management levels and this requires effective control and appraisal procedures, whatever kind of steering mechanisms are in force at government and university executive levels. This is an aspect which will be particularly examined in the following analyses, made by type of management classification.

1. Self-regulation and accountability implemented

In this group of countries, staff management is a university responsibility and is spread throughout the institution, from executive to departmental levels. One survey conducted in the United Kingdom in new universities (i.e. former polytechnics) found that conditions of employment (including negotiations with unions), disciplinary procedures and firing were the responsibility of senior management while recruitment and appraisal were mainly faculty responsibilities(1). A Staffing Committee at faculty or departmental level decides what staff are to be assigned to each unit according to the financial provision and level of teaching. A major strategy for better control of the use of academic staff is therefore through the annual budgeting process, combined with the costing of programmes in designated cost centres. This requires that teaching time (including preparation, lectures, marking and examinations), class size, support and space, are all analyzed and costed; any programme out of line with similar programmes can then be queried.

(i) Belgium

The Catholic University of Leuven operates a devolved version of this cost centre approach to staff management. Each faculty is given a certain quantity of units of account in its annual budget. One unit buys a temporary assistant, two a tenured professor, etc. The faculty must pay for excess promotions (above the norm set) by a reduction in number of posts but is also free to trade unused posts for credits to buy services, materials or space.

Usually teaching provision is guided by norms set at government or institutional level, using indicators such as:

- Student:staff ratios (SSRs) and class sizes, according to discipline; it has been found that a university can function efficiently with high class sizes in such areas as the Humanities and Commerce, while at present Engineering and Medicine, for example, need low ones).
- Ratios for the desired mix of different levels of staff.
- Workloads for teaching, research, administration and service by level and type of staff; for example, a professor may devote 35 per cent to research and service, while a Dean or Head of Department may spend almost as much time on administration.

Some flexibility in recruitment is provided by more short-term contracts for one or two years. Posts may also be moved between departments or faculties as demand increases or decreases. No departmental staffing is permanent(2).

Interest in effective staff management is high. Studies are being made of models, such as that by Phelps(3), which deals with the need for fairness in allocating teaching loads, since departments usually have particular educational policies and differ in the use of external staff. Another approach is through the analysis of the strengths and weaknesses of individual academic staff, in order to give management better information about their potential and needs for career development – or retirement(4).

Most staff management practice considers academic staff as *assets* from which the institution should ensure the greatest return. This involves getting the right people (more good teachers in particular) in line with objectives and ensuring their efficient use by analysis and control and their retention by career development and commensurate incentives or rewards. As has been seen in the previous chapters on finance and overall management, governments played a role in bringing about a more cost-conscious and flexible style of staff management also, in the shape of policy, norms, indicators and specialized agencies.

(ii) Netherlands

The experience of the *Netherlands*, which was one of the earliest, has many features in common with other self-regulatory countries. It was, however, the only *major* attempt to rationalize staff rapidly; other systems took a more gradual approach. From 1980, the annual budget of the universities was cut by two to three per cent, and they responded by not replacing retired staff and by introducing a new staff planning model for each department. Curricula were re-organized in independent modules exchangeable between departments, schools and the open university, which reduced staff needs. Extensive consultation produced a plan in which staff positions were reduced by 10 per cent and student/staff ratios were increased in some cases by 50 per cent. Redundant staff were either transferred to administrative jobs or took transfers to other departments, other universities, or retired(5). Norms for staffing were set which distributed full professors, associates, assistants and assistant researchers according to a ratio of 1:1.5:2.5:2. New categories of staff were introduced with a range of types of contracts from teaching only to teaching plus research. After 1990, there was no security of tenure for staff not covered by the budget. There is no permanent early retirement scheme and the principle of 'last in first out' will apply. It was political will which made the restructuring possible(6).

(iii) Australia

Government measures were forceful in *Australia* too. An agreement was reached on a new system that fixed staffing levels which cannot increase unless teaching activities increase. Teachers' pay is directly related to their workload, and deans were given more power to control staff. The net result was that departments reduced staffing levels(7).

(iv) Problems facing the universities

Such measures brought about a number of problems that had to be dealt with by university management. These were:

(a) Increased student:staff ratios, as illustrated in the data given in *Table 20*.

Table 20. Student:staff ratios in selected countries.

	1980	1990
Australia	14.6	17.4
Canada	19.0	22.4
United Kingdom	9.9	15.3

Source: UNESCO Statistical Yearbook 1992.

(b) An ageing staff profile, which created concern about sources of future recruitment and possible impact on research productivity. An international survey(8) found skewed age structures denoting a middle-aged profile. An example of this is Australia where almost half the academic staff are now 45 or over, compared with 30 per cent in 1980. Some individual institutions have much worse situations.

(c) Relative deterioration of working conditions, with higher SSRs and lower salaries. For instance, in Australia academic pay has fallen since 1970 by 30 per cent relative to other professions, and in New Zealand the decline has been of the order of 15 per cent. In the USA, growth of salaries in real terms stopped in 1989, and there were salary freezes or even cuts in the States of New York and Massachusetts(9). Promotion possibilities have diminished in most countries, creating a more competitive environment; in addition there is increased accountability to the public, less job security and a deterioration in physical facilities. Jobs in industry and commerce therefore now compare more favourably and universities are having to find ways of using external professionals in order to obtain certain types of expertise.

(d) Higher SSRs place more demand on teaching expertise and time if productivity and quality are not to fall. Hence there has been increased concern about teaching quality, including the ability to use new technology, with emphasis on teacher assessment and development, and the creation of appropriate incentives for higher performance. Concern for quality has also led to a demand for closer links with industry and the community, which has had an impact on staffing in certain countries.

Thus staff management accumulated many more responsibilities and was called upon to implement a variety of strategies that would allow universities to operate more successfully within the new constraints. It will be noted that in many cases, governments have offered assistance, either in the form of special funding or advisory units.

(v) Staff management strategies adopted

(a) *Slowing down the rate of increase or reducing staff numbers*

A strategy that was widely adopted early on was refusal to approve new posts, freezing vacancies, and voluntary early retirement schemes. Apart from the expense of redundancy payments, the disadvantages were that such schemes are most attractive to those staff with the best external earning opportunities and hence often the most dynamic and useful to the institution. Freezing vacancies also resulted in some staff having to teach in areas other than their own speciality, creating an imbalanced staffing profile and threatening quality. One scheme to counteract this in the United States involved part-time re-employment of certain retired staff, so that the university would not suffer the sudden and drastic loss of indispensable expertise, and would have time to plan replacement. Other strategies quickly followed these initial cost-containment reactions.

(b) Creating conditions of greater flexibility

Ensuring an appropriate staff profile in a period of rapid change requires that the institution acquire greater flexibility in management. Certain causes of rigidity have therefore been greatly weakened, i.e.

- *Academic tenure.* In most self-regulated systems, including the Netherlands, United States, and Australia, the proportion of staff with tenure is being reduced. In Australia between 1982 and 1991 the number of tenured staff decreased from 81 to 61 per cent, but the quality of staff, measured by Ph.D. attainment, rose from 60 to 72 per cent. In the United Kingdom tenure is being phased out as stipulated by the 1988 Education Reform Act.
- *Reduction in full-time permanent employment.* Generally the use of part-time staff is growing. In Australia, fewer than one in ten junior academics have permanent employment and the number of temporary staff has doubled. Part-time lecturers now comprise 40 per cent of all academics in the United States (Report by American Association of University Professors 1992); they tend to be used to teach English, foreign languages and mathematics to first-year students. In the United Kingdom between 1981 and 1986, numbers of full-time academic staff fell by 8 per cent while non-wholly university financed part-timers and temporary contracts doubled. A survey found that English Departments particularly rely on part-time postgraduates as temporary staff. Warwick University has a contract to develop training programmes for 20 postgraduate students, distributed among eight universities, who will be used to teach up to 150 hours per annum, for which they will be paid a small salary and receive their tuition fees. Such strategies are not without their drawbacks: returns may be negative in research and scholarship and a binary system can be created in which part-timers feel inferior. A survey in Canada showed that women formed 73 per cent of part-timers, are engaged in core teaching and cannot obtain research funding. In turn, full-time staff are burdened with all the administrative tasks(10).
- *Changes to staff regulations giving greater institutional autonomy.* Working conditions are relatively deregulated in the Anglo-Saxon systems; in Australia a response to some staff shortages has been to lower qualification requirements, while in New Zealand institutions may pay above salary levels to certain key staff in order to retain them. The USA and Sweden are also countries where universities may negotiate salary levels with individual staff on recruitment. Some institutions (United Kingdom, USA) are introducing performance-related pay schemes – see below under *assessment.*

(c) Insuring against an ageing staff profile

Apart from early retirement schemes, Governments have instituted measures to attract a pool of young talent. The main strategy adopted has been government-funded salaried Ph.D. posts, often called Research Fellows (implemented in Sweden, the Netherlands, Finland, Spain, Canada, Denmark, Australia).

(d) *Increasing teaching activity: strategies have included the following:*

- *New types of contracts*, such as for teaching only. In the United Kingdom, nine universities have introduced teaching-only contracts and more are to follow. The Netherlands too has a range of types of contracts, including teaching only. Also, as we have seen, part-timers or postgraduate fellows are often employed to teach first-year courses.
- *Increasing teaching loads* and ensuring that staff actually fulfil the loads specified. In the United States, senior professors have been asked to do more teaching and reduce the number of postgraduate students employed as teachers. Analysis of teaching loads over time has shown in some institutions that teachers teach less now than they did a decade ago. A few States have now specified the number of hours to be worked according to type of institution(11).

(e) Higher quality teaching

Strategies are much more complex, for example:

- *Appraisal of teaching.* By and large, university teaching has been considered *unprofessional*, i.e. not based on a qualification, and mainly learnt on the job. An exception is the United States, where in some cases future faculty are prepared by giving graduates a course on teaching. In Australia and the United Kingdom, a period of part-time teaching may precede formal appointment. However, the recent need to obtain the greatest value from the relatively smaller numbers employed has given impetus to both teaching appraisal and development.

There have been a number of innovations or experiments, such as directed small group student discussion and sample surveys of students, but generally combinations of self/internal/external, peer/student assessment are used. The participation of staff has often been stressed as being voluntary.

In Australia and the United Kingdom, all tertiary institutions are now obliged to review and assess staff performance according to guidelines laid down at national level. All staff are expected to undergo a career review annually or every two years, based on self-assessment which is confidential. In the case of a disagreement between a reviewer and the staff member, re-assessment can be carried out by a third party. The system has been generally accepted in both countries. Emphasis on assessment of teaching quality is very strong in the United Kingdom at present: a national Academic Audit Unit has been set up to review the quality of teaching and learning in institutions, and to conduct quality audits which would ensure that they conduct their own quality assessments(12). An example of the multiple procedures now involved comes from the University of Birmingham, which in 1992-93 underwent 10 different types of evaluation, which included teaching. It was the first to invite the Academic Audit Unit to visit; it also had to gain accreditation of its Law, Engineering and Medicine courses from professional bodies and receive the Higher Education Funding Council for England (HEFCE) assessment of its History Department. For this the Department had to complete a self-assessment covering admissions procedures, teaching methods, pastoral care, staff monitoring, resources and teaching innovations, after which a team of five assessors from other universities visited for three days to verify it. They dropped in on 30 classes, met the student counselling and careers services and staff development unit, and checked on library resources. At the end the assessors made a report, which included ranking on a 1 to 5 scale. In addition to these external assessments, the university has its own internal controls including annual staff appraisal and inspection by the Senate and five-yearly evaluation of curriculum design(13).

In Ontario and Quebec, Canada, the upgrading of teaching is very much on the agenda and universities are trying to find ways to put its assessment on the same level as research which at present preponderates. Present policy is to recruit those with an aptitude for teaching, and all new staff receive further training. Two universities already give merit increases for teaching equally with those for research, while others award prizes for teaching excellence. However, assessment procedures are not standardized; some universities use student evaluation, others peer assessment. Some use both, like the University of Ottawa, which also conducts surveys of former students.

Here, the individual staff member writes his own annual report covering the total annual workload for teaching, scholarship and service. The university's Centre for Teaching holds workshops and consultations, and will videotape teaching sessions. Over the four years 1990-1994, it has increased its activities from 15 to 70 per year. In this institution both tenure and promotion have been refused for poor performance in teaching(14).

In the United States, assessment by students is very common and has been used for a number of years, together with a variety of professional and teacher association evaluations, which inspect the entire range of resources in order to ensure good teaching much as in the United Kingdom quality assessment described above.

- *Staff development.* The main response in the United States, Canada, Australia and the United Kingdom to the need to assist staff to improve their teaching has been to set aside funds, design short courses and provide services or units within the institution to give advice on teaching methods and technologies. However, most depend on the staff member actively seeking assistance, and often only the younger members do this. However, in this area too, there has been a lot of innovation, and there is much experience from which lessons can be learned.

In Australia, Academic Development units have been established within universities for the last 25 years though approaches may differ. In the University of New South Wales, emphasis has been laid on training the head of department, who in turn meets new staff to plan their professional development, to clarify responsibilities, to monitor workload, and to explain goals and resource constraints. Four to six hours are now devoted to each new staff member in this way(15).

The United Kingdom, in line with its assessment system, has adopted a national approach, in addition to in-house courses. The universities collectively have established a Staff Development and Training Unit which provides training for all categories of staff, including top management. As regards teaching quality, this may involve:

- competence in a range of teaching methods from lecturing to preparing self-instructional materials;
- designing and evaluating a course;
- implementing an innovation in a department and analysing the reasons for success or failure;
- educational policy for a department or institution(16).

Most universities now have staff development units and their activities have recently increased with extra government funding. One example is the University of Surrey, which has received funds for a maximum of £650 per staff member per annum. This covers requests for seminars, workshops, job shadowing and short-term exchanges with other institutions. Significantly, the most popular in-house events are those dealing with management, e.g. time management, appraisal and communication skills and self-development topics.

- *Incentives to improve teaching performance.* There is still little incentive for good teaching in many countries; until recently, prizes for it were largely unheard of outside the United States. Although much of the behaviour of academic staff is voluntary, however, a reward system can motivate and a management system can orient and control. Those countries which have gone farthest in implementing assessment and development are also those which have introduced some rewards. These may derive from a national fund or from the university's own budget and may take the form of prizes, awards or bonuses and merit pay. There is a growing conviction that greater rewards must be given to teaching, and a number of research studies have been conducted to establish the most appropriate criteria, methodologies and rewards.

One study in the University of Sydney, *Australia*, addressed the vexed question of what constituted teaching excellence. Nineteen recipients of awards responded to a questionnaire on teaching effectiveness and responses were compared to replies from novices. The best teachers were found to structure the learning process, enhance the desire to learn and encourage individual and self-directed learning. They were found to use more complex and flexible concepts and were more inclined to adopt systematic, formal procedures for feedback and to use them to change their teaching(17).

In the past, teaching has not counted for as much as research as a qualification for promotion. This is often because its evaluation has been more problematic, since the quality of research publications and number of citations are relatively easier to measure. Anyway, the prospect of promotion may be an inadequate incentive when it depends on the occurrence of vacancies; bonuses and awards may also be necessary. Australia, New Zealand, Sweden, the United Kingdom and Finland therefore all now have a national fund for grants to enhance teaching.

The *United Kingdom's* experience in this domain has been controversial. The first move towards merit pay was accepted, and the Government withheld 2 per cent of its salary grant to provide rewards for high performance, in the first instance to Heads of Departments and above. Several institutions introduced merit pay for senior staff, for example a 10 per cent bonus for the achievement of objectives. However, the system of performance-related pay for all staff which was scheduled to be introduced in August 1993 is encountering resistance. Half the universities have not accepted the proposed one-off cash bonuses but instead are introducing incentives such as extra promotions, more money for additional responsibilities and extra funds for staff development. Staff in at least six universities have agreed to join *pools* to redistribute merit payments equally among colleagues, indicating that they value collegiality above a competitive merit system. It would seem that awards, well-known in the area of research, are more acceptable than merit pay as a first step in introducing reward systems for teaching(18).

United States academics are accustomed to being assessed and most departments have operated their own evaluation systems for many years. However, the trend is towards institution-wide systems incorporating merit pay increases, which are now quite common. The key issue in most of the schemes was how to combine professional development with assessment designed to assist institutional decision-making on promotions or dismissals.

United Kingdom universities tend to insist on the developmental aspects since promotion happens only at certain points in an academic career. In Australia, on the other hand, administrators feel that more flexible staffing requires a system of rewards, and see appraisal as a means of ensuring accountability(19).

A marked change in managing human resources has occurred. Whereas it was traditionally the case that individuals were responsible for their own development, this is now seen as a matter of departmental and institutional wellbeing(20). Where appraisal, development and incentive systems have been linked, as in the United States, Canada, the United Kingdom and Australia, considerable advances have been made in implementing this concept.

2. Self-regulation in transition

The universities in this group of countries were not subjected in the 1980s to as much governmental and financial pressure as, for example, the United Kingdom and Australia in recent years, but nevertheless SSRs rose, for example from 1980 to 1990 from 10.4 to 14 in Norway, and from 13.6 to 14.5 in Finland.

However, this situation has now changed dramatically in the case of *Finland*, which as from 1990 has had to cope with a declining budget. The process can be illustrated by the case of the University of Joensuu(21).

The search for flexibility, efficiency and devolution of staff management in Finland resembles the experiences of the self-regulatory group of universities.

Experience in this group of countries with staff assessment and development is, however, mixed. Some, like *Sweden*, have had national training courses for 20 years, but responsibility has now been moved to the institutions. All heads of departments are offered initial training. Universities with a strong interest in strategic planning usually have a parallel training programme for administrators, deans and department heads. The task of a head is no longer just to manage but to provide leadership and set goals, and several institutions are now running programmes for secretaries to take over daily administration so as to leave more time for leadership(22). Good lecturers are rewarded from a £2 million fund aimed at improving the quality of teaching. This is to be distributed by a Council which will investigate and reward good teaching practice and experiments, using staff appraisal, peer review and performance indicator systems(23).

In *Norway*, however, academic staff are reluctant to undertake further training. Though questionnaires are sent asking about needs for self-regulation in training, few answer and few participate. However, some programmes have been designed to give an understanding of management budgets, staff administration, leadership roles and means of communication. Reluctance to train is linked to lack of interest in appointment as head of department; such posts carry little prestige or career credit(24).

In *Finland*, the Council of Higher Education Departments evaluates research and teaching by discipline while the universities themselves have adopted a variety of approaches to evaluation, some creating special funds to encourage teaching and research excellence (see *Box 9*). Many departments use student evaluation. However, in this group a number of universities have not yet embarked upon teaching appraisal, which is seen as a complex and delicate process.

Box 9.

> In accordance with proactive policies which foresaw the need for retrenchment, staff resources were reallocated during the mid-1980s in a process of consultation and mild pressure, by means of combined measures (merging several posts and splitting them in a new way) based on analysis of the employment needs in the field, student/teacher ratios, indicators of teaching intensity, unit costs per teacher and academic performance of students. At that period, the main objective was the better use of staff time(25). In this case, since only senior posts (professors, lecturers) carry tenure, there was some flexibility within the system. However, under the staffing system operating in the 1980s, the filling of vacant posts was made by university Senate or, in the case of permanent full professor's posts, by the President of the Republic. After obtaining a new post, the department could retain it for ever, with no extra effective costs. In fact, because of the very centralized system, the departments did not even know their labour costs exactly. If a teacher had leave of absence without salary, the department or the university could not benefit from the savings. Consequently, there was not much cost consciousness at the departmental level and the opportunity costs were, due to detailed line item financing and the system of wages management, totally unknown in practice.
>
> In the new budgeting system, funds for salaries and wages for permanent personnel are budgeted to the university as part of the total fixed lump sum.
>
> At the University of Joensuu the reform was always explicitly considered as part of resource management, to integrate the use of human and monetary resources. While decision-making on non-academic staff has been delegated to department heads, collegial tripartite level (Council, Faculty, Department) decision-making was retained for academics. Centralized power was necessary due to future financial implications, possible contraction and the need to sanction the inefficient and combat cliques.
>
> Under the 1992 Law, universities obtained the right to create and discontinue tenured (civil service) posts. In addition, the strict formal qualifications for recruitment and promotion are being moderated and performance bonuses of 3 to 6 per cent are awarded on evaluation by Department Heads, Deans and the Rector. In particular, extra awards are given for administrative duties performed by academic staff but these are still not yet enough to make the posts really attractive.
>
> From the autumn semester 1992 on, the departments of the university implemented another new flexibility element in resource management: the university has been allowed to start a system of *flexible work loads*. Traditionally the system of defined teaching loads – different for each teacher category – has been very restrictive. In the new system, the work load of each teacher is defined as 1,600 hours a year, with the possibility to freely allocate it to teaching, research and other activities. No other restrictions are set for the departments. The working plans are made solely at departmental level, the Head of the Department approving the individual plans of the teachers. This kind of a system has already been piloted at two Finnish universities, at the University of Jyväskylä and at the Helsinki School of Economics and Business Administration. Teaching loads have not been changed much at these universities, but deregulation has made the introduction of *new teaching methods easier and more attractive*.

3. Self-regulation in difficulty

In Latin America staff costs are high as a proportion of the total budget: 87 per cent in Costa Rica and 91 per cent in Brazil. Most of the staff are part-time, paid on an hourly basis, and have more than one job. Few of them have permanent positions (e.g. only 11 per cent in the Faculty of Engineering of the National Autonomous University of Mexico (UNAM) in 1990). In this region, therefore, tenure is not an obstacle to flexibility in deployment.

There are, however, considerable other rigidities, particularly in public universities. In *Venezuela*, powerful teachers associations define and regulate functions and working hours. The Rector has to respect these employment contracts and internal resistance to the assessment of staff performance is strong. In private universities, contracts are renewed annually, so that there is a regular control process(26).

In *Brazil*, the principal obstacle to more autonomous management and the introduction of formula funding is that federal universities are not responsible for staff expenditures. Staff management, including recruitment, is done by the Ministry. There is no motive for institutions to develop policies to increase efficiency in staff management, and in fact they opposed proposals to give them the right to hire and fire staff(27). Other countries have begun what they see as a slow and difficult process to implement assessment and accountability as central values in university management. In Argentina, the Rectors proposed in 1989 the establishment of mechanisms for evaluation and two years later met to review what institutions had done. Most had drawn up proposals in various areas, and were to hold 'reflection days' as part of an initial sensitization process(28).

In 1991, *Mexico* announced its new policies for higher education, which included differential salary scales for academics, individual assessment and a programme for the evaluation of teaching performance. This is organized by the Ministry, and 30 per cent of the staff can receive a bonus of one to three times minimum salary, representing 6 per cent of the total higher education budget. However, the implementation of differential salary scales has proved difficult, since budgets are so tight and the salary bill represents 90 per cent of total funding(29). However, some universities are now introducing changes in staff management. In UNAM academic staff have more autonomy in allocating and using their time, and the degree and quality of participation of staff in academic activities now determines economic rewards and research funding through a 'Commission' set up for each academic unit(30).

The *University of Costa Rica* has autonomy in staff management and has established three types of employment contract: exclusive dedication (no other employment), extraordinary (some external employment) or discretional (for those on whom external demands are high). Staff can request the one they want. Central management sends questionnaires to heads of departments for staff evaluation; those with low evaluations are requested to make specific improvements. All new professors and those up for promotion are supposed to take a teaching methods course, but this is generally resented(31).

In *Cuba*, the main needs for teaching staff were satisfied by 1987, and a surplus in some areas began to appear, which allowed selection to be more rigorous by competitive examination for full-time posts. Part-time contracts have been maintained so as to be able to incorporate professionals from production and services. Legislation in 1988 made department heads responsible for the quality of programmes, the efficient use of academic staff, and adequate teaching skills(32).

In 1988, a particularly interesting project was carried out in *El Salvador*, where the University Council launched a case study on staff planning, which investigated the time spent by teachers in face-to-face teaching, on preparation, consultation, evaluation, post-graduate teaching, research, administration and further individual study. 88 per cent of time was given to undergraduate teaching, 2 per cent to graduate teaching, 1.5 per cent to research and service, and 7 per cent to administration. Time spent on teaching varied from 97 per cent in Law to 72 per cent in Economics. The student/staff ratio varied from 66:1 in Economics and Law to 5:1 in Pharmacy. It was observed that Engineering, Economics and Pharmacy under-used their staff while Law and Social Sciences overworked them. A quantitative model was developed to calculate full-time equivalent staff needs according to identified tasks and based on (i) optimally allocated time for each task; (ii) teaching method used; (iii) student enrolment; and (iv) time spent on preparation and other academically related work, such as research and service(33).

In Latin America, then, the first moves in staff management reform have been made in certain countries, though in others they face considerable resistance; in the case of El Salvador, sufficient institutional goodwill was generated to carry out what would be considered by most university staff to be a threatening analytical exercise.

The uncertain economic climate in Latin America is one factor impeding change, and this also applies to the next group of countries, those in Eastern Europe. Official statistics indicate relatively stable and favourable student:staff ratios, though salaries are now so low that secondary employment has to be sought.

Table 21. Studend:staff ratios in selected Eastern European countries

	1980	1990
Former Czechoslovakia	8.8	8.3
Hungary	5.8	5.2
Poland	7.9	7.1
Romania	13.2	14.0

Source: idem

The difficulties that these countries face in staff management are described in one report from *Poland*(34). Under the 1990 Act on Higher Education, universities now have autonomy over organizational structure, enrolments, admissions, hiring policies and salary levels, though not teaching workloads. However, such changes go against the habits of the academic community, which is accustomed to security of employment, remuneration for research regardless of results, and egalitarian treatment. There were plenty of jobs in the previously over-expanded structures of higher education and research, and hiring policies favoured conformists who did not necessarily have the best qualifications. From 1989 to 1991, funds allocated to education and research were halved; line-item budgeting persists, and Rectors therefore have little flexibility. There is little staff turnover, too many staff have tenure, and there are no individual evaluation procedures. The result is an aged staff structure, low salaries, and few openings for the young. The brightest graduates are not attracted to higher education but seek work abroad or in the private sector.

In Russia too, it was reported that more than 3,500 scientists and university lecturers left the country in 1992, the majority being young(35).

The governments in these countries are seeking to give higher educational institutions more flexibility in staff management. For example, in *Uzbekistan* a contract system has been introduced for recruitment of staff with a maximum of one year's duration. The salary structure is more flexible, and universities may give special incentives to exceptional teachers, extending to as much as double their regular salary. At the same time, staff development programmes have been introduced to supply new skills(36). However, only in special circumstances have they been able to achieve a leaner staffing structure, as in the case of staff from departments, whose role in the curriculum is being greatly reduced. The Slovak Technical University shed 250 teachers (15 per cent of its staff) in this way but the Rector is hampered by a strong Senate in reducing other over-staffed departments. The exception to this may be the Czech Republic, whose transition process is making more headway. Here it was reported that some faculties experienced up to 90 per cent staff turnover in 1989, but these were the younger staff and middle management remained largely unchanged(37).

Staff development has always been actively pursued in East European countries, and there has been some expansion of activity. In Poland, for example, television gives special programmes for university staff, while in Russia participation in staff development programmes is a criterion for promotion, and it is planned that 20 per cent of teaching staff should take part every two years.

However, there are few reports of universities tackling staff appraisal, though the University of Veterinary Science, Budapest, implemented in 1989 an evaluation system for academic staff that sets the minimum requirements for each position.

4. Centralized planning and control

a. Western European countries

A major difference between countries under centralized planning and those under self-regulation is that in the former university staff are often civil servants and their trade unions are monolithic and powerful political forces. Resistance to change may be strongly mobilized as happened in Germany. However, the policy of open admission to universities counteracts this conservative force. Student:staff ratios have grown and conditions of work have much deteriorated.

Staff recruitment may be by national competition (Italy, France, Spain) or, for lower levels, the department may put forward its preferences direct to the Ministry. In Germany and Belgium, state governments appoint professors from a list of three put forward by the university.

Table 22. Student:staff ratios in Western European countries

	1980	1990
France	21.6	24.3
Germany	12.0	18.0 (38)
Italy	25.8	26.2
Spain	16.3	18.6

Source: idem.

Under the system of four-year contracts implemented in France and Italy, the growth of staff is agreed between the university and the government according to a development plan. Control is exercised to some extent by norms, e.g. in France (1989) the ratios were 1 professor: 1.5 lecturers: 0.6 assistant lecturers: 0.5 monitors, while researchers are appointed on a supplementary basis. In Belgium, universities may appoint their own staff and the structure is less rigid, being set at 1 professor/lecturer: 1.5 assistants.

Many of the problems encountered by the self-regulatory systems are present in these countries too. Strategies have been somewhat similar, and Government action has tended to centre on obtaining more flexibility in deployment and reducing long-term commitments through fewer tenured posts and more part-time employment.

In France today civil service status has become harder to attain and teaching is being done increasingly by hourly paid staff. Three types of contract have been introduced: teaching, supervision of postgraduates and administration. Salaries have not kept pace with the cost of living, and bonuses had to be introduced for about 18,000 staff(39).

Recruitment in Belgium is now only to untenured posts, the system having been made more flexible by developing hybrid posts. The distribution of tenured to untenured has become similar to proportions seen in self-regulatory universities, i.e. 65 per cent full-time tenured; 5 per cent part-time permanent (mainly senior) and 30 per cent part-time temporary. The untenured may spend half their time gaining a Ph.D., but their post is not renewed after six years. Assistants now have to look elsewhere for employment and the problem of an ageing profile remains,

In 1991, one Belgian university reported that 46 per cent of its staff were aged between 50 and 59 and 16 per cent were over 60.

In Germany, as in Italy, civil service status has only ever been given to the two top levels of university employee. Long-term employment prospects of assistants in Germany have declined; only 25 per cent may now expect a contract, and their university posts are considered as a step to employment in industry. State policies include temporary support for fixed-term research appointments, temporary increases in staff in anticipation of retirements, and associate appointments below professor level so as to give staff more time to complete their Ph.D.s.

In Austria, universities may now decide for themselves on the recruitment of temporary lecturers. Spain for the first time permits the combination of a university post with other outside employment. Italy has introduced a post of Contract Professor to teach specific courses, while France has developed a system of exchange by delegation, detachment and positions *'hors cadre'*. In all countries a combination of state guidelines with a certain degree of institutional autonomy is seen to provide the best conditions for staff management.

Some countries are dealing with the problem of ageing by introducing compulsory retirement (Spain at 70) or a lower retirement age (Belgium from 70 to 65).

The need for more and higher quality teaching has also had to be met. In France extra hours of teaching are paid, and the 'monitorat' system trains future recruits. Some 45,000 graduate monitors are taught in 14 centres, and paid a small salary for teaching two hours per week. In 1993 an extra 12 million Francs were to be spent to increase the numbers.

Improvements in quality are being sought by the incorporation of highly skilled professionals in the staffing structure. France is providing incentives for researchers from the *Centre National de la Recherche Scientifique*, which employs 11,000 full-time staff, to move into university teaching posts for four years. At the Catholic University of Leuven, Belgium, the increase in student numbers obliged the university to ask some researchers (paid by the national fund or under contracts) to teach and these staff now have a dual status of researcher/part-time academic. In Austria, the Ministry appoints temporary university professors for up to five years on a supernumerary basis, in order to attract outstanding Austrian or foreign experts into the universities. In some countries staff from other public sectors are used for specific courses.

Assessment of teaching quality is included in the national institutional evaluation systems set up in Belgium and France, and is conducted by prior self-assessment followed by an external visitation committee. In Spain, individual teaching performance is evaluated every five years by a special commission within each university: the indicators are regularity and punctuality, keeping up to date, co-ordination between theory and practice, attitude to students, participation on faculty boards and in-service training. Assessment is linked to special pay rises. An academic with 12 years' service, if successful in the assessment, can receive a salary rise of 20 per cent. Academic pay is below what could be earned in industry, so the system attempts in this way to retain the best of its staff.

Evaluation by students is not widespread -and is resisted in Germany-but individual universities have set up internal appraisal systems which include students. One of the best-known examples is that practised in Leuven since 1977. The University Education Service has developed several methods for student evaluation of individual faculty, one for lecturing, another for practical sessions and yet another for the clinical teaching of medicine. The focus of the evaluation is to provide feedback to the instructor. The University of Complutense in Madrid has since 1988 evaluated academic staff by means of a questionnaire completed by students. An 'Interpretive Guide to Results' is provided to the individual afterwards to show the strong and weak points of their teaching and an external company, which staff consider will ensure objectivity, is used to analyze the data based on indicators. This method of assessment has reportedly been widely accepted.

In this group of countries, most action has been taken at the Ministry level. There is therefore not the emphasis given in self-regulatory systems to appraisal, staff development and incentives as part of *institutional* human resource planning, is missing, and, as a whole, much less change has occurred.

b. Africa

If universities in developed countries have suffered from financial constraints in the 1980s and 1990s, the impact of economic depression has been much more severe in Africa. Overall the budget share of higher education has dropped from 16.6 per cent in 1980 to 15.2 per cent in 1990 at a time when inflation increased and real wages in the region fell by 30 per cent between 1980 and 1986.

(i) The impacts on staffing

• *Student:academic staff ratios and growth in enrolment*

While the impact of financial constraint may, as in the developed countries, have been felt in the form of increasing Student:staff ratios (SSRs) in some countries, in others it has resulted in slow growth or decline in higher education enrolments, e.g. Malawi where university enrolment was 1,722 in 1980 and 2,330 in 1989, and Tanzania, which had 3,622 students in 1981 and 3,327 in 1989 as shown below.

Table 23. Student:staff ratios in selected African countries

Country	SSR 1980	SSR	No. students	Year
Benin	-	11.3	10,873	1991
Botswana	7.7	11.3	6,409	1992
Gabon	7.0	8.0	2,896	1988
Madagascar	50.2	49.9	42,681	1992
Mali	5.1	9.6	6,703	1990
Malawi	10.0	9.6	2,330	1989
Mozambique	3.3	6.0	3,482	1992
Nigeria	13.0	15.2	180,871	1989
Senegal	19.0	22.7	21,562	1991
Tanzania	4.1	3.5	3,327	1989
Uganda	(1985)10.8	9.2	2,327	1991
Zimbabwe	-	16.7	9,784	1991

Source: Idem

It can be seen that there are a number of countries with small university sectors which have low SSRs. This is a problem often associated with giving a broad range of courses to a relatively small enrolment, although some small universities (under 5,000 enrolment)

attain a relatively better SSR than others; the range is from 4 to 11 and there is evidently scope for better management.

- *The academic staff profile*

In Africa, staff management has been rendered more complex by the need to phase out large proportions of expatriate staff. These are more expensive, often short term and usually sponsored by a donor agency whose assistance may suddenly be terminated. According to a UNESCO study of the early eighties, half of the staff were then expatriates. As late as 1987, Zambia reported an expatriate staff of 46 per cent. The demand for such staff stems from a critical shortage of national staff in certain disciplines and for top administrative positions. For example, Malawi experiences staff shortages in Science and Technology and has a high percentage of expatriates in Engineering (52 per cent) and Science (48 per cent) and an overall expatriate staff of 30 per cent. The situation is similar in Zimbabwe. However, certain institutions or countries have largely overcome this problem; Tanzania's Sokoine University (teaching agriculture) is now 90 per cent self-sufficient in staff, and Nigerian universities report only 4-8 per cent and Ghana 8 per cent (1987) expatriates.

Africa's problems of age structure come from too young a profile. Most national staff are youthful and this has caused some universities to experience a decreasing proportion of senior staff: for example, Zambia has 61 per cent at the starting grade of lecturer and only 16 per cent at the two highest grades, from 25 per cent in earlier years. Kenya also reports that the rapid expansion of universities has left them without adequate numbers of senior administrators and teaching staff, while Nigerian universities have only 13 per cent at professor level instead of the officially prescribed 20 per cent.

- *Deterioration of working conditions*

Present working conditions of university staff in Africa have been the subject of a number of studies and workshops. They depict a gloomy picture of poor physical facilities, due to a number of years of low budget provision for maintenance and capital investment. In some cases even water and sewerage systems have decayed. Added to this are relatively low salaries (e.g. in Nigeria salaries in 1992 were one-tenth of their real value in 1985(40)), high teaching loads (e.g. Kenya, where double intakes have caused cancellation of sabbaticals and leave), little support for research, lack of training in management skills and few incentives for staff development. One of the consequences of low salaries is that university employment is considered to be only a part-time occupation.

- *High staff turnover and staff vacancies*

The World Bank(41) reports that some 23,000 qualified academic staff are emigrating each year. It has been estimated, for instance, that more than 10,000 Nigerian academics are employed in the USA alone. However, it is often a neighbouring country which beckons, e.g. South Africa attracts staff from Malawi, and the Universities of Botswana and Swaziland attract Zimbabweans.

For financial reasons, some universities in Nigeria have had to place an embargo on recruitment despite the exodus of lecturers. Zimbabwe, due to a cut in its teaching budget, has experienced a vacancy rate worsening from 28 per cent in 1988 to 34 per cent in 1992. Forty-eight per cent of posts are unfilled at the University of Makerere, Uganda. Zambia has been continuously short of certain teaching staff for some years and both this university and Malawi have found that most graduates sent abroad for training tend to leave for the private sector or abroad shortly after their return. Staff turnover is particularly high in accounting and business administration where the private sector pays higher salaries, as reported from Nigeria, Tanzania and Mozambique. Staff retention is particularly difficult in those disciplines most needed for the management of national economic development(42).

(ii) Systems of staff management

Although most African universities may have substantial autonomy in the operation of academic programmes, they may have relatively little in staff management. The extreme range is between the situation in French-speaking West Africa, where most university staff are civil servants, and universities like those in Swaziland and Zimbabwe, which may recruit, promote, assess and decide on staff development. The majority fall at some point between, with Ministries intervening at crucial points in staff decisions, particularly those relating to senior staff, or the granting of fellowships for study abroad. Staff management is, of course, everywhere constrained by government funding decisions.

Government guidance has for the most part been lacking, one exception being the Nigerian National University Commission, which set the science-arts ratio at 60:40 (in 1987 it was actually 52:48). Student/teacher ratios are prescribed for the various disciplines: at present, law, administration and engineering are grossly understaffed, while education is overstaffed; universities are trying over time to adjust their structures. The NUC also stipulates the proportions of staff at various grades, and some other countries have done likewise. (see below) However, for the most part guidelines have not been adequate, an example being Kenya, where norms were not set for non-teaching staff and their numbers grew out of all proportion to other types of staff and student numbers.

One investigation(43) in Francophone Africa found a lack of planning and information systems, undue dependence on rules and regulations, and an imbalance in staff structures. Other researchers(44) in Anglophone countries have also found a lack of adequate attention to institutional staff management, such as no clear job description being provided when a staff member joins a university. Such a lack of a major tool in effective staff management has resulted in under-use and mis-use of staff time. Despite sometimes low student/staff ratios, staff may not be given enough responsibilities to fill their time. A research study in Nigeria revealed that the staff declared that they spent 48 per cent of their time on administration and only 29 per cent on teaching(45).

The proper monitoring of staff activities and implementation of accountability measures for staff are rarely seen in African universities, and in the present situation it is necessary to look for more efficient ways of using staff. One study carried out in Zimbabwe found that though the average student/staff ratio was a reasonable 16:1, some departments could operate with a much higher ratio, perhaps as high as 80:1 in the Humanities. If an average SSR of 20-25:1 were adopted, staff could be paid better and teaching assistants hired to assist with marking or laboratory work. The study recommended that every post falling vacant should be reviewed, that the costs of study leave should be divided between institution and staff, and the number of sabbaticals each year should be limited. Contact teaching time should be increased and teaching prowess rewarded(46).

(iii) Management strategies adopted

From the literature and reports by visitors, the main strategy for staff management appears to be staff development programmes. Much less has been done in the areas of staff retention and incentives.

- *Staff development programmes*

Given the need to localize staff, many universities in Africa have had staff development programmes and agreements for links with universities in developed countries almost from the date of their establishment. Such links have grown enormously in importance, for example, in 1991 the University of Dar-es-Salaam had 50 agreements with foreign universities and the University of Zimbabwe 40. Such twinning arrangements are usually made between similar departments on a long-term basis, and used for the development of staff and programmes to meet local and departmental needs; they are essentially limited to disciplines and rarely serve to improve overall staff management.

Staff development programmes exist in most universities and are for the most part to enable staff to study at the Ph.D. level. Zambia, for example, has had a programme since 1973, having by 1985 trained 284 staff, with a further 163 still training. In Botswana, the university recently created a programme to train qualified nationals for positions in the university, but has not so far achieved its localization targets, because of to unrealistic requirements set in some departments, competition from private and parastatal sectors and the creaming off of the best science students for study abroad. Though many universities have made major efforts to plan staff development, their achievements are being eroded by high loss rates. In addition, only half the African countries reporting to UNESCO have their own post-graduate training facilities, and these find their graduates being poached by the others.

Moreover, career development in the sense of improving the teaching and research capacity of the academic staff already within an institution is not often to be found. Tanzania's Teaching and Learning Improvement Programme is one of the few explicit mentions of an effort to improve teaching quality. Competence in teaching, as well as research, is in Tanzania a requirement for tenure and promotion.

Helping African universities to help each other may be a more viable long-term strategy, particularly for the small ones. The AAU's Staff Exchange Programme aims at strengthening teaching and research and is designed to enable experts in specialized fields to share their expertise with others. The Universities of Ghana and Agiotage have signed an agreement to formalize co-operation. Another such initiative is that of the German Foundation for International Development (DSE) which in 1988 began a Medium-Term Programme on Staff Development in Eastern and Southern African countries involving ten partner universities in Ethiopia, Kenya, Malawi, Sudan, Tanzania, Zambia and Zimbabwe. It is acknowledged that it is unrealistic to assume that individual universities can expand existing postgraduate programmes to produce most of the top professionals required and that regional and international co-operation is vital.

- *Staff retention initiatives*

The main incentive for retention is adequate relative local salaries and some governments have been obliged to make significant increases. In 1988, Zambia gave a 50 per cent salary increase, but levels are still lower than in the private sector. In 1992, Zimbabwe and Swaziland both gave a 30 per cent increase to try to stop staff losses. Subsidized housing has been a traditional incentive for academic staff but due to the decline in capital investment, new staff have had to seek housing in the market. Though they are given a housing allowance, this only partially covers the rent. Generally traditional incentives have declined in value: among these may be listed research opportunities (equipment and funds are hard to obtain), travel abroad and sabbaticals (also much scarcer).

Newer incentives introduced are:

- compensation for staff who exceed a specified maximum teaching load (Ghana, Addis Ababa, Abidjan, Makerere);
- in Kenya university staff are allowed to import personal vehicles duty free: however, the benefits are limited to the few who have the money to buy;
- in Zambia, staff have been promised plots of land.

- *Staff management initiatives*

Some governments, becoming concerned about the state of staff management in universities, have tried to establish norms. Nigeria has set a ratio of 20:25:55 for Professors: Senior Lecturers: other staff, as well as SSR norms by discipline. Ghana has similar recommended ratios. Zambia introduced norms some years ago and in 1988 added an incentive to efficiency by permitting the university to use savings on the staffing norms for other purposes at its discretion. Tanzania in 1992 placed a moratorium on replacement of retired staff and departing non-academic staff in order to increase its SSR to a more reasonable level. Kenya recently set ratios for academic:non-academic staff.

The achievement of such norms has placed great strain on university staff management; in Nigeria, Sierra Leone and Tanzania, massive retrenchments have been necessary to rationalize staff levels to the size that will ensure the optimal mix of personnel, equipment and materials. Governing Councils, according to Mbajiorgu (1991), have been deterred by the high cost of rationalization. It has been estimated in Nigeria that the costs of most retrenchment programmes would outweigh the benefits: to save the annual salary of one excess staff member, the institution would be faced with an increased pension bill of 70 per cent of his last earned salary and an immediate lump sum payment of three times that salary as retirement gratuity. Moreover, where, as in Nigeria, a university has had to freeze recruitment for rationalization and financial reasons, despite the exodus of lecturers, as in Nigeria, its staff profiles are likely to become even more unbalanced by staff level and discipline.

In their efforts to fill gaps in staffing, African universities, as in the developed countries, have resorted to making more use of graduate and research fellows as teachers or tutorial assistants, but their time is limited and they are often lost on completion of a Ph.D. or shortly thereafter. The use of part-time qualified teachers has also been tried but these are in short supply. Zambia made an attempt to recruit expatriates to fill gaps on a temporary basis but this was largely unsuccessful due to low salaries.

There are few reports of attempts to analyze the use of staff time, teaching loads and performance, or to introduce new types of contracts. Exceptions were Burundi, which carried out a teacher rationalization programme and increased the teaching load by 10 per cent(47), and Nigeria. In the latter country, the National Universities Commission has set up a system of accreditation of higher education institutions which includes the appraisal of university staff. However, only 185 undergraduate programmes received full accreditation out of 836 examined between March 1990 and June 1991, while 572 received interim accreditation(48).

The situation of staff appraisal in African universities is very uneven. In Cameroon and Mauritius, for example, staff still resist teaching appraisal, while in Tanzania, Swaziland, and Zimbabwe, there are comprehensive procedures regularly carried out. For example, in Zimbabwe, each Department Board appoints two staff who attend classes without prior notice, student evaluation forms are discussed with the staff member and, after the annual examination results are known, external examiners review the outcome, course outlines, list of publications and services carried out. Only the University of Transkei, South Africa, reported the introduction of a merit pay system(49).

c. Asia

The range of staff management types in this region is as varied as the countries themselves. Some operate with high student:staff ratios which during the 1980s became even higher (the Philippines), others brought them down (Republic of Korea) while in others (Japan, Thailand and Malaysia) they have been stable and relatively low.

Table 24. Student:staff ratios in selected Asian countries

	1980	1990
Japan	11.5	10.2 (1989)
Republic of Korea	29.2	20.0
Malaysia	8.0	10.8
Philippines	23.0 (1985)	32.2 (1989)
Thailand	9.7	10.9 (1989)

Source: idem.

Some, the Newly Industrialised Countries (NICs), have been classified as more like those in the 'self-regulation in transition' group. They have staff management systems which incorporate most of the self-regulatory features, such as establishment of norms, appraisal, development and incentives. One example is Singapore, where a maximum of 40 per cent has been set for tenured staff, and the teaching load must be at least 5 student contact hours per week. All local staff are sent abroad for Ph.D training and on recruitment are given a teaching methods course and a handbook on teaching. Centres for Educational Development and Educational Technology assist them thereafter. Good teaching is motivated by incentives in salary, promotion, tenure and special awards, and quality appraisal is carried out by external examiners(50).

On a similarly favourable economic level but with a quite different style of staff management, Japan has a strictly egalitarian and national system of salaries but faculties control the selection and management of their staff. Professors are evaluated only on their research (a 1991 survey found that 60 per cent of academic staff say their first priority is research) and staff development programmes are unpopular(51). Conservatism is rife.

In India, staff management is difficult because of over-expansion, unionization, lack of accountability and a rational incentive structure, and the politicization of recruitment and promotion. The New Policy on Education (1986) stressed initial and in-service training for all academic staff and staff colleges were set up in universities for this purpose. In 1989 the first national test was held to assess the potential of staff for teaching and research. However, the criteria for 'tenured' appointments are still under investigation, and a recent survey revealed that one third of university teachers had not published an article and three quarters had not published a book. Less than a fifth did research, about two-thirds had never participated in any seminar or training programme and only a quarter availed themselves of study leave(52).

Different problems are encountered in China, where the student/staff ratio is extremely low (5:1) leading to high unit costs, and most staff are elderly (80 per cent over 50). The residential nature of universities and limited staff quarters restrict recruitment of young married staff. The small size of universities also makes efficient staff use difficult. However, a beginning has been made with a new appointment system which stipulates that all posts should be based on real need with a clear outline of duties, take account of set staffing ratios and be on a two to five year renewable basis. The new salary system is in two parts: basic living and supplement according to grade. This system was received with hesitation but has played a role in restructuring faculty. A bottleneck still exists of too many teachers recruited in the 1950s and 1960s, and waiting for promotion despite low achievement. Some universities employ postgraduate students as teaching assistants work, and others have junior posts with short-term contracts. Two national training centres for university staff have been established under a World Bank project, with sub-training centres in the provinces. The managerial system was generally well-known to protect job safety and inefficiency; promotion is based on seniority and it will be a long time before all those with tenure retire. A survey in Sichuan showed that most administrators lack management skills; they are usually low-level academics, and unlikely to implement new policies efficiently(53).

In other countries, the main problems are those of quality and brain drain, as in Philippines, Sri Lanka, Pakistan, and Malaysia. The Sri Lankan Government has raised the retiring age of academics from 65 to 70 to counteract losses. A significant proportion of young Ph.D. students who signed bonds to return from study abroad do not do so(54). In Pakistan study abroad and salary increments have failed to retain young talent, while Malaysia introduced a new salary and promotion scheme to stem losses(55).

In Indonesia, staff generally have only a first degree and promotion now depends on national assessment. This measures the performance of academic staff in six areas: (i) education and instruction; (ii) scientific publications; (iii) public service; (iv) institutional loyalty; (v) experience; and (vi) other activities. Each activity is composed of several items and each has a given credit, varying from 0.5 (for teaching load more than normal duty per semester) to 25 (for a cum laude doctoral dissertation)(56). This system is unusual; assessment and development have not been prominent features of staff management in the region, and are still not incorporated into a concept of institutional development.

d. Arab countries

In this region, SSRs have tended to increase where they were low, but to decrease where they were high, indicating some efforts on the part of Governments to bring their ratios into line with what were considered as more efficient norms.

Table 25. Student:staff ratios in selected Arab countries

	1980	1990
Algeria	8.9	14
Egypt	25.2 (1985)	17.4
Jordan	20.6 (1985)	20.5
Morocco	31.5	28.7
Tunisia	7.9	15.0
Saudi Arabia	8.6	12.7

Source: Idem.

According to one source(57), most universities suffer from inadequate managerial control, no agreement on objectives, lack of information systems and planning and an inability to know who is doing a good job. Teaching-learning methods are mainly lecturing and memorization. Resistance to reform manifests itself by stalling on implementation. A few institutions in Egypt, Iraq and Syria have programmes to improve teaching, but they have found that in order to overcome the sensitivity of senior staff, methods such as seminars to develop skills and exchange views have to be utilized(58).

Control is exercised mainly by Ministerial regulations on weekly hours and teaching load set according to rank. The figures in Egypt are eight hours per week for a professor, 10 for an assistant professor and 12 for a lecturer, which are higher teaching loads than usually found in European countries. Appointment to top posts is by the Minister while Faculty Boards recruit lower staff. The need for extra teaching is being met in Tunisia and Egypt by paid overtime, for which universities are given a special budget. In Egypt, retired professors may also be re-appointed as part-time staff.

5. Lessons learned

It is clear that the sensitive domain of efficient and effective staff management has not been firmly tackled in many countries. This section will review what is considered to be good practice, using the following structure:

(i) identification of requirements according to institutional mission, values and strategic plan;
(ii) recruitment of academic staff;
(iii) orientation and allocation of responsibilities;
(iv) provision of working conditions conduce to good teaching and research performance;
(v) appraisal of staff performance, incentives and further development of staff through in-service training;
(vi) evaluation of overall human resource performance.

a. Identification of requirements

In quantitative terms, academic staff requirements are usually estimated and projected on the basis of student contact hours in a particular discipline, level and methods of instruction (e.g. lecture, seminar, tutorial, individual advice, practical work, field visit, etc.). These requirements are commonly expressed in full-time equivalent terms. The norms vary in general from discipline to discipline and for different levels of study as well as teaching methods. It should be underlined that the establishment of such norms needs not only collection of detailed data on actual utilization of time by students and staff, but also consensus-building on these among the students, academics and managers.

In qualitative terms, it has been observed that often no clear job description is provided when a staff member joins a university. It is advisable that before a decision is taken on recruiting a new staff member, the real need for skills should be analyzed.

Ability specifications' involve defining and identifying factors that are 'essential' and 'desirable' to perform the job. There are three performance factors, each one of which has several elements which can be categorized as 'essential' and 'desirable' for the new staff, i.e.:

1. *Know-how:* job knowledge and skills, leadership and social skills, communication skills, knowledge of methods and techniques, general knowledge, work habits and career record.
2. *Commitment:* personal ambitions, personal values, attitude to others, and career record.
3. *Calibre:* maturity, learning and thinking ability, relevant aptitude and career record.

All elements of the above performance factors will have a variable utility for the job – some of them will be 'essential' and others 'desirable'. The manager should be able to specify them. The ability specification will, of course, take into account any legal requirements imposed by the State(59).

However, apart from quantitative and qualitative aspects, higher education now needs a greater variety of staffing modes to meet the new demands of its clientele. Standardized pay scales and working conditions for all employees can be barriers to this(60). Institutions, by negotiating with their Ministries, should seek greater flexibility in staffing. One means is the increased use of part-time and adjunct faculty, not only to contain costs, but also because such staff can bring variety and outside experience to the institution.

If financial pressures necessitate staff reductions, management should aim at an active redesign of the staffing profile of the institution than passive acceptance of the consequences of retirements and resignations. Allowing successful programmes to increase their workloads without appropriate additional human resources can also often be contrary to the long-term interests of the institution.

b. Recruitment of staff

In many countries the process of recruitment is not rational. It is important that the line manager (i.e. the head of department or institution) play a part in the decision since he knows the departmental requirements.

A major problem is how to attract the right applicants for the post. The job advertisement should include: (i) a brief note on the institution and its programmes, (ii) a short description of the needs of the job with possible future potential in an objective form, (iii) the ability specification defined earlier, (iv) the rewards in specific terms, and (v) instructions for applying for the job.

Recruitment is usually covered by regulations which stipulate:

(1) establishment of a selection board composed of representatives of the discipline, related disciplines, institutional faculty and department;
(2) public advertisement;
(3) selection of short list of four to six; taking up of references;
(4) interview;
(5) decision (adjournment is usual).

In addition to the interview, it is becoming more common for a multiple assessment process to be adopted for the selection of a candidate. The process involves a group of candidates taking part in a variety of activities set by a team of trained assessors who jointly evaluate a number of predetermined job-related abilities. The activities are designed to simulate the job for which assessment is being made. For an academic job, lectures/seminars are organized to assess the candidate's competence. The assessors are normally the potential superiors of the candidate and their combined judgment helps in decision-making. This method has been found to be consistently accurate.

It is common for lower grade staff to be appointed from among the university's own graduates (Japanese, USA and United Kingdom statistics show this). For upper levels, the possibility of promotion amongst the institution's own staff is also perceived as a good source of motivation. A study done at one USA university showed a firm internal market at upper levels, except for external affairs(61). However, it has been seen in the United Kingdom, where managerial change has been rapid, that estates and financial managers, computer experts and similar technological staff have had to be recruited from outside.

Where institutions embark on new activities and reforms, the infusion of 'new blood' is vital. Many of the IIEP case studies showed that new heads of institutions or new posts were often thought necessary to carry through a reform.

c. Orientation and allocation of responsibilities

Procedures for integration and orientation of young staff members are crucial. This is usually done by seminars, information handbooks, teaching methods courses and on-going mentor programmes. Delegation of some responsibilities and decision-making is an important requirement in establishing a collegial atmosphere and ensuring effective implementation of teaching/learning programmes.

d. Provision of conducive working conditions

Integrated institutional management is important in this, i.e.

(1) Financial management in the allocation of funds for equipment, books, support staff etc., and a salary structure which offers incentives. For instance, where there is no overlap between scales for different grades of staff, this provides a strong incentive for all those eligible to apply whenever a post in the next most senior grade becomes vacant. There is a strong case for an overlap of salaries between grades or (as in the United Kingdom civil service now) a continuous salary spine along which certain segments – which overlap at the top and bottom – are identified with specific grades of post.
(2) Space management for the equitable allocation of facilities.
(3) Staff management in the setting of teaching loads, administrative responsibilities, career development, etc.
(4) Research management.

e. Integrated system for appraisal of staff performance, incentives and career development

Most institutions of higher education have a long-standing tradition and practice of formal and informal appraisal of academic staff, but career development was usually considered the responsibility of the individual. There was also usually no incentive system, personal and professional recognition being the prime motivator. However, in a rapidly changing socio-economic and technological environment, career development is now very much a university planning responsibility. The task of management is to achieve both a productive organization and individual fulfilment. Ignoring the latter means that management will not be aware of problems and needs for improvement. These can be highlighted by appraisal processes, which can be used for such purposes as:

Academic staff management

- manpower skills audit;
- succession planning;
- planning of training;
- problem solving, to change behaviour and motivate;

It has been thought best to remove the appraisal process from any direct link to promotion by carrying it out on a regular basis (every two or three years) and not at the time of a regular salary increase. Ideally self-evaluation and some form of evaluation by clients should take place in addition to peer evaluation, using different peers for different aspects of the individual's job. The results are then considered in a formal interview with the line manager which is focused on providing staff development opportunities to solve the problems identified and to meet anticipated future needs.

Staff development activities are designed to be prerequisites for greater staff efficiency and not perquisites of past staff performance. They are not only opportunities to attend conferences and spend sabbaticals abroad but are increasingly conducted in-house or on a regional basis. Technical courses are often the responsibility of departments, but usually Staff Development Liaison Officers are appointed for each department who collate needs so that the institution may organize workshops, job shadowing and short-term exchanges with other institutions.

f. Evaluation of overall human resource performance

Staff managers need to obtain periodic, at least annual, feedback on the effectiveness of human resource management over time, between departments or between institutions. It is common practice to establish an information base from which performance indicators may be calculated in order to monitor the staffing situation in various domains.

A few examples of the data to be included are(62):

(i) Staff profile

- Proportion of vacancies to posts by departments;

- Proportion of vacancies filled internally;

- Breakdown of academic staff by level of qualification;

- Breakdown of academic staff by hierarchical level;

- Breakdown of academic staff by age;
- Proportions of full-time/part-time/consultancies, etc.

(ii) Utilization

- Student:staff ratios by department compared to norms set;
- Breakdown of working time (teaching loads, research, administration, services) by department;
- Proportion of teaching time accounted for by overtime or part-time staff.

(iii) Reward structure

- Salary levels/increases compared to posts in industry and cost of living index;
- Proportion of salary as fringe benefits;
- Proportion of salary as bonus or awards;
- Proportion of staff benefitting from residential facilities;
- Average periods elapsing between promotion or obtaining of tenure.

Figure 2 summarizes the integrated approach:

Figure 2. Data to evaluate human resource performance

1. Orientation	Induction of new staff and their commitment to institutional goals, identifying specific talents, providing information on opportunities to promote further learning.
2. Utilizations and appraisal	Matching individuals to the tasks needed to be performed, including extra-curricular activities. Annual self-assessment, and periodic appraisal by students, peers and line manager.

3. Development and incentives	Motivation mainly from personal needs and desire to extend talents, assisted within the institution by: mentoring (usually heads of departments); quality circles; teaching centres (for advice, materials, workshops); research teams; an active system of career development planning; some job rotation; incentives, such as special awards or prizes for teaching and research.

    (iv) Staff development

- Proportion of budget devoted to staff development;

- Proportion of staff taking courses by department;

- Proportion of staff taking sabbaticals by department.

    (v) Morale/attitudes

- Staff turnover per annum;

- Rate of absenteeism;

- Attitude survey information.

6. Challenges for staff management in the university of the future

The introduction of information technology in the management and delivery of higher education, links with government and industry, and increased interaction among universities and between universities and the community have called for much greater expertise in staff management.

Changes are occurring in:

- the composition of the student body (more adult students, part-time students, external degree students, business interns, etc.);

- the organization of instructional programmes: recognition of industries' own training programmes for credentials, recognition of work experience in awarding credits, course-oriented training regardless of level, flexibility in the hours and duration of instruction;

- the organization of the curriculum: problem-solving and interdisciplinary approaches.

The roles of academic staff will change. The professor will become the manager of a small educational system comprising staff support (researchers, course developers and programme deliverers) plus hardware and courseware (audio cassettes and discs) to meet changing academic goals. On the basis of diagnostic tests administered, a student may be prescribed a personalized course of study involving interaction with a collection of courseware materials, written papers, occasional lecture attendance and individual consultation with the professor, followed by an exit competency test. In this new role, academic staff would spend less time preparing and presenting formal lectures to large student groups and more time on keeping pace with the knowledge explosion, formatting the new knowledge in student-accessible coursewares and on counselling students. Staff managers in universities will have to cater for these new situations, and appraisal and staff development will be their main tools to bring about change.

References

1. Chaston, I. "Strategies of management in new United Kingdom universities". In *Higher Education Review*, Vol. 26, No. 2, Spring 1994.
2. Owen, V., former Deputy Director of Oxford Polytechnic, Visit February 1992.
3. Phelps, N.A. "A model for the allocation of teaching loads in academic departments".In *Higher Education Management*, Vol. 5, No. 1, March 1993.
4. Burna, S. and Arndt, T. "Faculty Portfolio Analysis", idem above.
5. Dijkman, F. et al. *Restructuring, reallocation and retrenchment: the Dutch universities*. Mimeo, May 1983.
6. Absalom, R. and Sutton, C. "Rigidity and change in staffing structures in higher education in Northern Europe". In *Higher Education Management*, Vol. 2, No. 2, 1990.
7. Times Higher Educational Supplement, 24 August 1990.
8. El Khawas, E. "Demographic factors in the staffing of higher education". In *Higher Education Management*, Vol. 5, No. 2, July 1993.
9. Altbach, P. "The Professor's Lot". *University News*, 1 June 1992.
10. Warne, B. "Erosion of an ideal: presence of part-time faculty". *Studies in Higher Education*, Vol. 13, No. 2, 1988.
11. Times Higher Educational Supplement, 28 January 1994.
12. HMSO, *Higher Education: A New Framework*, May 1991.
13. Times Higher Educational Supplement, 21 May 1993.
14. Beillard, J-M. "Evaluation of professors' performance with special reference to teaching". IGLU No. 6, April 1994.
15. McDonald, R. and Boud, D. "Training needs of academic departments in Australia". In *Higher Education Management*, Vol. 1, No. 2, 1989.
16. Piper, D. "Staff development in universities: should there be a staff college?" In *Higher Education Quarterly*, Vol. 42, No. 3, 1988.
17. Dunkin, M. and Precians, R. "Award-winning university teacher's concepts of teaching". In *Higher Education*, Vol. 24, No. 4, December 1992.
18. Times Higher Education Supplement, 25 June 1993.
19. Lonsdale, A. "Changes in incentives, rewards and sanctions". In *Higher Education Management*, Vol. 5, No. 2, July 1993.
20. Brown, H. and Sommerlad, E. "Staff development in higher education: towards the learning organization?" In *Higher Education Quarterly*, Vol. 46, No. 2, Spring 1992.
21. Holtta, S. and Pulliainen, K. *Improving managerial effectiveness at the University of Joensuu, Finland.* IIEP Monograph. Paris 1994.
22. Jalling, H. "Training departmental heads in Sweden". In *Higher Education Management*, Vol. 1, No. 2, 1989.
23. Times Higher Educational Supplement, 13 July 1990.

24. Knudsen, L. "Training programmes for heads of academic departments at the University of Oslo". In *Higher Education Management*, Vol. 1, No. 2, 1989.
25. Stenqvist, O. "Reallocation of vacant teaching posts as a response to economic retrenchment". In *International Journal of Institutional Management in Higher Education*, Vol. 10, No. 1, March 1986.
26. Albornoz, O. *Autonomy and accountability in higher education.* Prospects Vol. XXI, No. 2, 1991.
27. Klein, L. and Schwartzman, S. "Higher Education policies in Brazil 1970-1990". In *Higher Education*, Vol. 25, No. 1, 1993.
28. Alvarez, S. *Evaluation of quality as a means to transform universities: the case of Argentina.* IGLU No. 3, October 1992.
29. Samoilovich, D. *Evaluation of quality of higher education in different socio-cultural contexts: the case of Latin America.* Report of Round Table, UNESCO, Geneva, 1992.
30. Hirsch, E. *Improving the managerial effectiveness of higher education institutions UNAM*, IIEP, Paris, 1994.
31. Rojas, Y. Academic Vice Rector, University of Costa Rica Visit, 3 December 1993.
32. Trista Perez, B. Letter dated 22 July 1991.
33. Groot, T.M. *La carga académica, NUFFIC,* Netherlands, 1990.
34. Amsterdamski, S. and Jablecka, J. *Report on higher education and research systems in the transitional period.* Conference on the structure and legal order of higher education and research in Central Europe. Vienna, November 1991.
35. Times Higher Educational Supplement, 11 June 1993.
36. Buranov, V. Paper for IIEP Workshop on Education, Employment and Human Resource Development. Tashkent, August 1993.
37. Times Higher Educational Supplement, 29 May 1992.
38. Gobbels Dreyling, B. "Overcoming staff shortages and blockages". In *Higher Education Management*, November 1993, Vol. 5, No. 3.
39. Guin, J. "Reawakening of higher education in France". In *European Journal of Education,* Vol. 25, No. 2, 1990.
40. Okonkwo, I. "Structural adjustment programme and higher education in Nigeria". In *Journal of Educational and Social Change.* Vol. VI, No. 4, 1993.
41. The World Bank, *Universities in Africa: strategies for stabilization and revitalization,* 1992.
42. Blair, R. and Jordan, J. *Staff loss and retention at selected African universities.* Report to DAE, December 1993.
43. Kola Cisse, M. "Managing university based research institutions in Africa". In *Higher Education Policy*, Vol. 5, No. 2, 1992.
44. Bukhala, J. *Roles, functions and competencies of facilitators in professional development.* Report of a sub-regional workshop in Harare, June 1989, pub. DSE Bonn 1990.

45. Oshagbemi, T. *Leadership and management in universities*, De Gruyter, New York, 1988.
46. Blair, R. Paper for the British Council Workshop on Cost Reduction, September 1990, Lusaka.
47. Nsabiyumua, A. Visit IIEP, 26 December 1992.
48. Daily Champion, 13 December 1991.
49. Papers of IIEP Workshop on Institutional Management in Higher Education, Mauritius, September 1993.
50. Selvaratnam V. *Singapore at the Competitive Edge*. World Bank Technical Paper No. 222 Washington 1991.
51. Editorial. Higher Education Policy, Vol. 6, No. 2, 1993.
52. Moharty, S. "Professional development of teachers in higher education". University News, 22 October 1990.
53. Cao Xiaonan. "Policy-making on improvement of university personnel in China", *Studies in Higher Education*, Vol. 16, No. 2, 1991.
54. Times Higher Educational Supplement, 18 February 1994.
55. Times Higher Educational Supplement, 21 February 1992.
56. Soehito, S. *Staff and faculty development in Indonesia, RIHED*, Singapore, 1981.
57. Moustafa, M. "A faculty development plan for Arab universities". In *Higher Education Policy*, Vol. 5, No. 4, 1992.
58. Doghaim, M. *Teaching and training*. Paper for Second Collective Consultation of NGOs on Higher Education, UNESCO, Paris, 8-11 April 1991.
59. Scott, J. and Rochester, A. *Effective management skills - what is a manager?*, Sphere/British Institute of Management, London, 1990.
60. Windham, D. Paper, IIEP Workshop on Institutional Management in Higher Education, Paris, November 1992.
61. Johnsrud, L. *et al.* "University staffing decisions to hire or promote." In *International Journal of Educational Management*, Vol. 6, No. 2, 1992.
62. A more complete coverage is given in the IIEP Training Module on academic staff management, IIEP/UNESCO, Paris, 1994.

Chapter 8

Management of research and links with the economy

In most countries, research and/or scholarship[*] are accepted as being necessary university functions on the liberal grounds of fostering the spirit of free enquiry, and on the practical grounds that research helps to keep staff up to date or on the frontiers of new knowledge which, in turn, ensures the intellectual standards of teaching and self-renewal of staff. This concept spread from the German Humboldtian tradition to the United States and British universities in the nineteenth century. Latterly, other reasons for research as a university function have come to the fore, for example the need for universities to contribute to national or regional development by technological innovation and solving problems in the social sphere. This is particularly stressed in developing countries, where universities may employ much of the nation's high-level manpower. A survey of academics' views on the matter in Australia, where research is a traditional function continued to show support for the value of the research-teaching nexus for universities, indicating a belief that:

- teaching having inputs from research can transmit the most advanced knowledge; students expect it, and it maintains the reputation of the institution;
- an input from research methodologies develops in students a critical approach and attitude towards knowledge;
- research provides a stimulating institutional milieu and only an institution which carries out research can attract potential new researchers;
- teaching students, on the other hand, keeps researchers on their toes(1).

---

[*] Scholarship has been defined as a more limited research consisting of review of the state-of-the-art, theory construction, chronicling (in general keeping up to date) while research involves more active experiment testing, design, development and evaluation(2).

218

However, with the advent of mass higher education, increasing financial constraint, specialization and multiple disciplines, the nexus between research and teaching is being questioned. Universities are finding it difficult to muster the resources for research and research training and most of their students are in fact destined to be middle-level manpower, with only a few going on to post-graduate research. This has led to support for the concentration of research training in a small number of advanced research institutions. Some empirical studies comparing research productivity (publications) with teaching effectiveness (student ratings) produced no firm conclusions as to any necessary link between them.

In practice, the research function of universities differs according to government policy, by institutional policy and by department, though all institutions expect their academic staff to engage in scholarship in order to keep up to date. In reality, however, only a minority of university teaching staff are engaged in research. For example, in the United States two out of five do no research at all and more than half have never published a book. Even in France, where the government appoints teacher-researchers in all universities who by regulation are obliged to spend half their time on research, half the universities are not engaged in any official research(3). Some states, notably the East European, consider that universities are merely teaching institutions and that research should for the most part be undertaken by specialized institutes. Other countries are also thinking along these lines, because of the need to direct limited research funds into areas of economic growth. For example, Australia has a policy that research funds should not be spread thinly but be concentrated in those institutions where there is capacity and a good basic research record. Other universities are considered primarily as teaching institutions(4). It has been suggested that workloads should be adjusted; academic staff usually have 30 per cent of their time allocated to research whereas 10 per cent for scholarship might be more justifiable, with 30 per cent retained only for those actively engaged in projects. This would save nearly 25 per cent of present unit costs in universities(5).

An ever increasing proportion of the total research effort is being undertaken by public and private enterprises. For example, in 1985, universities in OECD countries spent only 15 per cent of total research funds but nevertheless had 23 per cent of research manpower(6). Such a situation is also found in developing countries as the IIEP research studies on the role of education in scientific and technological development showed. In Indonesia, in the field of communications and electronics, most research was carried out in state enterprises, who obtained the co-operation in some instances of state universities. The transnationals tended not to encourage local R&D and the amounts spent on research by local firms and private universities was low(7).

Not only are financial constraints, mass higher education and more rigorous national research policies having an effect on the research function in universities, but this function, previously accepted as a matter of course, is itself being questioned. Such pressures have resulted in a variety of institutional responses which are described below according to classification by type of university management.

1. The prevailing state of research management

There are common modes of carrying out research in universities, largely depending on the discipline. The classical organizational model for research is the chair (one person or a disciplinary group). Many chairs were originally funded by donations from individuals or enterprises interested in promoting specific fields. Traditionally, research in Humanities is an individual affair, the Social Sciences require team work while in science, technology and medicine, a special institute staffed by several professors of equal status and furnished with the necessary specialised equipment is the norm. An institute has the advantages of greater utilization of expensive equipment and multidisciplinary teamwork by staff possessing complementary abilities and hence more able to keep up to date in a particular field. It also tends to attract more funding. The disadvantages are adapting to the life cycles of research problems and of staff.

a. Self-regulation and accountability implemented

In these countries, as with university management as a whole, the management of research has been subject to particularly strong external pressure and change. The changes have in some cases been even more radical in this domain than elsewhere in universities. Government policies have decided the priority research areas, the increases in certain types of research graduate, the necessity for more applied activities and links with the economy, and the type of institution that is to be mainly concerned with research. They have taken some of the funds earmarked for block research grants in universities into their own hands for allocation; for example, in Australia 1 per cent of university funding is to go to the Research Council to support projects of high national priority(8), while in New Zealand a part of public research funds has to be competed for by universities and industry, with the results evaluated in audit reviews(9).

(i) USA

In the *USA*, universities became heavily involved in sponsored research during the Second World War and this has continued ever since. However, just 9 per cent of the total research effort (by funding) is carried out in the universities and even this is concentrated on a small number of doctorate-granting institutions, the majority of universities being teaching institutions with little research. Seventy per cent of funding comes from the government, 17 per cent from institutional funds and only 6 per cent from industry(10). Thus the governments (federal and state) are a major influence on decision-making, in particular for the 11 university campuses designated as science and technology centres, co-operating with scientists from government and industry, and funded by $25 million of government funds.

This being said, the larger universities have been able to develop their research and services by paying close attention to their specific missions in meeting local needs. SUNY (State University of New York) in 1987 launched a Graduate Education and Research Initiative to develop certain of its campuses as centres of excellence linked to research needs in the region. It has increased its external funding by 50 per cent over 1987-90 as well as set up 40 Business and Industry centres and 19 Small Business Development centres with 2,800 jobs. The University of Wisconsin(11), on the other hand, chose to link its research to services, e.g. its agricultural co-operative extension service is a partnership of basic researchers and extension agents who apply their findings to re-training. In fact, many institutions seem to fulfil their research missions by linking activities to services, and it is in this particular domain that the nexus between teaching and research is clearly seen. A number have set up corporate education partnerships with industry where research, curriculum development and teaching about new technology are interlinked. Some of the courses are subsequently inserted into existing degree programmes (see *Chapter 10* on *Educational delivery*).

United States universities have adopted an aggressive policy in their patent and licensing registrations. From 1980 to 1985 patents granted to universities were double those in the preceding five years, and certain institutions like MIT and the University of Arkansas have vastly increased their royalty incomes. However, the majority have not benefited to any great extent from patents.

(ii) Canada

Canada has many features similar to the United States. It will spend $200 million over 1990-95 in setting up seven centres of excellence to form the nucleus of research networks of university and industrial researchers. The National Council for Science and Technology awards grants according to project excellence and themes of national interest, while the Corporate Higher Education Forum exists specifically to promote university-industry research. Its awards carry high prestige and are strongly competed for. Provinces (as with the States) are also creating centres for interdisciplinary work with research agendas co-determined by industry. The growth of business centres and science parks has continued, numbering 11 by 1989. As in the United States, it is considered that research in new technologies, being complex, expensive and high risk, requires such co-operative structures to create a good organizational base and intellectual environment(12). Canada has devoted particular attention in its funding regulations to promoting favourable conditions for research: tax-free donations, the matching by the government of funds from the private sector, creation of industrial chairs, and subsidies for industrial liaison units in universities(13).

In both the United States and Canada, the management of research within institutions is given high priority, since success is crucial to the institution's reputation in the market for funding and students. Individuals and faculty teams do, of course, apply to state and foundations for grants but these are comparatively small amounts. Research is very much concentrated in centres of excellence and postgraduate training, where government and corporation priorities are the deciding factor. These trends have been noted with alarm by some academics and supported by others. It is said that professors are becoming more company-oriented and their teaching less productive, due to the fact that funded researchers can buy out their teaching time which is then assigned to temporary staff(14). On the other hand, there is support for the need to appoint special staff since some very fundamental changes are taking place in the environment. Decision-making within the institution has moved more to executive level. A report from Canada states "the impact (of corporate-university linkages) is that the influence of senates and councils has been eroded in favour of central management, and academic staff are weakened by internal divisions of interest". Nevertheless, the executive level has been aware of certain dangers from external influences and, as in the case of the University of Montreal, put aside half the funds collected from overhead costs of research contracts for distribution to projects which are of high quality but not able to attract funding. Other problems, such as restriction on the university researcher's rights to publish, or to register a patent have also had to be dealt with by seeking experts in negotiation and have, with experience, largely been overcome.

(iii) United Kingdom

Turning now to the European countries in this group, the trend is to tighter organization of the research effort at the national level. The *United Kingdom's* strategy has been set out recently in its paper "Higher education: a new framework" (HMSO, London, May 1991). There is a dual support system, with the HEFC funding the costs of basic infrastructure, while the Research Councils fund projects in the various disciplines as well as pump-priming initiatives. The Computer Board for universities provides specific funding in that field. The system of funding is characterized by competition, selectivity and accountability. In addition universities are expected to increase other funding: the EEC is rapidly becoming the largest single sponsor, while business is much more willing to seek collaboration. The greatest impact is experienced in the high tech fields of engineering, computers, medicine, agriculture, chemistry and biotechnology and the large programmes are carefully planned, high cost, complex and relatively few in number. To cite one example, the Pharmacology Department of Oxford University recently signed a £20 million contract with an American drug company(15). Universities are engaged in the whole spectrum of research from long-range basic to short-term quasi-market research (commercially funded) but most is medium-term, where the sponsors pay only the marginal costs of additional staff and equipment(16).

From 1985, universities were asked to make research statements covering present research expenditure as a percentage of total university expenditure; the ratio of full-time staff to research income; research planning machinery and practice; research plans and priorities; research by subject area (number of staff and students); books and articles representing the best research; and indicators of research performance. The results are published and universities are ranked on a scale of one to five, according to which government research funds are subsequently allocated(17). These rankings are not only useful for obtaining public research revenue, but also confer considerable prestige, thus increasing the possibilities of attracting funds from private sources, not only for research programmes but in the form of endowments, visiting researchers, and small industrial estates; they also, and most importantly, attract bright students. University executive levels have had to enter more thoroughly into decision-making on research activities in order to set priorities and goals in accordance with their own and government strategic development plans which outline the proposed nature of the university and its place among other centres of learning and research. New mechanisms for research management have been instituted, and influential research committees have emerged to set priorities. Some 'research-led' universities have carried out restructuring; the University of Sheffield in 1994 reorganized its Ph.D programmes into graduate schools, set up a Research Council, centres and institutes to which staff will be linked for work on multidisciplinary projects(18).

The United Kingdom government has been extremely active in providing incentives for links with industry, e.g. the Enterprise in Higher Education initiative, the Link Programme, and the £20 million a year Teaching Company Scheme which began in 1975, to use new graduates in joint industry/academic research projects. This is now expanding under the Ministry of Agriculture into food technology and under the Economic and Social Research Council into management. About one-third of the costs come from the enterprises involved. Universities benefit from the generation of teaching materials (60 per cent of projects), research publications (10 per cent of projects) and access to industrial equipment, as well as payment for part-time teaching staff to stand in for senior academics engaged in the research. They consider that the benefits outweigh the organizational costs and are more fruitful in the spin-offs they offer to teaching than other forms of co-operation(19).

This has also had an impact on management. Most universities have industrial liaison units to assist their staff. Other help has been forthcoming from the Committee of Vice Chancellors and Principals who in 1992 issued guidelines covering most aspects from intellectual property to cost recovery. A particularly successful innovation in this domain has been UnivEd, a company set up by the University of Edinburgh with 30 staff experienced in industry and law, to negotiate R&D contracts. It has signed 120 contracts with the EEC since 1988 worth £13 million. If a department is not doing much research, UnivEd will pay it a visit(20).

Salford University created a shadow administration consisting of a committee of faculty and industry in equal numbers to decide on research policy and create the structures to promote collaboration. Department heads are the key line managers but research is to be done in multidisciplinary centres(21). Some other universities have concluded that university-industry co-operation must be centrally managed and its board of management should include local business. The role of such a board is wider than a research committee, not only setting policies for contract research, consultancies, ownership of patents and intellectual property, but providing market research expertise and also setting the policy for continuous education and constituting teams for teaching. It should be accountable to the university executive and report periodically(22).

Industrial liaison is also promoted through Science Parks, 56 of which are now associated with higher educational institutions. They are usually high tech and allow manufacturing only on a small scale, many in the South providing marketing or financial services. Industrial links have brought a number of other benefits, not only financial. Heriot Watt University is creating an electronic campus through a partnership with business while Edinburgh acquired seven externally funded scientists for research on drugs, two of which were from the funder's country, Japan. As in the United States, there are a number of joint programmes, for example the Bradford University/Ford M.Sc. in Engineering. One undergraduate course was mainly taught by accountancy firms, and visiting lecturers are common, such posts bringing prestige and even honorary degrees!(23).

There has been a marked effect on income: research contract revenue grew from 9 per cent of current income in 1960 to 20 per cent in 1987. Income from services grew from 2 to 6.5 per cent(24). However, returns are slow to appear; it may take seven to ten years for a research programme to break even and 20 to 30 years for a science park to realize its potential (the Cambridge park generated 300 high tech companies in 20 years)(25).

Corporate money is changing university activities in that more short courses, short-term contracts and applied research are being carried out. For some staff this is a matter of concern, since over 40 per cent of business-financed research is in medicine and a further 40 per cent is in engineering and science – the arts and the social sciences are much less supported(26). In addition, the government funding systems themselves have become very selective. For example, research councils rejected a policy of spreading money thinly across all institutions and fields, but concentrated on a relatively narrow range, with engineering and bio-technology being the priority, followed by computing, information technology, physics and earth sciences, chemistry, pharmacology and building. There has been much criticism from humanities and social science researchers, who point out that the impact of their results is felt more on teaching, scholarship and in the social sphere rather than on publications and income generation, and that no allowance was made for size of departments(27).

These examples demonstrate just how much pressure is being exerted on British universities and how decision-making power has consequently shifted more to executive and government levels. The new forms of evaluation imposed mean that professors have to devote more time to the management of projects but, on the other hand, have generally been given guidance by specialized units and by research committees in contract negotiation and decision-making.

(iv) Australia

The *Australian* research funding system is similar to the United Kingdom's, i.e. some 6 per cent of operating grants is deemed to support research have some funds but the Research Council (established in 1988) allocates additional project funds which have to be competed for according to national priorities. It has both a large grant and a small grant scheme. The government has been the major initiator in changes in the way research is carried out, designating in the 1990s Co-operative Research Centres, Special Research Centres and Key Centres of Teaching and Research to promote concentrations and networks. Some universities are given few opportunities for major research(28). Funding by industry is encouraged by a 150 per cent tax concession scheme (1989) and research links by Collaborative Research Grants (1991).

Research-led universities are required to draw up research management plans, describing present effort, institutional goals, areas of strength, training activities and human resources available. Most institutions have established management structures to promote co-operative research, and have constituted research teams to form the requisite critical mass for projects. The ratio of postgraduates to undergraduates has also been increased. However, a survey of engineering and science graduate students showed that only half envisaged taking up research careers in industry since prospects were seen as poor. The Postgraduate Research Award (Industry) Scheme set up in 1990 for M.Sc. and Ph.D students and supervised jointly by university and industry has so far not been in high demand(29).

(v) Netherlands

The *Netherlands* has had a conditional research funding system since 1982 under which external peer assessment procedures are used to ensure the quality of research. Proposals must state the goals and social relevance of the project, give the estimated costs and show the reputation of the research team and its position in the national research network. The opinion was that whereas previously decision-making depended on proposals made by researchers, now the balance of power had shifted to the government(30). Eighty per cent of research is covered by this budget. The first group of projects carried out were evaluated to see whether the results promised had been fulfilled. Ninety per cent of them passed the test and universities have been asked to take action on the remaining 10 per cent(31). In 1989 the government decided to set up research schools as part of the university system in an effort to sharpen university profiles and concentrate both research and teaching programmes. These schools were also designed for the placement of trainee research assistants, a scheme begun in 1984 when 1,000 four-year posts were created in universities to re-train young researchers and create a pool of talent. Here, too, links with industry and the establishment of science parks have been actively pursued; for example, the University of Twente was involved in 170 companies (13,000 jobs) as of 1990. Within universities, similar management structures to those described above, i.e. co-ordinating committees working within long-term development plans, research liaison offices and, in addition to departmental research programmes, 'clusters' or teams, have been formed for multidisciplinary projects(32).

It will be noted, for this group of countries, that changes began to accelerate as from 1990, a little later than those for funding and overall management. They follow similar patterns, however: growth of government support agencies, greater power of decision-making at government and university executive level, and consequently less at departmental level.

b.   Self-regulation in transition

The *Nordic* countries have embarked upon changes in overall university management similar in many respects to those in the self-regulatory group, but this does not seem yet to be entirely so as regards research management. In Norway, the Central Committee for Research(33) deals with policy. It has abolished the distinction between basic and applied research, and has questioned the freedom of disciplinary research councils in deciding on grants. Since the government has stipulated priority areas (i.e. information technology, bio-technology, oil and gas, health and the environment, management) the Committee feels that funding should be centralized. Decision-making on research is mainly a disciplinary research council/department domain, the former giving grants both for research and for doctoral students(34). University expenditure on research is quite extensive, taking into account that teaching loads are light at 33 per cent of staff time.

In *Finland*, the Academy is the major sponsor of research and researchers apply direct to this body after obtaining the approval of the Department Head, except for very large and expensive programmes, which have to be approved by the University Council. Increased pressure has been exerted by the government for socially relevant research, which led to a decline in funding for basic, and hence university, research. Universities have become more dependent on Ministries other than Education and on private funding(35).

*Sweden*has gone farthest in instituting changes in the management of research. Government policy guides distribution of funds and, as in Finland, has stipulated socially relevant research, under which specialized institutes have tended to receive more of the funds; there are specialized boards in several ministries for this purpose. The latter, together with university funding to maintain a broad research capacity, and awards from research councils, constitute the three main sources of funds, a similar system to that seen in Australia(36).

Departments in Sweden are allowed some latitude in research decisions but the government has decreed that a board be set up in the university to stimulate research in new and important areas which are designated by its mission statement as a priority for that institution. About 40 per cent of institutional research comes under this heading, in addition to those projects of social relevance funded by specialized boards. Institutions who comply receive more funding. There are also reports of growing dependence on industrial financing, with consequent fears of influencing research topics, and conflicts over secrecy and property rights, as noted for the self-regulatory group.

The establishment of science parks is also a feature in the Nordic countries, a particular example being Chalmers University in Gothenburg, which since 1946 has produced 160 spin-off companies.

c. Self-regulation in difficulty

(i) Eastern Europe

In Eastern Europe, most research has been conducted in specialized institutes of Ministries and in the Academies of sciences. Teaching occupies most of the time of university academic staff(37) though officially 30 per cent is allocated to research. However, departments are now trying to compete for private contracts with the specialized institutes, technology centres and inventors' societies who have the advantage that they can carry out applied research more rapidly.

The structure of research set up in the past has created a vested interest in the status quo. Major reform is blocked by the powerful influence of the large numbers of researchers in academies of science, state funding has decreased and competition for these funds is resisted.

None of the four Central European countries of Poland, Hungary, the Czech and Slovak Republics, have set research priorities at national level. It seems that the market will be the main arbiter to the extent that institutions are forced to seek external research income(38) and will be the pressure that erodes the status quo. In Georgia institutions for private research have been established and in Russia, foundations with a special fiscal status.

National structural changes have taken place in Poland: the members of the Scientific Research Committee, which allocated the state budget as from 1991, are all elected. However, universities obtained only 31 per cent of their research funds from this source(39) so most funds have to be externally generated. Universities are now setting up mechanisms similar to those seen in the self-regulatory group of countries. The Polish Higher Education-Business Forum promotes relations between Rectors and leading private and state enterprises. The Warsaw University of Technology has established an Enterprise Development Centre to assist business to adapt to the new market economy and has opened a Business Management School in co-operation with French, United Kingdom and Norwegian schools(40). Such international links can be seen in most East European countries.

In Estonia, a law has been passed giving universities the key role in research; a Research and Science Foundation has been set up to establish priorities(41) and academicians have agreed to teach, under contract, in universities.

Reservations, similar to those expressed in West European countries, about linking university research to production are also being felt in the east, i.e. such research is not necessarily relevant to the institution's overall research and training priorities. In addition, fundamental research is stagnating and generally falling behind international levels, and increased reliance on this source of research funding has also apparently led to growing scarcity of modern equipment and facilities.

(ii) Latin America

In *Latin America*, there is no strong empirical research tradition and the funds for equipment, documentation and other services have not been available. Argentina, Brazil, Mexico, Colombia, Peru and Chile created national research funding agencies but these also in recent years have suffered budget cuts. For example, in Brazil funds for research declined in the 1980s to less than a third of the level a decade earlier. Equipment tends to be obsolescent and assistants cannot be retained(42). There is a general perception of the uselessness of university research, with research management needing special administrative staff to be responsible for evaluation and cost control(43). Another review concluded that there is a lack of national policies to make university basic research productive, since the teaching function dominates and the traditional bureaucratic model does not favour research. In addition there is long-standing distrust of universities in both the state and private sectors(44).

High quality postgraduate and research programmes tend to be concentrated in only a few institutions in capital or other large cities. Brazil, Mexico and Venezuela have expanded this level of education as a result of government policies but nevertheless research in recent years has become more and more divorced from postgraduate studies. Most is done in institutes, public laboratories and Ministry units(45). In Colombia the number of projects in institutes doubled over 1978-82 while university research remained stagnant and only half of university researchers find the finance they need(46).

Some governments have attempted to stem the decline by offering incentives; in Mexico a National System of Researchers was created in 1985 to allocate individual grants on evidence of high productivity. The two-three year grants are renewable only after evaluation by a disciplinary peer committee. Six thousand staff (out of a total of 100,000 professors) receive monthly supplements which may amount to as much as 40 per cent of their salaries(47). Venezuela (CONICIT) began a similar scheme in 1992 when 928 academics received an additional 18 per cent of their salaries after peer review of their work.

Attempts are being made in other ways by governments to bring universities into the national research mainstream. In Brazil, state-owned companies have set up research centres in proximity to certain universities, for example **PETROBRAS** and **ELCTROBRAS** are linked to the Federal University of Rio de Janeiro and cater for government programmes to train research graduates. There are also several technology parks at Brazilian universities: that at Sao Carlos has 36 high tech enterprises which may use the university laboratories and infrastructure. Once established they offer the university raw materials and facilities in return for practical training for students. There have been cases of private industry paying the salaries of collaborating professors but on the other hand, many high tech specialists are leaving universities for industry(48). The Mexican Government has also attempted to build a bridge between universities and industry with the establishment in 1985 of a Centre for Technological Innovation at UNAM which supports projects and training and arranges contracts between universities and industry. In order to motivate staff, UNAM altered its regulations to allow researchers to receive a percentage of the income earned(49).

Generally, in Latin America there has been insufficient appreciation of the need to actively manage research, particularly at institutional level. The case-study carried out in Peru for the IIEP research programme showed this clearly (*Box 10*).

Box 10.

> The Universidad Nacional Agraria La Molina Peru (UNALM), in a country of multiple micro climates, where half the household budget is spent on food, has the important goals of:
> - development of knowledge about national problems in agriculture;
> - technical innovation in agricultural production;
> - education and practical field training of students.
>
> UNALM's reputation in the 1950s and 60s was high. Close co-ordination between producers and university resulted in gains in development through the activities of three distinct regional centres and the university attracted high-quality staff and students. However, subsequent political instability, hyper-inflation and a depressed agricultural sector brought about a decline. UNALM is now seeking, with the assistance of donor agencies, to establish a more efficient research management structure to bring about a return to its former position. An analysis of research management and structure showed that the Research Office had not played a proactive role in planning and monitoring research. Due to paucity of funds, much research (as in Africa, for example) is donor driven. Most faculty are not now involved in research programmes since their salaries are less than other public employees such as the police, and they are obliged to seek secondary employment. Economic pressures have also influenced use of university land to generate revenue rather than purely for research. The problem-oriented projects conducted have been varied from small-scale individual, medium scale under departmental heads to large scale with multidisciplinary teams under a co-ordinator, but this mixed system had no uniform accounting and control procedures.
>
> The university has drawn up a new strategic plan defining specific targets and the means by which they will be achieved. To mention the most important of them:
> - *Strengthening of institutional information and capacity to plan, implement and manage research projects.* Basic data on the research process (e.g. utilization of facilities, faculty time allocation) and research results (e.g. publications, dissemination and extension) are unavailable. A key element is a concerted effort to implement an information system. In addition, each of the eight Faculties now has an Office of Research and Extension Programming.

- *A new commitment to multidisciplinary/participatory research.* Individual research may continue but greater emphasis is to be given to programmatic/strategic research requiring specialized inputs from various disciplines, producers and market agents to address the needs of small farmers in the highlands and low, humid forests, as well as the large export-oriented producers of the coastal region. Sustainability and environmental protection are fundamental principles.
- *Stabilization of the financial situation with income-generating activities and improved linkages to factor and product markets.* Examples are production and sale of certified seed and produce from experiments, and user fees for laboratory analyses of soil, plant and pest samples.
- *A new emphasis on co-operation with industry, commerce, government and international development institutions, including the carrying out of baseline studies and plan formulation.* Implementation is more collaborative, and includes representation of faculty, students, producers, market agents, government, voluntary organizations etc. This has resulted in diversification of donor support, i.e. the principal donors include two multilateral, six international private companies and six governments. In addition, the Food Science Faculty in 1989 appointed an external Visiting Committee of industrialists and businessmen to obtain feedback and propose changes. This innovation is to serve as a model for the other faculties.
- *Preparation of a new generation of scientists.* Beginning in 1994, approximately 20 students will be selected each year for M.Sc. and 10-15 at Ph.D level, every two years.
- *Incentives to encourage research and lessen secondary employment.* The government in 1990 set up a special fund for university development to improve faculty salaries, increase support staff, equipment and research.

Problems still have to be faced, i.e. lack of well-trained staff, particularly research programme leaders, the poor state of basic services, the inadequate monitoring of performance, some friction between the government and university over management of project funds, etc. However, UNALM is slowly but surely moving towards achievement of its targets. Pioneering research has achieved extraordinary results and international recognition, e.g. high yield crop varieties, tropical livestock breeding to increase milk yields, propagated species of tropical forages, new varieties of tomato and chili pepper and the collection and improvement of native species of fruit. A computerized network has been established by which researchers anywhere in the country can search UNALM databases for relevant information.

University research management is in transition to becoming a facilitator, catalyst and broker for collaborative action and narrow theoretical and disciplinary interests are giving way to improved response to markets and such externalities as environmental protection and sustainable development(50).

d. Centralized planning and control

(i) Western Europe

Research management in countries under central planning and control is being tightened. For instance, in *France,* the Ministry of Education is making four-year research contracts directly with faculties or institutes which must meet set criteria for quality, and the power of the universities' own science councils for research grant allocations is to be removed(51). More than half of researchers in the state sector and 60 per cent in the private sector are in the Paris region, and a nationwide research development policy is to decide on multidisciplinary research sites elsewhere to assist in the development of regional research networks. More than 2,500 scientists are to be transferred to the provinces by 1996. Most research in France (and in other centrally-planned systems) is conducted in separate institutes on university campuses, usually by CNRS (Centre National de Recherche Scientifique) personnel. However, in order to increase human resources for teaching, it is now proposed that CNRS staff should also do some teaching in universities and that only some of the academics in universities should carry out research. Universities are to focus on a few selected areas of excellence, networking with nearby institutions(52). The training of researchers has also fallen more directly under government control with the setting up of variants of the American graduate school, *Ecole doctorales* (found also in Germany as *Gradvienten Kollegen*, and in the Netherlands, as noted above).

Since 1984, universities can legally hold a minority stake in private companies and do so mainly in the field of new technologies. Links with industry in courses have increased, for example new engineering programmes in 1991 (alternating periods of work and study) and '*diplômes professionalisés*'(53). Eight or so science parks have been set up since 1969 as local authority initiatives; one, Sophia-Antipolis has 20 research centres and eventually formed the basis for the launching of the University of Nice(54).

The *German* Government has asked universities to be more entrepreneurial in research and training. Under a 1985 Act, professors may be given the responsibility to administer large research grants outside regular university activities and may employ staff funded by these grants. Both federal and state ministries have set out their research priorities. Funding in 1987 was distributed 40 per cent to individual grants, 29 per cent to collaborative research centres, 18 per cent to priority research and the remainder to special programmes to promote young researchers. Business funding has increased but has not been welcomed by all institutions(55). Thus research management still remains under the traditional chair. A survey found that only a third of a professor's time was spent on research, instead of the 45 per cent norm. The government has attempted to foster links with industry by funding research and technical transfer centres, but at most universities less than a quarter of research funds comes from private sources.

The *Belgian* 1986 Saint Ann Plan set aside 9 per cent of the higher education budget for research but requested universities to increase their funding from private sources. In 1987 interest-free loans became available to commercialize research results. Applications have to be made to a national committee to carry out projects and the decisions are made on the basis of an on-site visit. The process is very competitive and only one-third of applicants receive any funds. Top researchers must apply for post-doctoral fellowships for major research programmes. Thirty per cent of all staff time should be spent on research, but in a report from one university found that only 15 per cent of the staff were able to do any that was government-sponsored. The acute lack of space and cuts in government funding are major problems which the university has tried to alleviate by attempting to increase the amount of funds externally generated. For this purpose, it appointed a special Research Co-ordinator to explore needs, promote university research and disseminate information. Most universities have industrial liaison units, research centres for multidisciplinary work, and often science parks.

Other countries in Western Europe have continued to base research management on the department or chair. However, concern for quality has resulted in some evaluation mechanisms being instituted; as from 1990, the output of Spanish researchers has been assessed centrally for originality, contribution to the knowledge base, international recognition, publications and patents, according to which they may be accorded performance-related bonuses.

These centrally-planned systems reflect the same government concerns, for concentration, selectivity, multidisciplinary centres and regional networks, as in the self-regulatory countries. However, research generally remains a matter for direct negotiation between the Government and the researcher. There is also considerable government pressure to increase research funding from private sources, Belgium providing a case where a university has incorporated within its management structure a special unit to promote research links with industry.

(ii) Africa

In most developing countries research activity has had great difficulty in establishing a base, because the critical minimum mass of researchers in any particular discipline, the facilities, equipment, literature and international links are generally lacking. Among the many other factors militating against the building up of research capacity in Africa are government suspicion of universities and scholars, lack of academic freedom and respect for diversity of ideas, loss of indigenous talent, and problems in the dissemination of any research work done. In addition to all this, rapid increases in student numbers coupled with budgetary constraints have thrust heavy teaching responsibilities on staff, and made it difficult for them to devote much time to research(56). Many countries have established science policy-making bodies but their work has been affected by changes in government and stagnant or declining research funding(57). Contrary to what has been seen in the self-regulatory group, government is not a major guide and support for university research; spending may be as low as 0.1 per cent of GNP as compared to 2.5 per cent in the United Kingdom(58).

A recent report from the World Bank surveyed 14 African universities, and found a poor output of research, staff having second jobs and equipment being inadequate(59). Universities who could report on the percentage of research expenditure as a percentage of total budget were to be found in the more prosperous countries (Botswana, Nigeria, Zimbabwe) but even there internal funds allocated to research ranged from 1 to 4 per cent and external funds from 2 to 8 per cent (compared to 20 per cent for the United Kingdom). External funds are the major source of financing research and come either from foreign national or international donors. Only eight of the 14 institutions had developed a research management plan, one had an office to solicit external funds and eight undertook contract research, but only two of them on a full cost-recovery basis.

This situation was confirmed by the questionnaires completed for the IIEP in the Central African Republic, Kenya, Mozambique, Tanzania and Zimbabwe. Most research funds are obtained from international agencies. Only 10-20 per cent of staff carried out any research; most is linked to the obtaining of a Ph.D and is not socially relevant. The problems encountered by these institutions in undertaking research were:

- absence of research cultures and previous studies within the country;
- lack of postgraduate courses;

- inadequate funds, equipment, transport and books;
- inadequate contacts with industry and community;
- inefficient use of research manpower;
- absence of research leadership;
- inadequate or complete absence of data banks and data retrieval systems.

In Makerere University, Uganda, it was reported that research had virtually ceased. Only 24 papers for journals were produced in 1990, 12 of them in the bio-medical field.

Other studies support these findings. A paper produced for the Association of African Universities found that from 1986 to 1989 most university libraries had not been able to buy books and journals. Although universities have computers for research and teaching, they lacked material for basic elementary analyses and maintenance is not ensured. There is some expensive equipment, such as electronic microscopes, which should be used for interdisciplinary work but it is under-utilized and its existence is not widely known about. Teaching loads are double those in western universities. During 1988-89, 1,388 articles were published, 49 per cent of them in international journals, but three Nigerian universities accounted for 72 per cent of these(60).

National donors and enterprises fund little research and there is no local market for it. Even where specific efforts are made to stimulate demand, they are unsuccessful. For example, the University of Sierra Leone has a University Research and Development Services Unit for research and consultancy on a commercial basis, trying to sell the potential of graduates to the industrial community but it has so far achieved little(61).

What changes have universities instituted to try to combat the difficult conditions in which they have to try to carry out research? Most universities have the traditional mode of management, i.e. a Research and Grants Committee to advise on policy, identify needs for facilities, allocate central university funds and make an annual report on activities. A number of institutions are successfully collaborating with Ministries on problems of relevance to national development, e.g. the Obafemi Awolowo University (Nigeria) Geology Department has produced technical data for state mineral exploration, and the University of Zambia undertook research on such matters as primary health care, the sociology of a new industrial centre, and the ecological effects of a hydroelectric dam. Applied research with a particular focus on rural development is conducted in the Côte d'Ivoire Centre for Economic and Social Research, for example research on food production systems, agro-allied industries and technology transfer. Findings are disseminated via workshops for business and government officials. The University of Science and Technology, Ghana, has established a Technology Consultation Centre which plans to set up Intermediate Technology Transfer Units in each region of the country.

However, few universities have posts or units which actively promote research and collaboration with local industry. The University of Malawi created the post of Research Co-ordinator and the University of Ouagadougou an Assistant Dean for Research, to motivate staff to undertake research and seek external funding. Evaluations of these two experiences are not yet available.

In addition, it would seem that most universities do not know exactly what research and consultancy activities are being conducted by their staff. Quite a number of academics are involved in consulting activities but many of them are conducted on a private basis to supplement salaries, even though they use university resources. While internally funded projects have to be approved by the university, externally funded projects may be negotiated directly by departments with sponsors (reported from Kenya and Uganda). Hence management of the research effort is not controlled and codes for good research conduct are not yet highly developed. Where institutions have set up a university consulting company or industrial liaison office (six were reported), they tend, with a few exceptions, to be slow in reacting to proposals for joint ventures, are too bureaucratic and take too great a proportion of any revenue generated. The exceptions reported were the University of Dar-es-Salaam's engineering department, which has worked on designing sisal harvesters and solving problems of landslides for the rail-road(62) and the Engineering and Electrical Departments of Addis Ababa University, which have concluded successful consultancies(63).

Donor agencies have recognized the need to support researchers in Africa. An African Academy of Science has been set up to launch programmes to assist capacity building and help scientists to communicate with each other. One means will be the Academy's own journal, and researchers may also send their books to the Academy's publishing house. Universities in the islands of the Indian Ocean are also co-operating under COPESSOI (their permanent conference) in the realm of information circulation, exchange programmes, training and research aimed at development of the region. SAREC, the Swedish Aid Agency, is assisting capacity building in 160 research institutions in developing countries, of which six are in Africa. However, they have not been able to establish any groups and the number of scientists taking part is usually small, two being the most common.

Donor activity in the creation of centres of excellence has had some negative effects. Such institutions have provided a haven for high-level scholars but have contributed to a decline in the capacity of universities, which has discouraged donors(64). An IDRC study of 16 countries in Africa showed that donor agencies and governments prefer to establish parallel institutions for research or use foreign researchers. The comment was made that while these alternative arrangements provide the required research, they are not firmly linked to local institutions like universities or planning units of ministries, to ensure that their operations are rooted in reality. In most cases they tend to alienate existing capacity(65).

Another donor strategy, to establish research networks, may prove to be more useful to academic staff in universities. Networks are aimed at identifying experts, assisting in the obtaining of funds and arranging meetings and dissemination of research results. A number have been set up for different regions and different research domains, but again the criticism is that they are heavily donor-influenced. One network which has escaped this criticism is the Commonwealth Secretariat's network for renewable energy resources and local building materials.

Much remains to be done to promote university research in Africa, in particular the more active and efficient management and control of this vital activity at government level and within institutions. Experience shows that where research and links with industry have been successfully developed, structural units, planning mechanisms and management procedures were essential elements.

(iii) Asia

In Asia, governments have generally promulgated national research priorities and provided the funds for at least state universities to participate. They have stressed the role of university research in development and links with industry and have been highly successful in the case of the NICs, which set about improving research capacity and management in universities at very much the same time as some of the developed countries. Hong Kong has established a new University of Science and Technology to help local industry shift from labour intensive to investment and intensive, with a special research centre to carry out projects with industry and commerce(66). More recently, in 1991 a Research Grants Council has been established following recognition of the need to build up its local research base for manufacturing industry in an increasingly sophisticated and competitive situation. Hong Kong's Industry and Technology Development Council is also designed to promote research. In 1990 the Hong Kong University set up an Industrial Liaison Office and faculty are given time off from teaching when involved in joint research projects (of which there were 265 in 1990). A Teaching Company Scheme places graduates to work in companies abroad so as to acquire research experience. Progress has been rapid, and research publications are now on a par with the Republic of Korea(67).

The development of research capacity at the University of Singapore began a little earlier and in just over a decade, a complex and sophisticated structure was built up. The 1986 National Science and Technology Research Policy designated medicine, molecular and cell biology, and information technology as priority areas; 1 per cent of GNP is allocated to R&D. The university now has four Special Research Institutes in the priority areas as well as Faculty-based Research Centres. Links to industry are promoted by an Industrial and Technical Relations Office, an Innovation Centre, the Science Park and eight Research/Consultancy Centres for Entrepreneurship. Staff may earn fees up to 60 per cent of their annual salaries and an overwhelming weight in promotions is given to research performance(68). Businesses can subscribe to be members of INTROLINK and co-operate in R&D, receive literature, course curricula, seminars and assistance by consultancies(69).

China also began about that time to put its research management into more order – the universities being significant elements, since they receive 70 per cent of available basic research funding, as allocated by the National Natural Science Foundation, set up in 1986. Allocations are made according to peer review. Control at the national level is also exercised by the Institute of Scientific and Technological Information, which monitors output and publishes statistics on articles and citations. China's international ranking rose from 38th in 1979 to 15th in 1990(70). The policy adopted is essentially that seen in the self-regulatory group of countries but expressed in a different manner and with different emphases(71). Curricula give a third credit for course work, a third for independent study and a third for experimental work. This encourages small-scale invention by students and involvement of entrepreneurs in university committees. Continuing education is used as a window to increase mutual understanding between universities and enterprises, the former finding out the most pressing needs and the latter becoming aware of the strengths and assistance available from the university. Recently, in May 1988, more emphasis has been given to meeting the needs of industry by participation in technological development zones and in income generation. Universities may receive 10 per cent of the profits of factories founded by them and in the 27 development zones at least 200 of the enterprises were set up by universities. One example is the computer laser publishing system developed by Beijing University over 14 years: it is now being commercially produced in a high tech zone and bringing substantial financial returns. A major lesson from the Chinese experience is that enterprises need the continuing technical support of university R&D expertise to keep abreast of competition. The joint approach of teaching, research and production has been found to be a valid strategy for the training of researchers and technology transfer. Relations between the partners become ever closer, resulting in agreements to set up joint groups. For example, 400 multidisciplinary groups, covering the whole country, have been set up in the domains of agriculture and forestry to assist poverty-stricken areas to produce more rice, cotton, wheat, goats, rabbits, fruit, etc.

Science parks are also major co-operative ventures. The first was established by a conglomerate of 60 universities and colleges in Shanghai, in 1992, to sell research results and provide factory space for commercial exploitation.

The other larger Asian countries have experienced greater problems in funding and concentrating their research efforts and in overcoming the traditional gap between industry and university.

The Indian 1983 Technology Policy Statement emphasized indigenous development, adaptation of imports and linkage with financial institutions allocating resources. It delineated the main thrust areas for research such as self-sufficiency in oil seeds, dry-land farming, communications, and control of vector borne diseases. The New Education Policy of 1986 put emphasis on rural universities to serve as sources of guidance and innovation for development. The decisions on fund allocation are made at the apex – the Ministry of Finance allocates sums according to the various development sectors through particular agencies like the UGC and government departments. Experience has shown that initiatives to carry out this type of research may come from the researcher or from the university vice-chancellor, or the lending agency itself may approach the university[72]. However, it can only be carried out in the very best equipped institutions. A small survey[73] showed that financial support for research from industry is negligible except for the Institutes of Technology, though some had acquired a few gifts of equipment and sponsored research projects usually arranged on a personal basis. Companies were willing to sponsor research, but university laboratories were insufficiently well equipped. Only the Institutes of Technology provided consultancy activities to any extent and had drawn up a centralized list of the research interests of the staff so that firms might ascertain what expertise was available. As in Latin America, the obstacles to university-industry linkage were listed as mutual distrust, lower quality of research, and deficiency of facilities. In most universities only a few academics are engaged in research.

However, while university research co-operation with industry may have had difficulties in taking off, this was not the case for agriculture. India has been one of the countries, along with Indonesia and Thailand, which has particularly benefited from the establishment of agricultural universities. Impressive gains have been made in food production especially in wheat and rice areas. Improvements in credit facilities, marketing infrastructure and other sources have also been attributed to university activity(74). One particular report from the Haryana Agricultural University, India, shows that the university has released over 95 high yielding varieties of fruits, cereals and vegetables into the region. It has established outlying research stations and extension activities have supported state development departments to turn Haryana into an agricultural surplus state. Such a co-operative effort has required considerable planning and management. The university has a number of committees (e.g. a Variety Evaluation Committee, which identifies new types of paddy, sugar cane, cotton etc.) and multidisciplinary teams of compatible scientists are formed to work on the different crops. Transfer of technology is one of the most important activities and to increase the rate of transfer, the university adopted a whole village approach. A recent incentive given to researchers is that an individual or group may submit a specific project which if approved, they have the freedom to execute and receive due personal recognition for any success(75).

Some Asian universities are overwhelmed by the social demand for higher education. In Pakistan professors may officially allocate 40 per cent of their time to scholarship and research but increases in undergraduate enrolments meant that more time had to be given to teaching and some research funds were not used. However, the universities have the usual Directorate of Research to scrutinize individual proposals, with a policy of promoting applied research to assist local development.

In Japan, support to research in universities compares poorly with support to institutes and private company research, and heavy undergraduate teaching duties make it difficult for academics to do any(76). Government policy now advocates industry links, and to assist in overcoming university resistance, the Ministry of Education in 1991 established 14 joint industry-university research centres throughout the country to study clean energy, artificial intelligence, precision manufacturing and bio-technology. The universities are now signing substantial contracts with private industry.

In many of the other countries of the region, such as Malaysia, Indonesia and the Philippines, universities are basically teaching institutions. The industrial base is weak and unwilling to support R&D in the universities. However, there are signs of change with the setting up of technology parks, while certain universities have been given roles that specifically stipulate their links with the local environment, for example the University of Chiengmai, Thailand, in 1987 established UNISERV, a unit designed to promote sustainable industry in the region. It is staffed by a full-time Director and four administrators. The University Sains Malaysia's mission is to apply its intellectual and physical resources to industry, commerce and the community. An innovation and consultancy centre was created, the main user being industry in the nearby free trade zone of Penang. More than 600 firms have used its services and 108 major contracts undertaken. However, an obstacle is that the majority of firms which started as joint ventures with foreign companies have no policy of supporting indigenous R&D(77).

The Asian region at the moment shows a very wide range of university research roles, from mainly teaching institutions to being fully integrated in the development of the region, such as Haryana University and the universities in the NICs. Successful experiences illustrate the need for growth of structures and management.

(iv) Arab States

One study on higher education in the Arab States(78) reports that although legislation may state that research is an essential university function, it is given a low priority. This has been due to:

- the increasing proportion of university budgets taken by administration;
- shortage of qualified staff, both academics and technicians, due to the brain-drain;
- total detachment of universities from productive institutions and ignorance of problems in the local environment;
- absence of a research climate;
- lack of proper organization, materials and incentives.

This was confirmed by a survey conducted in the University of Kuwait, where 85 per cent of the departments said they had no contact with industry. The Office of Training and Consultancy has the function of promoting links but so far has been mainly concerned with organizing short courses(79). In Algeria, though most state research is done by the universities, with the exception of solar energy and nuclear research, the state budget for this has declined in the late 1980s to only a tenth of what it was a decade earlier. Research is organized in Research Departments or Units: in 1987, the 19 universities had 63 such units covering most disciplines with 600 projects in hand Little effort has been made to cooperate with industry(80).

2. Lessons learned

What can be learnt from recent trends in research management?

Current thinking on good practice in research management involves the following:

a. Policy-making and its dissemination

The main elements to be taken into account in policy-making and its dissemination are itemized in *Figure 3*.

Figure 3. Policy making and its dissemination

National level:	Setting priorities.
	Selectivity, concentration, designation of centres of excellence.
	Promotion of networks.
	Funding mechanisms to steer research activity, postgraduate courses and university-industry links.
	National agency to set policy and promote links to industry.
	Accountability procedures which stimulate research.
Regional and local level:	Definition of needs for social development, promotion of links and stimulating funding.
Institutional level :	Defining the mission of the university, i.e. decisions to concentrate on certain spheres, on basic, applied or development, and what can be done to assist regional development, etc.

b. Research management policy

(i) Staff

Generally research is not required, but all academics are expected to engage in some scholastic or research activity. This is encouraged by the practice of setting norms for the division of time between research, teaching and administration.

In the United Kingdom the latest survey indicated that university staff devoted 36 per cent of their working time to research (the stipulated norm is 30 per cent) and 35 per cent to teaching, while in the former polytechnics, which receive very little research funding, academic staff devoted 21 per cent of their time to research. Thirty to forty per cent seems to be the general rate in universities around the world, though this, on its own, has not been a sufficient condition for research to be actually conducted. Staff who are not engaged in research are now being given teaching-only posts.

(ii) Promotion criteria

The most important criteria for promotion in the past have been research publications, patents, dissertations, participation in scientific conferences, etc. The situation is beginning to change now with the division between teaching and research universities and with staff appraisal and development practices which concentrate much more on good teaching.

Research staff policy is also concerned with:

- Provision of a pool of young researchers from which permanent staff may be recruited. This is often done by providing part-time work to students completing Ph.Ds, the establishment of special posts for non-teaching researchers and funding of relatively long study visits.
- Retention of high level staff capable of leading research teams. This is a major problem in developing countries. Some universities (e.g. Dakar) pay a bonus to those having a Ph.D., and offer more favourable sabbatical and conference opportunities.

(iii) Finance

Is a basic allocation to be made to each department or will research funds go to those who are producing the best work? It is felt to be good policy to provide small amounts of 'seed money' for new and untried lines of research and for research which assists local enterprises, and may attract money from the private sector.

(iv) Contracts and consultancies

In particular the monitoring of such activities and their contribution to university overheads. Donor-assisted research often involves the provision of equipment, buildings and training, with long-term burdens on university finances which may have to support them when the project is completed.

c. Designing an appropriate management structure

This structure might incorporate:

- a post at high level, with responsibility for overall institutional research management, its promotion, data collection, information system, and analyses;
- a Council or committee to draw up policy and plan proposals, decide on fund allocation and conduct periodic monitoring of activities;
- a post or unit for liaison with local economic activities to establish needs for research and training. This depends on the institution, its goals, size and research capacity. A dynamic technological institution may establish an industrial liaison centre to disseminate information on the university's capabilities as regards research, consultancies and short courses, to arrange exhibitions, lectures and visits, to oversee contractual arrangements and to solicit funding. Another institution, with research activities more in applied and specialized fields, may find it more suitable to make a staff member in each faculty or department responsible for the promotion of research in the department.
- a technology transfer or innovation centre;
- multidisciplinary teams;
- an economic activity park or zone to assist the development of local entrepreneurs and commercial exploitation of university R&D.

d. Management procedures

(i) A code for good research practice and ensuring that it is adhered to

In Australia, for example, universities must now adhere to a code of good conduct for research which requires record keeping, preservation of data, close supervision of work, peer review and public presentation of findings. Institutions applying for public research funds have to certify that they have instituted procedures which ensure that they have followed the code.

(ii) Criteria for the selection of projects within a co-ordinated overall research programme

Each university sets their own, usually influenced by government policy, and uses them as guidelines for researchers. Some at present being used are:

(i) the activity should aim primarily at professional contribution to a field rather than personal gain;
(ii) it should not be used for a degree thesis;
(iii) research money should not be used for holding conferences;
(iv) the researcher or team has proven competence;
(v) the researcher or team are likely to stay at the university long enough to complete the research (age structure of team, possible retirement or transfer);
(vi) the research should accord with university policy, so that:
- a balance is kept between previous well-established lines of research and opening up new areas;
- some opportunities are available which allow 'freedom to enquire' as opposed to meeting national or regional priorities for research;
- multidisciplinary team work is encouraged;
- it is related to the teaching programme.
(vii) the feasibility and sound methodology of the research are demonstrated;
(viii) the future implications of the research for the university, including time, policy and cost implications which may arise only after several years;

(ix) cost. Is new apparatus required? Is it likely to lead to unforeseen demands for finance? Where it is to take more than one year, it should be phased and costed in each year.

At each level of evaluation of the research proposal (Department/Faculty/Council), there are different emphases in the criteria used. At departmental level, the interests of the researchers take priority, whereas university and national interests take precedence higher up in the selection process. The latter are likely to be paramount in developing countries, but are also important in developed countries.

(iii) Information on the procedures to be followed in applications:

The procedures followed usually consist of individual or group preparation of a project which is at a stipulated time in the university calendar presented to the Departmental Head for review of scientific content and requirements for resources of finance, space, facilities and staff. It may then go to the Faculty Head and on to the Director of Research for inclusion in the agenda of the Research Council or committee. If it is approved there in principle, the proposal may still have to undergo some revision. For instance, the Research Director or Industrial Liaison Officer may suggest it be sent to selected funding agencies. If they are interested, they will enter into negotiations which may change to some extent the methodology or expected outcomes of the project.

(iv) Procedures for on-going control, evaluation and possible re-orientation of research programmes:

Usually Department and Faculty Heads evaluate in turn before reporting to the Research Council. Part of the evaluation is to investigate whether research is being used in teaching programmes and involving students, and that time schedules are respected.

Monitoring requires a central information base on all research programmes in progress, their balance between theoretical and applied, between disciplines, and between contractual and institutional research. Such an information base should contain the indicators which may be required by university management, ministries and funding agencies, such as patents obtained, publications, academic distinctions, amount of research income generated from external sources, percentage of staff time spent on research, linkage between teaching and research, and contributions to regional or national development.

e. Improving the research environment

(i) Planning the physical and material conditions under which research may flourish:

This requires that the university include in its budget sufficient resources for the buying and maintenance of equipment and facilities, with training to staff in the proper utilization of the more complicated and sensitive equipment installed where this may be used by students and personnel other than the researchers. Included among favourable material conditions is the organization of the accelerating growth of new scientific and technological information in the form of computer services, and library and information systems research and development.

(ii) Improving the dissemination of research

Seminars and Workshops, exhibitions and demonstrations are normal features of university life that contribute to a stimulating environment. The organisation of national, regional and international links with other researchers is vital, particularly in developing country institutions. These can be arranged through twinning agreements between faculties and departments or in projects whereby researchers from other countries are incorporated into a team, or by regional groups interested in similar problems.

Some developing country university researchers have difficulty in finding outlets for publications and need guidance on the possibilities, such as the AAU network. Language problems may also impede international dissemination of research results. Certain universities could do very useful work in preparing comprehensive abstracts of research articles produced in their own region which could be exchanged on a reciprocal basis with similar institutions in other countries or with international bodies and donor agencies.

References

1. Neumann, R. "Perceptions of the teaching-research nexus: a framework for analysis". In *Higher Education*, Vol. 23, No. 2, March 1992.
2. Neumann, R. "Research and scholarship: perceptions of senior academic administrators". In *Higher Education*, Vol. 25, No. 2, March 1993.
3. Staropoli, A. Evaluation of Research, Xth General Conference, IMHE/OECD June 1990.
4. Lynn, Meek V. "The transformation of Australian higher education from binary to unitary". In *Higher Education*, Vol. 21, No. 4, January 1991.
5. Elton, L. "Research, teaching and scholarship in an expanding higher educational system". In *Higher Education Quarterly*, Vol. 46, No. 3, 1992.
6. Taylor, M. "Implications of new organizational patterns of research". In *Higher Education Management*, Vol. 1, No. 1, March 1989.
7. Sanyal, B. and Moegiadi. "The role of the educational system in the technological development of electronics and telecommunications in Indonesia", IIEP Research Report No. 74, Paris, 1989.
8. Times Higher Education Supplement, 16 December 1988.
9. Times Higher Education Supplement, 19 May 1989.
10. Department of Education and Science. *Aspects of higher education in the USA*, HMO London. 1989.
11. Corry, J. and Gooch, J. "The Wisconsin idea: extending the boundaries of a university". In *Higher Education Quarterly*, Vol. 46, No. 4, 1992.
12. Bell, S. and Sadlak, J. "Technology transfer in Canada: research parks and centers of excellence". In *Higher Education Management*, Vol. 4, No. 2, July 1992.
13. Crespo, M. *University/business relations in a comparative perspective*. IIEP Paper, October 1982.
14. Buchbinder, H. and Newson, J. "Corporate-university linkages in Canada: transforming a public institution". In *Higher Education*, Vol. 20, No. 4, December 1990.
15. Times Higher Education Supplement, 16 October 1987.
16. Thomas, D. "Teaching and research in United Kingdom universities". In *Industry and Higher Education*, Vol. 7, No. 1, March 1993.
17. Cave M. et al. *The use of PIs in higher education*, Kingsley Publishers, London, 1988.
18. Times Higher Education Supplement, 22 October 1993.
19. Williams, G. and Mader, C. "Ménage à trois". In *Times Higher Education Supplement*, 28 June 1991.
20. Times Higher Education Supplement, 12 February 1993.
21. Wasser, H. Spring "Changes in the European university: from traditional to entrepreneurial". In *Higher Education Quarterly*, Vol. 44, No. 2, 1990.
22. Kelly, J. "Establishing a university-industry programme". *In Industry and Higher Education*, Vol. 6, No. 3, September 1992.

23. Williams, G. "What can higher education realistically expect from industry?". In *Industry and Higher Education*, Vol. 6, No. 4, December 1992.
24. Cottam, D.. "University-industry collaboration: overcoming the barriers". In *Industry and Higher Education*, Vol. 4, No. 4, December 1990
25. Watson, J. "Problems in partnership". In *Higher Education in Europe*, Vol. XVIII, No. 1, 1993.
26. Williams, G. and Mader, C. Idem.
27. Philimore, A. "University research policies in practice". In *Research Policy*, Vol. 18, No. 5, October 1989.
28. Marsh, A. and Turpin, T. "The Australian university research system". In *Higher Education Quarterly*, Vol. 46, No. 4, 1992.
29. Powles, M. "Graduate students at the interface between universities and industry". In *Higher Education Policy*, Vol. 7, No. 1, 1994.
30. OECD. *Evaluation of research and resource allocation*. 17th Special Topic Workshop, November 1984.
31. Ackerman, H. "The Dutch case". *La Evaluacion Academia. Colombus documents on university management*. Vol. 1. UNESCO, Paris, 1993.
32. Van Haarlem, R.*Sponsored research*. EAIR Paper, 13th Forum, September 1991.
33. Wasser, H. "Changes in the European university: from traditional to entrepreneurial". In *Higher Education Quarterly*, Vol. 44, No. 2, Spring 1990.
34. Aamodt, P. et al. "Norway: towards a more indirect model of governance?" In *Neave, G.* (ed.). Idem.
35. Stolte-Heiskanen, V. "Research performance evaluation in the higher education sector: a grass-roots perspective". In *Higher Education Management*, Vol. 4, No. 2, 1992.
36. Ahgren-Lange, V. "Changing demands on university research in Sweden". In *International Journal of Institutional Management in Higher Education*, Vol. 6, No. 3, November 1992.
37. Savelyev, A. "Trends and problems in the development of higher education in the Soviet Union". In *Higher Education in Europe*, Vol. XVI, No. 3, 1991.
38. Amsterdamski, S. and Rhodes, A. "Perceptions of dilemmas of reform 1993". In *European Journal of Education*, Vol. 28, No. 4.
39. Szefler, M. "Science Policy in Poland". In *Industry and Higher Education*, Vol. 6, No. 4, 1992.
40. Dietrich, M. et al. "Co-operation between business and higher education in Poland, 1992 and 1993". *Industry and Higher Education*, Vol. 6, No. 3 and Vol. 7, No. 4.
41. Times Higher Education Supplement. 1993, 3 September.
42. Klein, L. and Schwartzman, S. "Higher Education Policies in Brazil from 1970 to 1980". *Higher Education*, Vol. 25, No. 1, 1993.
43. Drysdale, R. *Higher Education in Latin America*. Mimeo World Bank, March 1987.

44. Casas Armengol, M. "State of Research in LA Universities, CRESALC" In *Higher Education Analytical Abstracts*, Vol. 9, No. 1, January-June, 1988.
45. Vessuri, H. "Higher Education, Science and Engineering in Twentieth Century Latin America". In *European Journal of Education*, Vol. 28, No. 1, 1993.
46. Acebedo, J. *Postgraduate Research in Colombia in Universitas 2000*, Caracas, Vol. 11, No. 4, 1987.
47. Kent, R. "Higher Education in Mexico: from unregulated expansion to evaluation". In *Higher Education*, Vol. 25, No. 1, 1993.
48. Times Higher Education Supplement, 2 March 1990.
49. Parker, L. *Industry-university collaboration in developed and developing countries*. World Bank, Washington, PHREE 92/64.
50. Smith, F. and Estrada, J. *Changes in research management at the Universidad Nacional Agraria La Molina, Peru*. IIEP, Paris, 1993.
51. Times Higher Education Supplement, 2 March 1990.
52. Times Higher Education Supplement, 11 February 1994.
53. Chevailler, T. et al. "University-industry relations in France". In *Higher Education Quarterly*, Vol. 47, No. 1, 1993.
54. *Universités*, April 1991.
55. Peiseht, H. et al. *Higher education in Germany*. CEPES, Bucharest, 1990.
56. Times Higher Education Supplement, 29 March 1991.
57. Kola Cisse, M. "Managing university-based research and research institutes in Africa". In *Higher Education Policy*, Vol. 5, No. 2, 1992.
58. Saint, W. Technical Paper No. 194, Washington, 1991.
59. Blair, R.D. *An assessment of progress and potential for financial diversification at selected African universities*. World Bank, December 1991.
60. Houenou, P. *Training of 3rd cycle and research graduates in African universities*. Paper to AAU Dakar Meeting 26-27 June 1991.
61. Mbajoiorgo, M. Paper for AAU *Innovative responses to the problem of under-funding of universities*, January 1992.
62. AAU study on Cost effectiveness and efficiency in African universities, May 1991.
63. Ayiku, M. *University and productive sector linkages in Africa, AAU*, Accra, November 1990.
64. Coombe, T. A consultation on Africa: Report to the Ford Foundation, December 1990.
65. IDRC Nairobi. Status of capacity building and education research and policy in Sub-Saharan Africa, 1991.
66. Times Higher Education Supplement, 11 March 1987.
67. World Bank. Higher Education in Hong Kong, PHREE/92/70.
68. Selvaratnam, V. *Singapore at the Competitive Edge*, World Bank Technical Paper No. 222, 1994.
69. Chou, S.K. "Promoting industry linkages and technology transfer". In *Industry and Higher Education*, Vol. 7, No. 4, 1993.

70. Hayhoe, R. and Zhong, W. "Chinese Universities and Chinese Science". In *Higher Education Policy*, Vol. 6, No. 9, 1993.
71. National Centre of Educational Development and Research. Paper, Beijing, 1992.
72. Sharma, G.D. and Sanyal, B. *Funding mechanisms of thrust areas of higher education in India*, IIEP Research Report. No. 82, Paris, 1990.
73. Ansari, M. and Sharma, T. "Industry and Universities in India". In *Industry and Higher Education*, Vol. 5, No. 3, September 1991.
74. Bawden, R. *et al. Agricultural University for Twenty-first Century.* Paper for WCEFA Jomtien, March 1990.
75. University News, 5 November 1990.
76. Yamamoto, S. "Research and development versus traditionalism at Japanese universities". In *Higher Education Policy*, Vol. 6, No. 2, 1993.
77. Ratnalingam, R. *et al.* "Technology transfer at University Sains Malaysia". In *Industry and Higher Education*, Vol. 7, No. 1, 1993.
78. Ratnalingam, R. *et al.* "Technology transfer at University Sains Malaysia". In *Industry and Higher Education*, Vol. 7, No. 1, 1993.
79. Salahaldeen, Al-Ali, "The development of industry – higher education relations in Kuwait and the United Kingdom". In *Industry and Higher Education*, Vol. 8, No. 1, 1994.
80. Djeflat, A. *L'option scientifique et technique dans le système educatif, et les transformations du secteur productif en Algérie*, IIEP Research Report No. 84, Paris, 1990.

Chapter 9

Management of space

Scarcity of space was not perceived as a major issue in institutional management until the mid-1980s, but the advent of mass higher education, changing demands, high construction costs and the reluctance of governments to invest in new facilities, have brought it to the fore, particularly in developing countries. There are few higher educational institutions now where space is plentiful and cheap to maintain; many universities have been trying to economize by cutting down on the maintenance of the buildings they already have, and few have managed to acquire new ones.

In this situation, some university managers, while attempting to use their physical space more efficiently for full-time, part-time and summer courses, have adopted a number of strategies for using less space, by increasing the throughput of students and reducing drop-outs, and by using different methods to reach larger numbers of students who require space at the university only intermittently. It is likely that these will become more and more important in the future (see *Chapter 10*).

Success in providing adequate space and facilities is evidently linked to admission policies, and the infrastructure and resources provided, which are often decided externally by the government in developing countries. At university level, however, the ability to plan and innovate in the provision of courses can make a great contribution to ensuring that the best possible use is made of what facilities exist.

Space management in universities around the world has not attracted much attention in the literature, although it has been the subject of a great deal of practical work, such as the use of computers in integrated time-tabling and space allocation. IIEP therefore sent a questionnaire to a small sample of universities in each region (40 in all) to establish the prevailing state of space and its management. Most of the information in the following section is based on responses to this questionnaire; most responding institutions considered their cases to be typical of universities in their country.

1. Space management problems

a. Self-regulation and accountability implemented

In Europe, space management and maintenance are major preoccupations, many institutions reporting cut-backs on expenditure for maintenance of buildings and libraries and consequent deterioration. Evidently, increases in student numbers and in research (particularly externally financed) have put heavy pressure on space. Three countries specifically mentioned the problems of finding adequate space for advanced research (Netherlands, United Kingdom, Australia). Old buildings are unsuitable either for modern teaching or for research, and funds are generally unavailable for modernization (United Kingdom). With the increase in class sizes, there are now not enough large rooms for lectures. Furthermore, rooms for visiting faculty and intensive courses are also hard to find. Deciding whether demands for space are justified and the difficulties of re-allocation were mentioned as major management problems.

North American universities cite much the same difficulties, such as the obsolescence and unsuitability of old buildings, the deferral of long-term maintenance, and the changes in curricula which are taking place, together with the sometimes unreasonable expectations of individuals, and the inability to adapt existing space to accommodate different functions.

b. Self-regulation in difficulty

In Latin America, overcrowding is endemic due to the mass demand for university education, but most countries have allowed the spread of private institutions to take up some of the strain, the exceptions being Uruguay, Bolivia, Panama and Paraguay. However, the ability of private universities to select their fields of activity is a fundamental reason for their success; the hardest tasks have been left to the public sector, which has to provide education in the more expensive disciplines(1). Hence public universities are still overcrowded and obliged to open their facilities from early morning until late at night, operating a shift system; in Argentina there are three shifts a day from 8 a.m. to 11 p.m., and Mexico either two or three shifts depending on the location. In Venezuela, inadequate facilities and weak logistical and support services have been cited as amongst the major problems of universities by the Association of

Rectors, who made a plea that the Government should regulate increases in enrolments(2). The development of new professions, specialization of activities and continuous changes in schedules also complicates space allocation, as reported by universities in Chile and Mexico.

In Eastern Europe, the problem of lack of funds for maintenance and modernization is widely cited. In the Czech Republic, the sporadic growth of the university in diverse buildings around the city has made effective space management difficult to achieve.

c. Centralized planning and control

The over-crowding and high drop-out rates in *European* universities with open admissions are well known: France and Italy have experienced frequent student demonstrations and have devoted their main efforts to expanding available space by establishing regional branch campuses or satellites in neighbouring towns. The situation in Germany is similar: as of 1992, there were 1.8 million students in higher education but only 850,000 study places. Universities have resorted to various strategies to obtain extra space; for example, the University of Essen rents a church for its largest lectures, and the University of Wuppertal a cinema. High drop-out and repetition rates are a feature of French and Italian open admission systems, where administrators calculate that only about one third of enrolled students will be on campus at any one time. Campus activities are considered to be only a part of the learning experience, the remainder taking place in the community, in contrast to English universities where most activities, including social and sporting, are on campus. However, the media has shown that those who do wish to attend a lecture in a French university, for example, may have to queue 2-3 hours to be sure of a seat.

Countries in *Africa* generally had to stop building new universities before the provision of tertiary education had reached as high a level as in other developing regions. The cost of building has even led to inability to complete capital projects already started. In Uganda's Makerere University, no physical expansion has taken place for 20 years, sanitary and related facilities are overstretched and not enough practicals can be given. Madagascar reports much the same situation while the University of Abidjan now has 22,000 students in buildings designed for 7,000. The University of Chad, which was built for 700 students, had 2,600 as of 1992. Students have to arrive early and queue for a seat at lectures. Another example is the University of Bangui which was established in 1969 with 300 students in Law and Sciences and has expanded to 4,000 students in eight faculties in 1991 without new buildings being added.

Heads of units manage their own buildings and those with inadequate facilities write to request the use of classrooms from others. One unit has no building of its own, and is dependent on other units while the Science faculty must use the laboratories of another school. Sometimes the allocation of rooms depends on the relations existing between the heads of the basic units(3). In Kenya, staff have had to repeat the same lecture eight times because halls are not large enough(4).

However, difficulties of space have brought an end to expansion in some countries: reports from Sierra Leone, Sudan and Nigeria(5) indicate that in recent years universities have limited their student intake due to inadequate facilities. Nevertheless, overcrowding and poor facilities seem to be the general situation in the continent, exceptions being the University of Botswana, where current space under construction equals existing space, and some specialized institutions like universities of agriculture.

The situation varies in the *Arab States*. There is overcrowding in many of them but articles in the press have spoken of new universities being established in Tunisia, Kuwait, and the Gulf States, while the King Saud University only recently moved to a new campus that meets expansion requirements for some years ahead. One study from Tunisia found that while the average space for f.t.e. students, at 8.3m², was within international norms (e.g. the United Kingdom has been set at 9m²), there are large disparities between universities, and in Science one institution might have only 3.3m² while another as much as 18m², indicating that admissions procedures do not take much account of space criteria.

In the *Asian* region, one may find situations similar either to Latin America or to Africa. Examples of the latter are India, Sri Lanka and Bangladesh where, under pressure of demand, admission capacities have been far exceeded. In India at least 50 per cent of students do not complete their studies(6). As to the former, such countries as the Philippines, Indonesia, Korea and Japan have large private tertiary education sectors and have allowed state universities to enrol only those numbers which can be adequately accommodated. Thus the problem of space has been kept under control. However, the private universities where fee increases are regulated by the government, as in the Philippines, were obliged to seek means to earn more with the same amount of space, and many give evening courses.

One Asian country, China, reports very particular problems of space management, the difficulties arising from the campus model chosen for all universities, since in addition to teaching rooms and laboratories, there must also be housing, schools, clinic, stores, printing press and factories. Management of maintenance is poor(7) and low classroom and laboratory utilization rates are general (47 per cent and 62 per cent respectively) due to the small size and specialization of institutions(8).

Countries in the region which are in a better financial situation mention other problems, for example the increasing number of different classes due to growth of specialization, the inappropriateness of the buildings due to age, and the fact that teaching staff want to form their own territories and permanent space, which causes problems for re-allocation (Thailand). In Singapore additional buildings are being constructed but there is a shortage of land to expand further.

2. The type of university facilities which have to be managed

The IIEP questionnaire sought to establish the type of existing university space, i.e. the traditional campus model with teaching, laboratory and sports facilities plus student and staff residences, or some other type. Only six institutions classified themselves as other than the campus model. These were an African university which was still in temporary buildings, a Finnish and a Mexican university which had neither staff nor student residences but otherwise a compact campus area in which teaching, laboratory and office facilities are situated, an English polytechnic, and Czech and Mauritian universities which have buildings scattered throughout the city, causing, as they stated, higher running costs and loss of efficiency in day-to-day management.

There were significant differences in the proportion of staff and students housed on campus. This aspect of space management has been the subject of some debate and change in recent years since housing is a major cost factor in university budgets, particularly in developing countries. For example, in China housing is offered not only to staff and students, but also to retired personnel, in addition to clinics and schools for children. *Table 26* shows the variations which exist. It can be seen that high proportions of students may be housed in Africa and in some cases in Europe but generally only small proportions of staff, except in Africa. Institutions in Asia and Latin America offer relatively little staff or student housing. These differences are related to the traditional campus model in the case of the United Kingdom and Belgium, and to need in Africa, where suitable local housing for students and staff close to the campus does not exist. Both the United Kingdom and USA governments are urging enrolment of more local students to reduce on-campus residence.

Table 26. Proportions of students and staff housed on campus in selected universities

		Students housed %	Staff housed %
	Self-regulation and accountability		
Europe	Netherlands	30	5
	United Kingdom	80	1
	United Kingdom	48	0
	United Kingdom	40	0
	United Kingdom Polytechnic	20	1
Oceana	Australia	10	0
	Australia	5	0
North America	USA	33	1
	USA	20	5
	Canada	25	3
	Canada	18	1
	Canada	N/A	0
	Self-regulation in difficulty		
Europe	Russia	37	10
	Russia	70	50
	Czechoslovakia	30	0
Latin America	Chile	3.2	0
	Mexico	0	0
	Guyana	0	0
	Central planning and control		
Europe	Belgium	70	N/A
Africa	Sudan	100	50
	Saudi Arabia	100	1
	Zambia	85	70
	Ghana	62	56
	Botswana	70	0
	Uganda	60	50
	Nigeria	45	50
	Madagascar	54	15
	Central African Republic	25	0
Asia	Singapore	20	6
	India	12	0
	Thailand	5	5
	Philippines (private)	17	30
	Hong Kong	17	19.7

Source: Based on responses to a questionnaire sent to a sample of 33 universities.

3. Utilization of buildings

The second set of questions referred to the intensity of use of buildings, i.e. the number of weeks during the year in which the university is open for full-time studies, the hours per week in which teaching activities are scheduled, and the use made of facilities during vacations. Again the variations found are rather wide (see *Table 27*). It can be seen that intensity of use does not correlate with the type of management system but rather with culture and climate. This is, however, a domain where governments of self-regulatory systems are pressing for change (as described below).

Table 27. Building norms: space allocations per student in full-time education

Belgium	Humanities	10m²	Biology	20m²
Finland	Arts	8m²	Natural sciences	23m²
Russia	Arts	8m²	Natural sciences	18m²

Institutional space allocation norms:

Canada	Classrooms	1.3m²
United Kingdom	Classrooms	1.5 to 2.5m²
	Laboratory	9.5 - 15m²
Russia	Laboratory	8 - 12m²
	Residential	6 - 8m²
Czechoslovakia	Classrooms	2.5 - 4.5m²
	Laboratory	3 - 5m²
	Residential	15.5m²

Source: idem.

The total hours per year during which teaching activities take place range from a low of 900 in India to highs of 4,000 plus in the USA and Chile. The former confirms articles complaining that Indian professors will only work short hours but climate obviously is a factor, since total hours are low also in the Central African Republic, Thailand and Sudan. However, hours are not always low in hot climates, for example, in Latin America one private university in the south of Brazil reported that it closed only one month in the year (February), when it ran extension courses, but in the summer had special opening hours in the mornings and evenings only. This may be compared to Venezuelan public universities, which close entirely in the summer.

259

The fact that some institutions in Australia may open only half the year and that the Saudi Arabian, Ghanaian, Ugandan and United Kingdom institutions function for little longer points to the tenacity of Anglo-Saxon tradition. In the United Kingdom, this has been broken by the former polytechnics, which are much more efficient in their use of space and are eroding the distinction between term time and vacation. This is spreading to the other universities. Aberdeen's Radical Plan of May 1986 to cope with budget cuts suggested extension of the teaching year from 30 to 40 weeks, so that students would complete their four-year degree in three years. It was rejected by the Senate, but the HEFC is now putting pressure on all the United Kingdom universities to extend the teaching year(9).

The Pearce Report on the United Kingdom situation, published in June 1992 (10), pointed out that the key to development was the ability to accommodate increased numbers. It showed how marginal increases might be made by increasing length of day and term, remodelling and rationalization, or more radical improvements brought about by changes in the teaching year, modularization of degree courses and consequent changes in the employment and conditions of staff. It recommended, amongst other things, that funding criteria should include efficiency of space use and the existence of estate management strategic plans.

Although North American universities do, for the most part, make greater utilization of facilities, state boards are continuing to press for greater efficiency. In January 1994, the University of California Board of Regents drew up a series of proposals(11) that they wished to see implemented, which included: year-round operation; lengthening the instructional day and week; and expanding the uses of the summer session.

In order to see whether change had actually taken place in the use of physical facilities, we referred back to the IIEP research project on Planning the Development of Universities for which a survey was conducted in 1970. One question was about the number of weeks the university was functional for instruction. We found that Australia, India and the Arab States had not changed whereas Canada reported at that time 38 weeks (some are now 52), Mexico reported 30 (now 38), and Spain reported 32 (now 44).

There are distinct possibilities for improvement of space use. Only five of the institutions surveyed made full use of their buildings during vacations. No use or little use was made of university buildings during vacations in Botswana, the Central African Republic, Ghana, Madagascar, Thailand, Mexico, and Zambia, all of which have long vacations. In other countries 10-30 per cent remained unused. Facilities are used for examinations (Asia and Russia) while in the majority there are conferences, short courses and sports events. Summer schools are a feature of North American institutions. It was pointed out, however, that research and administration continues all the year round, particularly in developed country universities.

4. Space management procedures

An attempt was made to find out how space was allocated and how much attention was given to it. Again, the classifications by 'self-regulation' and 'centralized planning' proved not to be a decisive factor in this area. External policy may have affected building norms but government pressure has not so far achieved a general change in institutional space management, though there are a number of exceptions.

a. Self-regulation and accountability implemented

Among the self-regulated countries, responsibility for space management in North American universities tends to lie at a high level, such as Associate Vice-President in the case of one Canadian university. Here comprehensive information is collected and analysed: the buildings on the campus are listed by age, total space of primary occupants, and facilities. The amount of space per f.t.e. staff and student and for offices in all disciplines is calculated (e.g. an engineering student has 214 square feet while an arts student has 25.6 square feet). Instruction occupies 24 per cent of the campus space, research 9 per cent, library 7 per cent, housing 17 per cent, health and sports 5 per cent, etc. Staff are given guidelines on space management and standards that make clear that 'all space is owned by the university' which is responsibe for its allocation; the longest period of allocation is one year. Requests for new space requirements must be made on a specific form listing the purpose, dimensions, and facilities needed, such as heat, cooling, electricity, water, and telephone). The physical resources of this university are evidently subject to a very high degree of control.

Centralization of space management is not the norm in Europe, except for Russia. It can be found to some extent in Australia. The Swinburne University of Technology operates with only 77 per cent of the official space norm. All teaching facilities are allocated by a central office, but specialized space is under the control of the Dean of the various faculties. Utilization is checked every semester by staff filling in a record, that has to be verified by the Dean. The central office also checks against student registration and timetable(12). In Russia there is central planning of auditoriums, classrooms and laboratories, while faculties allocate their own workshop space.

In European self-regulating universities, systems of space management vary. Faculties or departments are given a building or space, either only annually or on a long-term basis and either partially or wholly. One institution stated that "Each department has core rooms which it timetables but there is a pool of rooms centrally allocated which varies from year to year". In another, central allocations are long term and rearrangements are usually linked to major changes such as a new building or closure of a department. These statements were made by United Kingdom institutions.

The most radical change, that of renting space to departments, was reported from universities under self-regulation policies. For example, a Dutch university indicated that faculties are now being charged rent for space. The problem had been that new faculties needed more space while old faculties did not want to give up any of what they had. Under the system of renting, all departments now use only such space for teaching and research as is really needed. Space which becomes surplus to requirements reverts back to central management, which rents it to other occupants. A Finnish university, two United Kingdom universities (self-regulation) and a Belgian institution (Flemish) stated that they would shortly be changing to such a system. The Finnish university explained that at present there were empty rooms in the evenings, Monday morning and Friday afternoon and that peak demand was around noon. The new computerized system would set different rents for different hours or days to try to even out demand. Pricing would also give an incentive for early cancellation if a room is not needed.

The norms set may either be institutional norms governing space per student or national norms (as in Finland and Belgium) for overall building space applying to disciplines or groups of disciplines. Some examples are as shown in *Table 27*.

Most of the institutions had norms, and these were generally adhered to (+ or – 10 per cent). The exceptions were in Australia, where there was overcrowding, actual space for the Humanities and Science in one university being reported as $4m^2$ per student. In the United Kingdom, where the official norms were being increasingly ignored, though universities are now expected to operate with an overall average of 9 square metres per student compared to the former 10.3 square metres (Pearce Report, idem.).

In North America, institutions were equally divided between the practice of retaining the previous year's allocations with adjustments for changes in curricula and entire annual or semester re-allocation; in Europe only one institution (in the United Kingdom) conducted entire re-allocation. However, in either case computers were used for time-tabling and space allocation by all universities except two.

The amount of control over space management also varied. Every university in North America had a Space Planning Committee which met monthly in four cases and four times a year in the fifth case. In Europe six institutions had such a committee but four did not, while they meet only annually, or three or four times a year. However, all had a Buildings/Facilities Officer in charge of allocation and maintenance, and a regular inventory was made.

A more comprehensive survey was made by the UFC of estates management in all United Kingdom institutions in 1991; it found that half of them had drawn up estate strategy development plans and had space audit management committees to oversee use of space, and three-quarters had a formal estates and building committee, though a fifth did not have up-to-date records. One interesting finding was that research occupied one-third of non-residential area on average, and that this space is used much more intensively, for a longer day and for 50 weeks a year.

The final question concerned any special arrangements made in recent years by the university to cope with space problems. The most radical responses were given by (i) US universities, including shifts, reduction of staff:student ratios, use of computer-assisted learning to replace lectures; (ii) the United Kingdom polytechnic, where a great deal of imaginative management thinking has had to be done. Lectures in the past taught groups of 20 to 40 students but, now have 80 to 200. One solution was the purchase of folding stadium-type seating placed in the largest hall for lectures. Another was the use for at least half the courses of study packs which radically reduce the number of lectures required. Increasingly, classes are divided into two seminar groups and employ peer assessment. The tutor shares his time between the two groups, which meet to compare outcomes. The Polytechnic has had to redirect funds to obtain large lecture rooms backed up by lots of smaller rooms, more word processing and printing and up-to-date libraries. Staff also need to be trained to produce learning materials for these purposes, in order to ensure the maintenance of quality and level of output.

Keele University recently began the practice of renting space to basic units and found that demand for lecture rooms fell considerably: tutors now meet small groups in their own rooms. A further three institutions reported extension of teaching hours and standardization of starting times and length of classes to facilitate time-tabling and space allocation. A Dutch and an Australian university were the only fortunate ones to be able to acquire new buildings for lectures and for informatics; several complaints were made about the difficulty of finding space for personal computers.

Universities in the United Kingdom are being urged to consider implementing other models of the academic year which involve lengthening the teaching period from 30 to 48 weeks(13). By this means 50 per cent more students could be taught and first degree courses could be completed in under three years.

Many new systems of higher education delivery are specifically designed to be space saving. To give one example, the United Kingdom's Open Polytechnic is the joint effort of eight existing polytechnics which combine distance with institution-based studies in Business Management, Law and Languages. Similarly, in Long Island University in the USA, students alternate trimesters of work and study after an initial year at university. The subject of new educational delivery systems is dealt with more fully in *Chapter 10*. Those responsible for space management now have to keep in mind the possibilities of planning courses using a combination of distance, technological, commercial/industrial and university facilities. This is a fundamental change in university management thinking.

It is evident from the above that space is considered as an important aspect of overall university management in some but not all institutions - there are a number which are practising ad hoc or even crisis management of space in Europe.

b.   Self-regulation in difficulty

In Latin America, the management of space and facilities has provoked little discussion in the literature; with the shift system, however, management has been flexible in expanding time schedules so that buildings are often heavily utilized. Students are not expected to live on campus and many work for a living while studying. With such a system, much wastage occurs in drop-out, and problems of space arise from repetition.

Permanent allocation of rooms to departments seems to be the general rule, though in Guyana certain rooms, and in Chile 35 per cent of available hours in auditoria and laboratories, are retained at the centre. The Mexican university re-allocated its rooms annually and used a computerized system.

Norms were used, and set at a low level, e.g. in Chile the norms were as given in *Table 28*.

Table 28. Space allocated in a Chilean university

Lecture rooms	0.9 - 1.2m² per student
Laboratories	2.2 - 3.5m² per student
Residential	12.5m² per student

Source: idem.

In the Chilean and Guyana universities, inventories of facilities and equipment were regularly carried out, and both had a Space Planning Committee. However, the utilization of space is difficult to control in the usually large universities of Latin America. For example, at the beginning of an academic year, the University of Costa Rica rented classrooms in a nearby high school, only to find they had not been used. The teachers had themselves managed to find space on campus which had not been reported by the Faculties as available for use.

c. Centralized planning and control

In centrally planned countries in Europe as a whole, the pattern usually is that faculties are allocated their own core building/rooms on a more or less permanent basis but subject to central regulation on norms. The faculties then conduct their own space allocation and time-tabling exercises, which are much easier to do on a small scale. Available space per f.t.e. student has fallen; for example there is 4m² per f.t.e. student in the humanities, compared to double that figure in Finland. France and Italy have been spurred into implementing measures to cope with the large numbers in the first years of tertiary education. Italian universities are setting up satellite campuses in neighbouring towns; the University of Turin has three faculties in Alessandria, two in Novara and one in Vercelli. Students may now choose a two or three year diploma course instead of the four-year degree, which suffers a 70 per cent drop out(14). France similarly offers a new tier of colleges providing shorter courses so that not all new baccalaureat holders will demand a university place. The Ministry has also opened up university branch campuses in the provinces for the first cycle of higher education to relieve universities of some of the heavy pressure of new entrants.

In *Africa*, according to the questionnaire completed by nine universities, the practice is also to permanently allocate rooms to faculties and departments. In one Nigerian university, space allocation is almost non-existent; student numbers have increased while the number of classrooms remained the same, and teachers merely take classes where they can find a space. Four institutions retained the previous year's room allocations with adjustments for changes in curricula and student numbers while in four other cases, departments re-allocated space annually. A computer was used in only one instance. Four universities stated that norms were set for space but they are not adhered to and are sometimes exceeded by 100 per cent. The remaining universities did not have any set norms.

There was a Space Planning Committee in three cases, which met only once or twice a year, but all had a Buildings/Facilities Officer. An inventory of space was carried out regularly or irregularly in four cases but not at all in five institutions. The first inventory ever made is now being completed at the University of Botswana.

Space management evidently requires improvement. The University Rationalization Committee in Ghana calculated that the utilization rate could be increased by 35 per cent if a central time-table were instituted for shared use of rooms and daily sessions were extended. The AAU study on cost effectiveness and efficiency in African universities (May 1991) stated that African universities did not keep data on space allocation.

Nevertheless, there are some obstacles to using space efficiently, as the University of Zambia pointed out, though it is aware that large lecture theatres are used only 60-75 per cent of available time, other teaching rooms 50-60 per cent of the time and laboratories in the afternoons only. The real limiting factor on the expansion of student numbers to use this space efficiently is the shortage of residential accommodation for students, since very few can find housing off-campus. Nevertheless, the main response of African universities to overcrowding seems to have been the adoption of off-campus residence for students, and this is reported from Uganda, Sudan, Tanzania, Ghana, Kenya, Malawi, Mauritius and Zimbabwe. Universities are also being urged to charge the full costs of on-campus accommodation to both staff and students.

The University of Dar es Salaam attempted to extend its teaching hours but classes at 8 a.m. and those after 6 p.m. were poorly attended, because of the transport problems of non-resident students. The time-table had to be compressed, and free periods removed. The university in Madagascar has extended its teaching day to use rooms at meal-times and at the weekend and also rents rooms in other public buildings. In Makerere University, the central administration has lost control over space since there is no up-to-date inventory. Rooms are hoarded once

Management of space

allocated and under-utilization exists side by side with overcrowding. Four staff residences were taken over to open new programmes(15).

Space management is more effective at the University of Botswana(16), where a time-tabling Committee allocates classrooms on the basis of the previous year, with adjustments for additional courses, change in class sizes and specific requests for room change. It does from time to time take space from one faculty and allocate it to another.

More complex space-saving strategies have been reported in a few instances. The University of Gezira, Sudan, has tried to overcome space limitations by establishing a core curriculum for first-year students and using interdisciplinary approaches to maximize use of classrooms and faculty. It has also introduced shifts and modified its buildings. A Nigerian university has a double intake system in the form of full-time and long vacation programmes, and the University of Ghana introduced shifts, also using rooms for lectures which were not originally meant for this purpose.

The most radical re-organization occurred in the Kenyan universities which in 1987 began a double intake system. The IIEP research programme conducted an in-depth study at Kenyatta University(17) in order to analyse the experience and establish the relative advantages or disadvantages of using space so intensively in the context of a developing country see *Box 11*).

In *Asia*, permanent allocation of rooms to departments also seemed to be the general rule, though in Hong Kong large/medium-sized lecture rooms are time-tabled centrally. The use of norms was common practice (except for the Indian Inistitute) and they were adhered to. Examples are shown in *Table 29*.

Box 11.

> In 1984 the Kenyan Government decided to change to a 8-4-4 educational system, i.e. secondary education was reduced to four years and higher education increased to four years from the previous three. This meant for Kenyatta University that it would in 1990 have to enrol two groups of students, those under the old A level system and the new secondary leavers. The university had six years to plan how it would cope with the additional influx. A three-semester year and double intake system was decided upon.
>
> Committees were established to plan the curricula - for the new intake a preparatory year was envisaged while the A level group would follow the existing curricula. Departments were asked to establish their staff needs and the physical facilities that would be necessary, e.g. ten more science laboratories, etc. A Facilities Committee then put forward a building programme for the classrooms, laboratories, hostels, library, cafeteria, sewerage system and print shop.
>
> The teaching day was extended to 7 a.m. to 8 p.m. and Saturday mornings. Tutorial groups were discontinued. Staff recruitment was accelerated and numbers increased from 369 in 1986 to 682 in 1990, the student:staff ratio rising from 1:11 to 1:13, which is quite reasonable, but the majority of the new recruits were young.
>
> A Project Implementation Unit was set up to monitor the carrying out of all the work necessary but in the event only one-fifth of the funds needed for infrastructure were released by the government. Implementation became crisis management.
>
> Prior to the double intake, 79 per cent of students were accommodated in hostels, and only 37 per cent afterwards. Meal-times in the cafeterias had to be lengthened and meal cards introduced to stipulate time and cafeteria.
>
> Since the lecture halls were not large enough, some lectures had to be repeated four times and conditions of work were very difficult. As a result, thirty per cent of the staff left during the period 1987-92. To combat this, promotion criteria were relaxed and tutors of primary teacher training colleges and secondary schools were recruited to swell the ranks. The lack of staff to supervise has caused an increase in examination irregularities, and while the cost per student has fallen from Kpounds1,882 to Kpounds1,378 from 1986 to 1990, it now takes an extra year on average for students to graduate. However, the greatest demerit of the exercise particularly for the older senior members of Kenyatta University, was the decline in standards.

Management of space

Table 29. Space allocation in Asian universities

Thailand	Lecture room Laboratory Residential	1 - 1.5m² per student 3.5 - 10m² per student 8m² per student
Hong Kong	Lecture theatre Classrooms Laboratories depending on subject	1m² per student 1.9 - 2.3m² per student 2.8 - 9.5m² per student
Philippines	Laboratories Residential	2m² per student 6m² per student

Source: idem.

Allowances for laboratory space are much less than in developed countries.

All institutions responding to the questionnaire carried out an inventory of facilities and equipment on a regular basis and the Filipine, Hong Kong and Thai universities reported the use of a Space Planning Committee. The latter has been instituted only recently at the Philippine university in order to solve the problem of department 'territories'. To provide more space, Hong Kong University intends to extend its teaching day by half an hour in the near future.

More intensive use of facilities was the strategy chosen by a private university in the Philippines in order to keep pace with rising costs and maintaining its standards and reputation(18) as described in *Box 12*.

Innovations in university management

Box 12.

> Recognition of the long-term implications of an inflation rate of 30-40 per cent per year and a government ceiling of 15 per cent on tuition fee increases forced the De La Salle University to reflect on how to avert future financial difficulties. An outline of a possible strategy was first drafted in a graduate student's thesis in 1974. University facilities lay idle for 12 weeks a year while there was continual pressure for admission and it would be possible to change from two 18-week semesters to three 14-week trimesters. Students would have to spend more hours in the classroom but those who opted for all three sessions could obtain a degree in three years instead of the usual four. A pilot experiment was conducted in a graduate school in 1978-79 after which the results and implications were discussed in workshops. Parents and students were consulted and in 1980 sub-committees studied possible effects in various domains, such as administration, study time, curricula. Subsequently programmes were revised to eliminate overlaps, to update and prioritize content. At the same time, government approval had to be obtained, which took almost a year.
>
> The Academic Council eventually gave its approval in 1981 and a Task Force for implementation as well as a Trimester Evaluation Committee were set up. The faculty were paid for the extra trimester's work, amounting to a 50 per cent increase and thus accepted the change; admissions were computerized to lessen the administrative workload. Students expressed anxiety about the extra study load, while parents were mainly concerned about the convenience of vacation times, but resistance gradually subsided. In 1982 the university was obliged to make a report to the Ministry of Education, evaluating the change. Examination results, drop-out and attendance had not suffered to any appreciable extent. At this time too the university implemented a series of courses for the academic staff on teaching, communication, the university's mission, etc. in order to improve delivery methods.
>
> By 1984, the trimester system had been institutionalized, bringing a substantial increase in revenues (+ 56 per cent) and a 48 per cent increase in f.t.e. day students. The successful implementation was attributed to:
>
> - *internal* source of change;
> - lengthy gestation, discussion and planning period;
> - combination of central leadership and consultative mechanisms;
> - use of existing decision-making and accountability structures plus the creation of new ad hoc committees, research studies and fora;
> - willingness to revise and adjust at each stage;
> - existence of incentives;
> - creation of goodwill by open communication with staff, students, parents and government
>
> Despite the care taken, one problem arose that had not been correctly estimated; the impact on the non-teaching staff workload was heavier and had to be accomplished much faster than foreseen. This resulted in a strike three years afterwards which was resolved by a salary increase.
>
> Nevertheless, the experience reinforces the conclusions drawn from other IIEP studies: that change in one area brings with it quite radical changes in other areas. In this case, a trimester system brought reform of curricula, modernization of admissions procedures, improvement of teaching methods as well as giving useful experience of implementing reform by participative democratic process.

5. Lessons learned

Space is a major institutional resource, and its management must be continually responsive to overall management if the institution is to be able to achieve its strategic goals. For example:

- expansion of student numbers: this might necessitate a longer annual pattern of work, longer days, shifts or double intake, or reduced teaching hours and more self-directed learning, in which case space needs change;
- generation of revenue: the organization of evening or vacation courses for the community, hiring out conference facilities in a planned package of large and small rooms, catering, hotel and transport facilities;
- demonstration of the efficiency of management as required by funding agencies.

Space and facilities may be fixed assets, but in terms of their utilization may be very flexible. Improvements in building methods and architectural planning provide for movable walls and easily extendable buildings, which are becoming features of university building design. Management is capable of organizing utilization so as to accommodate increasing numbers of students and widely divergent needs. Flexibility can also be attained through patterns of work, space allocation procedures and educational delivery systems.

a. Patterns of work

From the small survey conducted by the IIEP, it is evident that space is not used intensively in many universities and that wide variations exist. However, it is also clear that intensive use necessitates efficient management and control (see above examples in the Philippines and Kenya). How intensively is it possible to use buildings, particularly in those developing country universities having few of them, while still offering a quality education and maintaining adequate conditions? An examination of university calendars shows some of the advantages or disadvantages of different patterns.

A common university calendar within a country is usually felt to be useful for arranging summer coaching, continuing education and refresher courses, and conferences and related professional activities of interest to academic staff. A common and customary pattern allows all those concerned to plan well in advance but a university could change its pattern of work and still retain certain holiday periods which coincide with other institutions in the country. For example, in both Australia and the Philippines, some use a trimester pattern, while others use the semester, and in Latin America, universities in different parts of a country may adopt different dates for their semesters to suit their local climates.

The trimester system with one long and two short breaks has often been preferred. The long break allows time for summer activities, and no teaching session is so long that it creates pressure on students and staff. However, it has been found by universities switching to the semester system that students benefited from the longer and less interrupted sessions and that some completed their programmes more quickly; in addition, it facilitated sandwich-type programmes or double intake. It also allows staff to take six months' sabbatical leave instead of a whole year. The trimester is the typical European calendar while the semester has been adopted by Latin and North American universities. However, the drawback of the North American pattern is that it treats each semester as an independent unit requiring fresh enrolment; this requires an efficient and computerized system of standardized re-enrolment if the administrative workload is not to become very much heavier.

Year-round teaching on a twelve-month calendar is difficult to arrange given staff holidays, summer courses, delays in obtaining books and materials at the start of a new academic session, and the work required for updating or writing new curricula. The difficulties of very intensive utilization of facilities are shown by the double intake system in Kenya where staff were not able to take leave and maintenance work was neglected. Nevertheless, year-round and seven days a week teaching is conducted in some institutions, and it is evident that more intensive use will become general.

b. Space allocation procedures

Maximising utilization of existing accommodation requires:

1. *A responsible officer and unit in charge* which have the necessary status and support from the head of the institution. This unit should participate in decision making together with academic and financial officers, and should have computing expertise.
2. *An accurate inventory of facilities*, updated annually. Space availability is often assessed only when there are complaints that there is not enough. Institutions often then find that their time-tabling habits have led to uneven use being made of space. Usually, inventories look only at rooms and laboratories, but offices, libraries, sports facilities, entry halls and lounges should also be covered. Total space resources should be considered in utilization plans and spaces should be classified by basic size, shape and facilities. The Pearce Report (idem.) has noted the following as being the minimum information that should be available:

(a) Details of all property owned, leased, or rented by the institution: its land holdings; current alternative use and replacement values; and legal issues such as planning constraints, etc.
(b) Details of physical condition, linked to a planned maintenance programme.
(c) An assessment of functional suitability of rooms, buildings and sites for current, and potential alternative use.
(d) Details of service costs.
(e) Drawings, sufficient for remodelling and space allocation.

3. *Periodic analysis of use of facilities by* both time and station utilization and station utilization. If only 15 students use a room for 25, then it is under-utilized.

4. *Some centralized allocation of space.* Certain authorities advocate central allocation of space and elimination of 'ownership' so as to control under-utilization. But a wholly centralized system has sometimes failed because it could not handle the array of different information. It has been common for a block of rooms to be allocated to each teaching unit, the advantage being that people feel in control and can manage their facilities flexibly from day to day if necessary. This does tend to lead over time to under or mis-utilization. However, a compromise is to allocate a certain number of rooms to departments but place as much space as possible in a common pool to be centrally allocated, including in particular the large rooms and general-purpose laboratories.

Given the differences in instructional and research technologies within an institution, equality of space provision will rarely be equitable or efficient. Careful study should be made of the needs of specific disciplines for laboratories, studios, conference rooms, etc. While no allocation system will satisfy everyone, an open, participative process in the establishment of space standards will be the best means of minimizing discontent. Periodic re-examination and re-allocation of space should be instituted as a means of avoiding departments feeling they have acquired 'ownership' of space beyond that justified by their actual needs.

5. *Encouragement of space use over a longer day and Saturdays.* A fixed lunch hour should be avoided so that rooms can be used all day and the cafeteria will not be overcrowded. Consider several smaller informal snack bars instead of a large refectory-type cafeteria. Promote the use/renting of facilities during vacations.

6. *Mechanisms to motivate economic use of space.* One method is for departmental budgets to include payment for space used, with ability to transfer some funds from space to buy more materials.

7. *Strong interaction between room programming and course time-tabling.* Maximum utilization of space requires negotiation between departments. Standardization of teaching time units and starting times will be necessary; otherwise there will be 'dead' periods and students leaving one class will disturb others still in class. Laboratories cannot achieve a

high utilization rate because of preparation, repairs and maintenance and a 75 per cent utilization rate seems to be the maximum achieved. Consideration should be given to multi-purpose laboratories: many basic laboratories can be adapted to a variety of needs if ample storage space is provided for the different types of courses.

8. *Investment in new buildings.* Avoid if possible building small ones. Locating several departments in a larger one reduces capital and operating costs. Also avoid, if possible, tailor-made rooms, but seek a variety of room sizes, which will be readily adaptable to different functions, and also obtain the most up-to-date features such as movable walls and easily extendable buildings.

9. *Maintenance.* Neglect of space and building maintenance has been prevalent in universities in most parts of the world in recent years. This item of expenditure has been the easiest to cut, but this has often been a major error. Neglect of buildings multiplies future expenditure since, in many cases, costs will be heavier and sanitation and health problems can arise. Reducing cleaning accelerates wear and tear and cutting down on air conditioning or heating interferes with learning, work schedules and hiring out of premises(19).

10. *Policy.* A clear policy on space management needs to be defined and disseminated to all staff in order to encourage efficient utilization. This is useful for external as well as internal purposes, since the availability of space or buildings depends on a number of decision-makers, including regional and national authorities. The ability to show clear analyses and demonstrate managerial efficiency is critical if the relevant Ministry departments are to be convinced about further investment needs. A flexible long-term development plan with provisional costings should be drawn up and periodically updated. Such plans need to consider the possibilities of mergers of departments and institutions, of satellite campuses, of programmes alternating work and institution-based studies and other changes that may stem from new delivery systems. Sharing of facilities is also often an unconsidered alternative for many institutions. In all areas, but particularly the vocational and technical ones, opportunities usually exist for sharing facilities with private sector firms, public agencies, or non-profit organizations.

References

1. Levy, D; "To what extent are private universities in Latin America successful?", *Universitas 2000*, Vol. 13, No. 2, 1989.
2. Association of Rectors, *Bases for formulating a university policy*. Venezuela, 1987.
3. Dolingo, F. IIEP Term Paper 1992.
4. Rees Hughes *et al.* "An essay on the implications of university expansion in Kenya in Higher Education", Vol. 19, No. 2, 1990.
5. Times Higher Education Supplement, 29 January, 1988.
6. Saxena, R. "Governance of Indian universities" In *Higher Education*, Vol. 20, No. 1, July, 1990.
7. World Bank Report, May 1986.
8. Min Weifang, "Higher education finance in China" in *Higher Education*, Vol. 21, No. 2, March 1991.
9. Clarke, K. IIEP Current Issues Seminar, Paris, 20 May 1992.
10. UFC, London, United Kingdom. *Capital funding and estate management in higher education* (Pearce Report, June 1992).
11. Curtsinger, S. What the Reports are doing to save the system. Article for university journal, 1993.
12. Sharma, R. *Manager of Planning and Information Service*. Swinburne University of Technology, Australia. Visit IIEP, 1993.
13. Flowers Report to HEFCE, April 1993.
14. Times Higher Education Supplement, 9 November 1990.
15. Aligaweesa, A. Paper for IIEP Workshop, Mauritius, September 1993.
16. Botihole, E., Paper for IIEP Workshop, Mauritius, September 1993
17. Mwiria, K. and Nyukuri, M. *The management of double intakes: a case study of Kenyatta University*, IIEP, Paris, 1994.
18. Bautista, O. et al. Change from a semester to a trimester system at the De La Salle University, Philippines. IIEP Research Report No. 94, Paris, 1992.
19. Bland, D. *Managing higher education*, Cassell Education Ltd., London, 1990.

Chapter 10

Educational delivery systems

The preceding chapters have shown that major improvements are being made in management and administration, including reductions in cost per student per annum; increases in student:staff ratios; streamlining, strengthening and devolution of managerial structures; establishment of performance indicators; mergers to achieve economies of scale. However, all these trends, which have taken a strong hold in self-regulated systems and are now spreading to centralized systems, are only the *beginning of the process of achieving cost-effective mass higher education*.

What is the next step? Major economies which will provide the means of offering an opportunity for higher education to all who wish it still remain to be achieved. They can only be found in radical changes to educational delivery systems.

This domain of university activity generally falls under the management of academics at the departmental level, since educational delivery methods differ by discipline. Certain subjects lend themselves much more easily to modular or package types of instruction (e.g. Business Administration), while others remain very much in the conventional mode of lectures, tutorials, and laboratory work (e.g. Engineering). Thus in many universities, educational delivery systems may not have been discussed centrally or considered as a part of overall university management. This is not the case for those few having specific roles assigned to them under government policies, such as the introduction of distance education in countries which have only two universities (Uganda), or where centres of population are remote from one another (Australia). All in all, educational delivery may be said to be one of the most decentralized of university activities. Its management is therefore the least well defined in either the literature or the history of institutional experiences. Understanding of how to manage alterations to the curriculum and its delivery will have to advance considerably before the executive level can feel confident about entering this jealously guarded area of individual or programme privilege. This being said, university management in many countries is, at the present moment, having to face this challenge and therefore the subject has also to be taken up in this book, however tentatively.

1. Changes in educational delivery systems

Innovations in educational delivery systems in universities have come about for a variety of reasons. According to our review of the literature, these, in order of frequency of citation, have been:

(i) Expansion of demand for traditional higher education, with constraints of financial and physical resources.
(ii) The availability of new technology that can be put to use in education.
(iii) The internationalization of higher education.
(iv) New partners in education and changes in clientele: employed, part-time and mature students.

a. Meeting expansion of demand with fewer resources

The most radical response to increasing demand for higher education has been the Open University-type institution. The one in the United Kingdom now produces one in twelve of the country's graduates, each at one third of the cost of a traditional university graduate. The influence of the Open University has been significant, not only in the spread of such institutions to other countries, but in the development of the use of videos and computerized programmes in modular instruction, and learning packages which have increased the extent of independent learning and reduced staff:student contact hours in traditional universities.

Open University-type institutions now operate in more than 90 countries. In the developed countries the primary advantages have been listed as being that it is low-cost higher education which can be offered as a second chance to older sections of the population, or in conjunction with employers as recurrent education, and that it overcomes the constraints of remote location, employment or disability(1). Each country has been able to adapt it to meet its own particular needs; in Ireland, for example, the aims were to meet needs for recurrent education and to equalize educational opportunities. It has been found to be particularly suitable for economies in transition, where it has taken root quickly, as in Thailand, Singapore, Hong Kong, Korea and China(2). It can serve any clientele, it is learner centred and can use the existing resources of universities who are natural partners in such types of education.

Many universities which offer traditional full-time degrees are also engaged in different types of distance education. Several offer dual or mixed-mode courses as well as full-time courses, some students taking the same courses as full-time students, but being on-campus only for part of the time. The University Sains Malaysia, has operated such courses since 1969. Here the students complete 75 per cent of the course content by distance study plus an annual three week school and then spend their last year on campus so as to ensure that standards are maintained. Print, library services and telephone, with regional study centres for tutorials and laboratory work, constitute the educational delivery system. These students cost 27 per cent less than the full-time ones, but 15 per cent more of the former drop out.

Such a dual mode system is also organized in Australia, for example at Deakin University, but here a number of universities collaborate in the preparation of the learning materials(3). At the Swinburne University of Technology, a new campus was set up in 1993 to organize courses. One third at home by distance learning, one third at a local study centre and one third at the university. Dual mode systems have the advantage of compensating for some of the weaknesses of distance education, by preserving the capacity to criticize and process knowledge(4). The main characteristic of distance education, however, is that learning takes place largely in the physical absence of any teacher. Its methods have therefore had a major influence on practice in traditional universities under pressure from expansion and financial constraints. Modular and credit systems, unpaced courses, mixed assessment, use of group learning, networking, audio conferencing: all these innovations in educational delivery are now being adopted by universities. Many instructors have been and still are reluctant to abandon their investment in teacher-centred education and may see the new technologies as a threat to their job security or professionalism, but attitudes are changing. Already the previously unthinkable question is being asked – can traditional university courses survive(5)? Course design and delivery are shifting from the institution to the individual. Lajeunesse(6) lists the essential tools of any modern system of higher education as: new modes of teaching, in particular distance education; co-operative teaching; and university-industry collaboration in alternance programmes. It will be useful to take a look at what is happening in the various groups of countries classified as before.

(i)   Self-regulation and accountability implemented

In North America universities have operated modular credit-based systems for some time, but higher education institutions in the United Kingdom, New Zealand and Australia have only recently begun to see their advantages and to make moves to adopt such systems. Modularization(7) *has been marked out for a leading role in the future development of a mass and lifelong system of higher education in Britain.* Most significant in educational terms has been the *parallel development of systems of credit accumulation and transfer* within and between institutions of higher education in Britain and now Europe, and across other sectors of education, training and employment. Modularization is also an aid to efficient management, since it helps break down unit costs, and therefore in the allocation of resources and the audit of their use. A UFC survey in 1991 found that two-thirds of United Kingdom universities were operating a modular degree, either for all programmes or only in some. Conversion has tended to take place department by department with science faculties in the lead(8).

Such systems provide the basis for further innovation, and institutions adopting them have been rewarded by the HEFC in their annual grants. Further incentives were offered; in 1992 some 5 million pounds was set aside for initiatives in the use of modern technology to teach larger classes and a further million for flexible courses, task-based learning, small group work and the use of postgraduates as teaching assistants. In 1993 five consortia of higher educational institutions were given funds to develop mass teaching techniques. One university was awarded a contract to provide workshops for over 3,000 staff which dealt with:

- ways to escape formal lecturing by adopting active learning techniques and encouraging more student participation;
- strategies for cutting down time needed for assessment, such as peer tutoring, where students are encouraged to mark each other's work;
- ways to find more opportunities for student discussion which decline as seminar sizes increase;
- new methods of independent learning, such as tutorials led by students;
- examples of how to redesign courses to cope with larger numbers.

Experience revealed that different disciplines need different methods for teaching larger classes. A follow-up survey found that nearly half the lecturers attending the workshops had changed their teaching methods and a quarter had changed their assessment methods and redesigned their courses.

Overall it is reported that tutorials are being phased out and the size of seminar groups increased(9). Induction programmes provide study skills packages which shift the emphasis towards learning how to learn.

Group learning has attracted much attention since modules of knowledge need to be integrated by discussion(10); it also promotes individual accountability and social skills. Permanent course groups can create long-term relationships and commitments, and help to reduce drop-out(11).

    (ii)   Centralized planning and control

Although most of the universities in these countries have had to cope with mass higher education for many years, large-scale innovation in teaching methods does not seem to have taken place. Lectures, with individual guidance for a thesis, are still standard practice. In France, innovative teachers are trying to introduce more discussion between teachers and students and between students, and to provide more aids to independent work(12). Most changes have been aimed at reducing drop-outs and repetition and assisting entry into the labour market.

A modular course structure was to be adopted by October 1993. Its aims were to help students wishing to change courses to continue their studies or to study part time(13). However, only a few of the *grandes écoles* have a unit for learning or teaching developments, and most courses are subject to the control of a national body.

In Italy, a 1990 law stipulated that each faculty was to set up a tutor system and counselling centre to try to combat the 70 per cent drop-out and long duration of studies. Students who pass their exams on schedule with high marks may have their fees cut by 50 per cent, while poor results will be penalized by higher fees. In Spain, the Polytechnic University of Barcelona gives a certificate on completion of 135 credits in order to set students a lower and more realistic target, and offer at least some recognition to those who cannot complete their programme.

Wastage, particularly in expensive disciplines such as Engineering, is hard to accept in a developing country. This was the case for the Faculty of Engineering, UNAM, Mexico, whose high drop-out rate was thought to be due to low level mathematics and science in secondary education, low motivation, impersonality of staff:student relations and a system of open admissions which allows students to choose their own programmes. The Faculty tackled the problem with a new system of group tutorials (one hour a week in groups of 20); encouragement to take a properly sequenced study plan and to make use of student support services for weak subjects, such as computerized programmes in basic science and mathematics; and by keeping full records of progress. Another programme was designed for students who had dropped out and entered employment, which included obtaining grants from their employers as an incentive to complete degrees. A greater proportion are given the opportunity to participate in research projects. Evaluation showed that the number of repeaters has declined and students are completing their degrees in a shorter time. The graduation rate rose from 33 to 40 per cent and is now the highest in the Faculty's record(14).

The problems of implementing reform of curricula and teaching methods in a bottom-heavy continental European university are well illustrated by the IIEP case-study of the Catholic University of Louvain (K.U. Leuven), Belgium see *Box 13*).

This experience underlines the need for sound and consistent executive-level policy, and the importance of providing expert professional support in areas such as teaching and learning methods in mass education.

A great many of the developing country universities are also very traditional in their educational delivery methods, though the continuous assessment, semester and credit-based system is to be found where the North American model was followed. It has also been adopted by a number of institutions in India, and in Ghana, where the basis exists for easier reform of educational delivery methods.

b. New technology in higher education

The use of new technology in higher education was pioneered by distance learning systems, and has only recently been taken up to any great extent for campus programmes. Pressure to increase teaching productivity led to research into the use of computer-based learning, and this was found to be effective when properly supported by an open learning infrastructure, particularly in subjects such as mathematics, statistics, computer science, and electrical engineering. Multi-media courseware for foundation courses freed a substantial amount of lecturer time. The advantages of this type of learning were found to be that:

- it can be individualized to suit the student's pace and needs;
- it can simulate experience;
- it provides deeper learning by doing;
- it provides information-handling skills;
- delivery of education is automated;
- it is cost-effective *in the long run*.

Box 13.

> K.U. Leuven is the oldest catholic university still operating; it has a large number of programmes and 25,000 students. Its organization conforms to the traditional continental faculty type, each faculty and department being responsible for the development of programmes and delivery methods and equipped with a Permanent Education Commission for this purpose.
>
> After the 1985 law was passed giving universities more flexibility on teaching loads, the Rector decided to establish 15 think tanks to consider the implications for increasing efficiency. The think tank in Educational Innovation subsequently submitted in 1986 its recommendations on educational delivery and learning, in particular proposing increased self-study as an alternative to the high number of contact hours and passive methods of student learning.
>
> In April 1988 a concrete proposal for rationalization was drawn up. The Rector's letter to the staff on proliferation of courses (e.g. 72 in statistics alone), stressed the necessity to rationalize subjects by merger and closure, set up a credit point system of course equivalences, organize programmes by modules, devote less hours to formal lectures and more to intensified study supervision. The faculties, in response, asked for more specific guidelines (i.e. target figures for contact hours, etc.). In June 1989, a document was issued setting 10 subjects and examinations as the maximum in an academic year per programme. Higher quality was to be sought by new teaching methods.
>
> Rationalization planning was implemented at faculty level by task groups, which achieved a reduction of 7 per cent in hours of formal lectures and 3 per cent in contact hours. The number of subjects and examinations was reduced from an average of just over 11 to 10.
>
> An evaluation of the reform was carried out which concluded that Faculties had carried out the rationalization according to the quantitative target set, but despite having asked for the latter, they then felt they had not been given the requisite freedom to exercise their professional expertise. Implementation was strongly influenced by the relevant departmental culture. Some faculty departments did not co-operate as regards equivalences. Little attention was paid to the qualitative aspects: some departments waited to receive guidelines; most left it to individual initiative; only a few took collective action to promote self-study.
>
> Thus, by itself, external and executive-level pressure was insufficient to achieve complete realization of the reform. A core team inside each department should have been designated to carry out more radical qualitative measures. In addition, once the targets had been reached, the task groups at faculty level were disbanded and support for the process fell away. The inconsistent policy of the Academic Council in making concessions to certain departments was also instrumental in reducing the pressure for reform(15).

The teacher (as noted in *Chapter 7 on Staff management*) now plays the role of interpreter, guide and course developer(16). Information technology can also be used for more efficient student tracking and assessment, saving teachers' marking time(17).

(i) Self-regulation and accountability implemented

Certain technological universities have tended to lead the way, often funded by special government grants. The United Kingdom's HEFC Teaching and Learning with Technology Programme is an example. Grants have been awarded to consortia of universities to introduce technology to the teaching of specific disciplines; for example images can be drawn from the university's photograph or slide collection and imported into a PC for further processing for chemistry courses. The QUEST programme (Quality in Engineering through Simulation Technology) devised computer-based units constituting 25 per cent of the technical course content; they reduced formal student contact time by 20 per cent, were flexible, self-paced and available 24 hours a day. In the Arts, a large number of museum and art collections are now on videodiscs and can be found by topic on a data base.

Eventually all higher education institutions in the United Kingdom will be connected via information super highways (SuperJANET) for the transfer of academic material. The possibilities for future organization of higher education are already being recognized: a blueprint has been drawn up for a University of the Highlands and Islands, where students would be linked with their tutors and classmates only by computer and video. Courses would be bought in and the university facilities would, in effect, be made up of existing colleges in the region.

Such systems already exist in slightly different forms in multi-campus institutions in the USA, Canada, New Zealand and Australia, where large proportions of the populations are dispersed in rural areas. For example, the Memorial University, Newfoundland, Canada, has a geographic coverage of 150,000 square miles and half a million people. It has set up an audio-graphic teleconferencing network reaching 160 sites and can access other networks to share programmes. The principal tool used is the telewriter or long-distance blackboard. A home-based package of manuals, assignments, and textbooks form the educational delivery system, plus teleconferencing and two summer schools. At present, approximately half the first degree programmes are in this mode. A problem has been in finding funds for the equipment, for libraries in regional centres and for the additional staff, comprising the network operational and technical delivery group, the production team, an administrative group and the academic staff for course development and teleconferencing.

New Zealand also has an unevenly distributed population and devised its own system, called Unitel, on 30 sites. Its courses are given in much the same delivery mode as those in Canada.

The Australian Government has been a prime mover in promoting technology for educational delivery to remote campuses. It is funding the Open Learning Agency of Australia Pty Ltd., which is being developed by a consortium of universities, and involves the broadcasting of the first year of certain university courses. Students will not need to enrol but will be able to sit first-year examinations, gain the necessary credits and then enter a university. Subjects requiring sequential learning will not be offered. 'Telecottages' equipped with television, telephone, computers and faxes will be set up for rural areas.

The possibilities for combining different types of study methods and co-operation between different institutions are boundless; universities are breaking new ground every year. In the United States, the Association for Media-Based Continuing Education for Engineers, a non-profit consortium of 34 engineering universities, has produced 700 video-based programmes, while the National Technological University, a private co-operative effort of 25 engineering schools, provides high-quality continuing education leading to an M.Sc. and broadcasts via four channels on a 24-hour day schedule.

(ii) Centralized planning and control

In France, multi-media courses and computer assisted teaching are used to a certain extent, but information about them is not widely distributed. Many programmes have been assembled by teams in biology, physics, chemistry and English, and simulations are used in physics, statistics, medicine and management. Obstacles are the diversity of needs, lack of funding and training of teachers[18].

Certain developing countries have been quick to perceive the advantages of new distance learning technology. One of the earliest was Thailand, where the Sukhothai Thammathirat Open University was set up in 1979, and 400,000 students were enrolled by 1990. It makes use of regional learning centres and a mass communication network. This has meant that students who cannot enter university because of enrolment restrictions can still study. Though it diffuses political unrest, it has created another problem: an excess of Humanities and Social Science graduates[19].

Indonesia's Satellite system for higher education began in 1983 under SISDIKSAT which connects members of eastern island universities. The main activities are sharing seminars, information exchange and demonstrations that include other user groups outside the universities with an emphasis on course exchange between members. A formative evaluation of the system, which included student and faculty questionnaires, has shown that: (i) everything takes more time than anticipated: planning, purchase of equipment, testing and installation can take several years; (ii) equipment should start simple and should only be made more complex if time, staff, money and skill permit; (iii) the mistake of concentrating on hardware at the expense of software is invariably made; (iv) a strong organization is needed at the centre of the network to co-ordinate, mediate and implement; (v) the system is particularly appropriate for the upgrading of teaching staff; and (vi) the introduction of an innovative system does not mean that users will adopt innovative ways to utilize it(20).

India's experience in using television to improve university education has also been positively evaluated. In 1984, the UGC launched the Countrywide Classroom project, which operates on all working days from 1-2 and 4-5 p.m. Programmes are targeted to undergraduates in small towns in rural areas. The Inter-University Centres provide facilities such as education media and libraries(21).

The largest distance learning system is in China. It was set up by international satellite with 2,000 receive-only earth stations. One channel operates 17 hours a day, 11 for training teachers and six for adult education. Two channels relay educational programmes including those of the TV University and the Peasant Broadcasting School. 15,385 video viewing centres have been set up to show tapes sent to students.

Distance learning systems are continuing to spread. Some examples are: Japan's University of the Air (1986); Egypt's Open University(1991); Cuba's 'Directed Teaching' at ten higher education institutions; Russia's proposed open university, which is being designed to modernize the present higher education system. Certain universities could not operate without such technology, for example, the Universities of the West Indies and the South Pacific, which cover huge regions, with multiple centres, each equipped with teleconferencing studios.

The new technology enhances the interdependence of higher education institutions; for instance, the University of Science and Technology, Hong Kong, is organizing direct access to the supercomputer and seven libraries of the University of California by an intercontinental link. The Australian Open University and Broadcasting Corporation are sending selected programmes of a consortium of nine universities to Asia via the Indonesian satellite and the EEC is funding the use of the Olympus satellite for nine hours a day of broadcasting over two years in order to promote this technology in Europe. A new global degree – "Master of Distance Education" is being developed by an international consortium of higher education institutions in Australia, Canada, India and Britain to be offered through OUs in each country(22).

This brings us to the third of the factors providing impetus to changes in educational delivery systems: the internationalization of higher education.

c. Internationalization of higher education

International links have been organized both by consortia of universities and by individual institutions. A major initiative has been the European ERASMUS programme under which 25,000 students are to benefit from study periods in other member countries, receiving grants from the European Union. Priority is at present being given to building up a network of co-operation between universities.

In 1994, the five Educational Ministers of the Nordic countries signed a common treaty on higher education. Students in these countries can apply on equal terms to any university in the region since the languages spoken have common roots and do not constitute a barrier, the Finns tending to be bilingual with Swedish. Each host country will pay for the students it enrols but can limit total intake.

A country which has been particularly active in internationalization is Japan, going so far as to establish the new Kibi International University to create 'international people' (with interdisciplinary studies in international relations, and trade, travel and study abroad). Japan has also established overseas colleges, the latest being a new women's college in north-east Spain which is offering courses in languages and social customs. Japanese universities switched to an autumn start in 1987 so as to bring them into line with international practice and they have been buying buildings on other campuses to establish overseas branches. The links between Japan and the United States are particularly strong. Since 1980 more than a 100 American universities have sent teams to Japan to explore the establishment of campuses there and 120 Japanese institutions have conducted mergers or purchase of United States institutions so as to be able to offer study abroad and language courses. Experience has shown that there are some problems of negative reception, acceptability and control(23).

Joint courses by developed and developing country institutions are flourishing, particularly in Malaysia, where economic growth has produced a rapidly increasing middle class whose demand for places in the state system could not be satisfied. The government therefore authorized the development of private colleges which established joint arrangements with institutions in English-speaking countries (United States, United Kingdom, Australia, Canada, New Zealand). After students have completed one or two years' study at home, they move to a foreign institution to complete their degrees. Similar arrangements have also been made by state institutions for some programmes. An example is the link between Canada's Carleton University and Malaysia's Sunway College; in this programme students in Business Administration, Engineering and Computer Science transfer to Carleton after the first year. A similar arrangement has been made by a Yorkshire consortium of universities which won a contract with Malaysia to take 1,200 students, involving one year at the University of Malaysia and then direct entry into the second year of a British course.

In the reverse direction, Australian universities are increasingly setting up campuses in Asian countries; for example a consortium of 11 universities has an agreement with the Malaysian Government to build a college within the country to teach the first year of Australian degrees. The economic motivation for this trend is very strong, governments wanting to stem the flow of money abroad. Similar arrangements exist in other Asian countries. A consortium of British universities is giving a foundation course and first year of B.Sc. in Karachi, Pakistan in co-operation with well-equipped schools. China also has a number of agreements with foreign sister universities. Examples are Dalian and SUNY, Buffalo, in business administration and a new Masters course in Business Administration which will be taught jointly by Lancaster University and the University of Xian, with Chinese students in Lancaster for their third and final year. Canada's Concordia University has set up a joint doctoral engineering programme with the South-East University in Nanjing, China, and a management education linkage with Tianjin University.

There are also examples of setting up entire courses in developing countries. Manchester Polytechnic has launched a degree course to be taught entirely overseas. One hundred and twenty Sri Lankan students are enrolled in a course in applied computing at a private institute in Colombo, which is a replica of the one at Manchester and is set up with a private company which has been supplying computers in Sri Lanka for some years. Computer experts are one of the few types of manpower which are scarce in Sri Lanka. The Royal Melbourne Institute of Technology and the Singapore Institute of Management offer a joint Master's degree in Finance in Singapore while the Victoria University of

Technology organizes a graduate diploma course in computer science in the Hong Kong Polytechnic. The International University of Alexandria was set up in October 1991 to give French language 3rd cycle courses in management, environmental science, finance, nutrition and food technology to experts having three to seven years of professional experience. Its main aim is African development and it will eventually enrol 500 students per year(24).

d. New partners in education and changes in clientele

Higher education authorities are beginning to accept (i) that much higher proportions of their students will be adults (mid-twenties up); (ii) that mature students do not need to study for as long a period as teenagers in order to obtain the same qualification; (iii) that work experience may, like the practical experience given to full-time students during courses, count for credit towards a degree, and (iv) that business and industry are bona fide partners in the process of undergraduate, postgraduate and continuing education.

The United States is in the vanguard of this particular trend with Corporate Partners Programmes. The process involves working with a company to review its training programmes and establish a partnership to link resources, avoid duplication and assist one another. Courses conducted by the company, if equivalent to those in the university, are awarded credits. Business requirements are inserted into existing degree programmes. The Director of Partnerships is often funded by the companies concerned(25).

There are large numbers and an enormous variety of courses which alternate work and study. Long Island and Northeastern Universities have courses where employers provide part-time professional jobs, and students alternate trimesters of work and study after an initial year spent entirely at the university. Other courses allow students to continue in employment, such as the off-campus graduate engineering programme at Columbia University, which is conducted at work sites by a two-way video link or videotapes. Students register by telephone, assignments are sent by express mail and instructions are sent by E-mail. The advantages of this method of delivery are that students can select a course irrespective of their location, while faculty can develop useful research relationships and new course inputs, and use leading engineers as adjunct faculty.

Partnerships have also begun in the United Kingdom. The Partnership Degree Programme at Portsmouth Polytechnic allows people to study while working full time. Students will be evaluated on both course work and work experience, and projects will be negotiated with employers.

Students may have time off for lectures, but will have to work in the evenings.

As from 1992, two-year degrees were introduced in some former polytechnics, the numbers being limited in the first experimental phase to 500 mature students. The teaching year will have to be extended to 45 weeks, an example of the ways in which new educational delivery methods are changing space requirements.

Australia is also considering new doctorates whereby professionals will be able to obtain degrees based in part on workplace experience. Co-operative ventures, known as Centres for Professional Development, between higher educational institutions and technology-based industries and education, health and community services are spreading.

Victoria College conducted a survey of needs amongst companies in its region and devised a course on Technology Management to meet them, which would allow employees to continue in their work and study at their own pace. Employers stipulated that the course should result in a recognized tertiary education award, and a new B. App.Sci. (Technology Management) was created. Two colleges, one company and a foundation were the major sponsors and representatives from each were on the management committee. Tutorials conducted at work sites, response to queries by E-mail and prepared learning materials formed the mode of educational delivery. Many of the students did not have the normal requirements for entry to higher education. However, evaluation of employers and students showed good progress and satisfaction with the relevance of the content and the convenience of study methods. Faculty had learned to use a new approach and had broadened their perspectives. A consequence of the experience has been a high demand for such courses to be delivered in industry and the development of long-term arrangements in larger companies(26).

Such co-operation between university and industry can also be found in continental Europe. France has just announced 56 new courses within the structure of the Institutes Universitaires Professionnels to boost the output of engineering graduates. Students are selected after completion of the first year at university and are given a further three years of education in which half the teaching is done by business and industry(27).

The tailoring of teaching programmes to suit potential customers is now considered a major source of innovative ideas in teaching, learning and curricular design(28). University staff have gained considerable experience in adapting their methods of work and content in the light of what both external experts and clients have to say.

In Africa and the Arab states, there is some reason to believe that innovation in educational delivery(29) methods has not taken place to any great degree(30), the lack of funding for technology and training being an obvious factor in impeding any such development.

However, in certain self-regulatory countries there has been a determined onslaught by governments to bring about change which, apart from giving lower costs, has, as in the United States, allowed both the economic sector and clients to have very much more influence on how and what higher education is provided. It is becoming clear to universities that educational delivery modes have major implications not only for the provision of effective and efficient teaching and learning, assessment and examinations *but also for managerial efficiency*. In the future, therefore, the executive level must expect to make more demands on the base units in this domain. As yet, the requisite organizational structure, on the lines seen for staff and research management, is not apparent to any extent, though executive-level management has been instrumental in the change to modular credit systems, designation of cost centres, teaching methods and educational resource units.

2. Lessons learned for improving educational delivery

This chapter shows the way that universities are equipping themselves to meet mass but very diversified needs in the future. A major lesson is that base units cannot be left to respond to the challenges alone. Success and progress are achieved by the support of government agencies, executive-level guidance and planning and flexibility of implementation at departmental level. Responsibilities should be defined in order that duplication of effort is avoided as much as possible. The following programmes of action at different levels could improve educational delivery.

a. International and national levels

- policy guidance on efficient modes of educational delivery;
- organization of shared production of core educational materials and resources, including induction packages on learning, how to learn, and computer-based learning packages;
- dissemination of teaching materials;
- research on mass teaching techniques;
- teacher training in new modes of educational delivery;
- formative and summative assessment of software;
- international universities;

Educational delivery systems

- student mobility arrangements;
- grants to assist setting up of courses in developing countries.

b. University executive level[1]

- fora for discussion and information dissemination;
- strategic plan: the information base for decision-making on provision of courses; would include:

A periodic intensive needs-assessment survey in what fields and how many; what is the potential market?

Evaluation of existing facilities (including computers, videos, E-mail etc.), what is the teaching and technological capacity at what levels? What is the gap between what can be produced and what needs to be produced? What is the state of the communications infrastructure, postal services, radio, TV, in order to establish whether distance learning may be incorporated.

Evaluate the structure and personnel to produce and disseminate materials. (With desk-top publishing, it is not difficult for developing countries to set up a production facility with trained staff). Seriously consider regional and bilateral agreements with existing universities of repute. The co-operative model spreads the initial fixed costs of course production and draws on the academic strengths of each participating institution, allowing access to a greater range of specialities:

- planning of teacher and technological staff training to improve educational delivery;
- planning of technological infrastructure;
- increased role for educational resource units;
- encouragement of research on educational delivery;
- control of efficient educational delivery in a cost centre, information and reports;
- decision-making on courses to be set up in other countries.

---

1. Academic Vice-President/Deputy Vice-Chancellor responsible for keeping the university up to date.

c. Departmental level

- adaptation of national/regional core programmes/materials to local needs;
- research and experiments;
- orientation of staff in teams according to their capabilities in specific roles such as course direction, materials preparation, technology expertise, etc., and recommendations for training;
- adaptive and open to working in partnership with external bodies training their staff at higher education level;
- feedback to executive level on success/failure.

References

1. Curran, C. *Institutional models of distance education*. Paper for OECD, IMHE 29th Workshop, December 1990.
2. Ebert, D. "Issues in distance education". In *International Journal of Innovative Higher Education*, Vol. 7, Nos. 1 and 2, 1990.
3. Kool, B. and Jenkins, J. (ed.), *Distance Education*, Kogan Page, London, 1990.
4. Kaye, T. and Rumble, G. *Open universities, a comparative approach*. Prospects Vol. XXI, No. 2, 1991.
5. Duke, C. *The learning university*. Oxford University Press, Buckingham, United Kingdom, 1992.
6. Lajeunesse, C. *What are the essential tools of a modern system of higher education?* IGLU, 2 April 1992.
7. David Watson et al., *Managing the modular course: perspectives from Oxford Polytechnic*, Milton Keynes, Open University Press, 1989.
8. Times Higher Education Supplement, 20 December 1991.
9. Times Higher Education Supplement, 31 July 1993.
10. Jacques, D. *Earning in groups* London, Kogan Page, 1991.
11. Johnson, D. et al. *Co-operative learning: increasing college faculty instructional productivity*. ASHE-ERIC Report No. 4, 1991.
12. Bireaud, A. *Les méthodes pedagogiques dans l'enseignement superieur. Editions d'organisation*, Paris, 1990.
13. Times Higher Educational Supplement, 29 May 1992.
14. Hirsh de Trejo, E. *Improving managerial effectiveness of higher education institutions: the case of UNAM, Mexico*. IIEP, Paris, 1994.
15. Vandenberghe, R. et al. *Rationalisation of curricula at K.U. Leuven, Belgium*. IIEP, Paris, 1994.
16. Mayes, J. *Technology-based learning*. Paper for EAIR 15th Forum, September 1991.
17. Times Higher Education Supplement, 19 November 1993.
18. Bikeavud, A. idem.
19. Minnis, J. "Distance education as social policy in Thailand". In *International Journal of Innovative Higher Education*, Vol. 7, Nos. 1 and 2, 1990.
20. Johari, R. et al. "Higher education via satellite: the Indonesian DE satellite system". In *International Review of Education*, Vol. 32, No. 3, 1986.
21. Khanna, S. *An important innovation*. University News, 30 September 1991.
22. Times Higher Education Supplement, 27 July, 1990.
23. Chambers, G. *Profiting from education, Institute of International Education*, New York, 1990.
24. Tabatoni, P., IIEP, Current Issues Seminar, January 1991.

25. Nugent, M. *Critical success factors and benefits of corporate education partnerships*. Industry and Higher Education, June 1992.
26. Beeson, G. *et al.* "A co-operative approach to providing relevant higher education in the workplace". In *Innovative Higher Education*, Vol. 6, Nos. 1 and 2, 1992.
27. Times Higher Educational Supplement, 24 July 1993.
28. Becher, T. and Kogan, M. Idem 1992.
29. Bubtana, A. "Financing Arab Higher Education: a search for new alternatives". In *Higher Education Policy*, Vol. 5, No. 4, 1992.
30. Sanyal, B.C.; Martin, M. *Institutional management in higher education*, Report of a sub-regional workshop, IIEP, 1994.

Part V

Prospects for improving management

Chapter 11

Taking stock: the prospects for improving institutional management in developing countries

The time has now come to take stock of the changes which have taken place in the management of higher education institutions around the world and to try to place these in perspective. Subsequently, the possibilities for improving university management in developing countries will be considered, together with the lessons drawn as regards good practice in implementing change, as shown by the case studies carried out for the IIEP research programme.

1. Taking stock

Higher education – and its management – is a product of social, cultural, political, organizational, and economic history: each system, and even each institution, is unique. The need for change within higher education occurs through the recognition of the effects of changes in each of these contexts at the international, national, and sub-national levels. However, there has usually been no mechanism in higher education to make it respond automatically to contextual changes, except in those institutions subject to market forces. Universities were and are, almost without exception, highly conservative social institutions in terms of their internal structures and operations. A combination of bureaucratization, unionization, and traditional forms of protection, such as tenure and academic freedom, have combined to insulate them from the need to adapt. This endured up to the 1980s for some and even later for others. Many of the attempted reforms of the 1970s were frustrated by the academic community in Western Europe, and the same situation is repeating itself in the 1990s in Latin America and Eastern Europe. Government intervention is needed because higher education systems may, if left to themselves, change too slowly to serve society's broader needs.

Although higher education always has been subject to external influences, these have recently gained considerable momentum and have multiplied. The most important are mass social demand, the emphasis on social inclusion of previously marginalized populations, the new demographics of labour supply, the technological impacts on labour demand, the internationalization of information and markets, changing fiscal conditions, and public and political attitudes to higher education and the justification for its continued public support. The characteristic of this coming decade is that in a number of countries in the developed world the ability to resist these pressures has been reduced; the successful systems and institutions of the next century will be those that can adapt to new demands while retaining the best aspects of existing structures and processes.

A special contextual pressure on higher education is the competition for funds from other forms of education (especially basic education and non-traditional forms of post-secondary education), from other social sectors (especially health, nutrition, and population control), and from the economic, or 'wealth-creating' sectors. Higher education must be prepared to show value for money not only in terms of outputs, such as number of graduates, research products and service activities, but in terms of how these outputs produce societal outcomes, which may be social, cultural, political, or economic, that are valued sufficiently to justify its relative cost.

If university managers are to recognize the need for change and to make proper use of the practical reforms described in this research, they must be able to comprehend such contextual factors, and the imperatives they imply. Among those managers must be included those responsible in government departments for higher education, especially in centrally-planned systems. A number of governments in developing countries have neglected to provide the directives and guidance that have been such a prominent feature of the self-regulatory systems. What has become clear is that a system of multiple-level integrated management, possibly involving government, universities association, university executive, faculty and department, can be quicker to change than one which locates decision-making at mainly one level. This is shown by the sheer extent of change which has taken place in the self-regulatory groups as opposed to the centrally planned. Some countries, including France and Italy, have acknowledged this, and attempted to reinforce institutional management and to introduce self-evaluation in order to improve the capacity of the institution to cope with local needs and problems.

It is true that many institutions in self-regulatory systems had a tradition of catering to a minority elite, good conditions of residence, research and other facilities, and had high average costs per graduate. They were institutions which, if they were to meet social demand for higher education, required to be streamlined and made accountable. On the other hand, centrally-planned systems, apart from Germany, had lower costs and poorer conditions of study and work, but, at least in Europe, offered greater opportunities of access. The challenge now for the self-regulated institutions is to maintain quality and expand supply, while for the centrally-planned systems it is to increase effectiveness of performance and responsiveness to changing needs.

It has been shown that governments may adopt different policies, and that the institutions themselves may adopt unique solutions to overcome perceived threats to their viability and reputation. What is particularly striking is the change in universities to extreme awareness of context, to looking outward rather than remaining preoccupied with strictly disciplinary and academic values. As one case-study author put it, a major contributory factor in the University's financial problems was a failure to monitor external factors, such as developments in government funding policies and their effect on the University, and performance indicators such as levels of resource utilization at the university as compared with other universities, available from published information(1).

This is one of the fundamental differences between the two ends of the management spectrum of self-regulation - central planning. It is one which is now leading ministry officials from the latter systems to enquire into formula funding, incentives, decentralization, and other mechanisms which allow greater flexibility of institutional management(2). The other fundamental difference is the cohesive and integrated nature of university management in self-regulatory systems, involving finance, staff, research, services, space and educational delivery at executive, faculty and departmental levels. Again problems arose due to:

- a failure to ensure close linkage between academic and financial planning and to recognize that *virtually all academic decisions carry resource implications*;
- absence of robust planning and budgeting arrangements, linking budgetary allocations to agreed plans, and monitoring performance against them;
- absence of effective financial control arrangements, under which all kinds of expenditure would be covered by approved budgets with designated individuals as the budget-holders, individually responsible for ensuring that budgets are adhered

- to, or at least able to explain why this is not possible because of external forces;
- an over-reliance on forecasts of income and expenditure, instead of close monitoring of actual figures, both during the financial year and at the end of it once the final accounts were available;
- absence of effective internal information systems and communications, both between different central offices and between central offices and academic departments;
- absence of effective mechanisms and expertise to allow senior officers to detect problems at an early stage.

An integrated management system is now indispensable to the proper functioning of universities within the self-regulatory environment. However, the environments of centrally-planned systems have also become increasingly unstable and their institutions have difficulties working as a cohesive whole where staffing, research and space decisions are not under the control of the executive; examples have been given of direct liaison between individual departments and ministries about staff, research and buildings.

The problems of centrally-planned systems have been recognized and a number of strategies devised to give more flexibility in use of resources and to strengthen the executive level. The straitjacket of financial constraint for certain developing countries seems insurmountable without external assistance, but the majority do have some scope to equip their universities with improved management systems that will make them viable partners for the international higher educational network of the twenty-first century. The following section examines this possibility more closely.

2. The possibilities for improving university management in developing countries

a. Role of the government

Change is costly and often frustrating. Strong political and moral will is needed to overcome the paralyzing effects of resistance, low motivation, poor use of resources and low productivity. How far the government is able and willing to go has to be judged and timed correctly, and has in practice varied greatly. In some countries very specific and hard policies have been imposed; in the United Kingdom, for example, departments were penalised for low submission rates as a percentage of Ph.D students, with the result that in 1993 69 per cent of these were completed within four years, rising from 25 per cent in 1980. The Netherlands has a slightly less severe policy of withdrawing funding for Ph.Ds after a stipulated number of years, while other countries may merely include it as a performance indicator which influences research funding. Generally, however, steering has been by incentives rather than penalties.

Also essential is the information base by which to judge and time the introduction of policies and measures. The development of information systems in self-regulatory systems has been rapid and striking. Australia publishes reports of over 50 indicators of performance and diversity(3) while the United Kingdom HEFC has more than 70(4). Even Finland has ten. The objectives of analysis differ according to the goals of the higher education system. Those for Australia are intended to serve a number of purposes: first, to add to existing market information to assist both international and domestic students in making informed comparisons between institutions; second, to enable the devising of strategic plans, and to compare themselves with other institutions as an input to their strategic planning; and third, to contribute to public accountability. In both Australia and the United Kingdom, it is stated that when comparing universities, it is important to note that *each university has a unique mission* and that it is government policy to encourage diversity in institutional offerings, in order to broaden student choices and promote flexibility of labour supply.

Centrally-planned developed countries, such as France, have always amassed a large amount of information, but have not analyzed it in order to compare performance, to rank institutions and to increase competition. Programme costs by institution were not known. Most developing countries, however, lack good working information systems, though some, such as Korea, Nigeria, and Ghana, are beginning to establish them.

Another major ingredient of change in the self-regulatory systems is the preparation of everybody concerned. Reforms have usually been accompanied by a great deal of media activity: rhetoric comes first, new values precede new structure or methods(5), such as the establishment of task forces, publication of official papers and meetings, countered by dire warnings from academics of the decline of the higher educational system. These are all part and parcel of the process of change. Governments armed with information and overwhelming arguments about value for money, financial constraint, and mass social demand, have managed to rest their case over to the public. Other systems have to be prepared for this debate, though in some Asian countries accustomed to centralized planning, it may be less noisy than it has been in developed countries. On the other hand, the process in Latin America is not only antagonistic, but excessively protracted, thus weakening the move to reform.

This leads to a fourth major element of successful change: good relations and collaboration between governments ministries and universities. It is evident that close collaboration has been necessary for improving the management of finance, information systems, evaluation, staff and research, in countries with self-regulatory policies. Improved collaboration has been assisted by the establishment of university associations in countries where they formerly did not exist. This has enabled the universities to give collective opinions, which prepare the ground more solidly, even where there is no unanimity and the debate continues.

Ministries and institutions share the responsibility for creating an environment for dynamic institutions. Improved institutional management requires the sympathetic support of Ministry officials knowledgeable enough to avoid official procedures which work to the detriment of good everyday management, as in the case of Makerere University. Practical collaboration might also break down the government distrust of the capabilities of university management, noted for African and Arab institutions, while also ensuring that universities understand the constraints on the Ministry. With sympathetic and well-informed government support, universities have shown that they can make very difficult decisions to cut departments and staff and also embark upon less costly educational delivery systems and new directions of research. Innovation in management is cumulative and provides a favourable environment for *academic innovation*.

Other important elements of the government's role in change have been referred to in *Chapter 5*, and include:

- Pilot projects, and their utility in enlisting support in the higher educational system.
- Technical support, in the form of training and expert consultancy agencies in specific domains of university management.
- A clear agenda, objectives and timing.
- Incentives in the form of funding for equipment and bonuses to management staff.
- Evaluation and feedback mechanisms giving information for adjustments and directions for the implementation of further reforms.
- Detailed accountability procedures, with early publication of results showing institutional performance.

- A clear realization on the part of governments that they form an integral part of university management.

Attention to these will greatly increase the possibilities of successfully introducing change in institutional management in public universities. Moreover, in developing countries, it has generally been the government which has initiated change, a few examples being:

(i) Institutional management

- slimming down of university decision-making structures, and merging of departments (three or four African universities).

(ii) Financial management

- savings made on staff to be used at university's discretion (Zambia);
- promotion of income-generating activities by staff and students (most countries).

(iii) Staff management

- output-based payments based on number of lectures (Uganda);
- appraisal of staff (Indonesia);
- staff development programmes (but with little government funding);
- department heads responsible for efficient utilization of academic staff and adequate teaching skills (Cuba).

(iv) Research

- Centres for Technological Innovation which provide support services for projects and arrange contracts between universities and industry (Brazil);
- regional research centres to circulate information, arrange exchange programmes, etc. (Africa and Asia - often donor agency-supported);
- technology parks (Malaysia, Singapore, Latin America).

(v) Space

- shifts (Ghana, Sudan, Kenya);
- extension of teaching day (Hong Kong).

b. Role of the institution

The essential characteristics of a university management capable of adaptation and improvement in efficiency and effectiveness can be summarized as follows:

- good working relationships with funding and support agencies;
- clear and concrete strategic mission;
- strong executive-level management responsible for guiding work in the major domains: finance, staff, space, research, academic (including education delivery);
- channels for reception of information from outside, such as governing board members from industry and commerce, posts for industrial liaison, fund raising, overseas students, a planning unit which collects and analyses socio-economic data;
- information base, use of performance indicators for institutional and departmental comparisons, and to measure progress;
- budgeting procedures linked to planning, working on actual costs and devolved to departments to whom all costs are charged;
- departments as managers and performers;
- flexibility in all domains: finance (possibilities of transfer and carry-over), staff (variety of contracts), space (central control of most facilities), educational and research activities (innovation in teaching methods, continuing education and consultancies), all within the framework of the devolved budgeting procedures and mission.

Such an adaptive system is not without its dangers, as many Ministry officials will be quick to point out. It has a tendency, by its emphasis on management and information, to increase the proportion of administrative staff, and efforts have to be made to restrain this. In addition, academics are required to be managers, which encounters some resistance and need for training, although there has been a radical change in the attitudes of some, particularly younger, staff. The existence of an institutional mission and accountability has also tended to build up allegiance to the institution as opposed to concern only with establishing a reputation in a particular discipline. A reasonably balanced decision-making structure also builds up confidence and motivation – which was one of the advantages of the former collegial system.

The implementation of such a type of management in centrally-planned systems encounters obstacles. As much as three-quarters of the resources may lie outside university budgets, and government contacts about staff and research funds may be made direct with faculties, undermining the institutional executive level. Such difficulties are being met by the drawing up of mission statements, contracts, information systems, evaluation and accountability procedures, all of which strengthen the executive level and weld the different faculties into a cohesive institution.

None of this, however, can overcome to any appreciable extent the low motivation and paralysis existing in institutions suffering from the effects of inflation, arbitrary funding cuts, and political instability. Such measures would, however, assist the staff to ensure that the institution functions as well as it can, and assure donor agencies that their assistance is truly worthwhile.

3. Implementing change within institutions

The 14 case studies carried out by the IIEP research programme produced a wealth of information about the ways in which change has been effected. The findings can be summarized as follows:

a. The impetus for the change

In all cases the impetus came primarily from financial constraints, followed by the need for improved managerial efficiency and effectiveness demanded by the government and/or the market.

b. The source of the change

The sources of proposals for change were (i) experience elsewhere, and (ii) theory, applied and adapted to the institution. Most developing country universities have staff with experience of training workshops and study abroad, but when they return home, they find a situation where most academics are not expected to interest themselves in administration or management. New ideas therefore have no outlet, unless the staff member is, say, an Academic Vice-President. Universities need to stimulate sources of change, by the circulation of information on management and research in other institutions and countries, and regular forums for the discussion of management issues and connected university problems. There were long incubation periods, of two to ten years, for most changes, demonstrating that institutions need to create awareness that change is a natural and beneficial process, and that what was done previously is not necessarily the best practice.

Change is more acceptable when all those affected feel they have contributed and have been involved, and ideally they should themselves be the source of the change. Where this cannot be the case, they should included from the beginning.

c. Planning the implementation of the change

   (i)   As far as possible, plans should reflect wide consultation within the University and command a broad degree of support; this does not preclude early emergency action. Neglect of some seemingly uninfluential actors could have harmful repercussions later in the process.
   (ii) The process should not be hasty or inflexible – adjustments in the light of concrete evidence will have to be made. A dogmatic stance tends to create more opposition. However, consultation should not become an excuse for procrastination, and there comes a point where it is the role of senior management to give leadership and to act decisively. The continued vitality and commitment of leadership over the period of the change is essential. A management team composed of key members of the staff, who are trusted representatives of the rank and file and not only of the upper hierarchy, has been found to be a critical element in success.
   (iii) Plans should be formulated so as to indicate the time scale for achieving each phase, and the individual who is to be responsible for it. Before making a change, thought should be given as to whether *other* official policy changes are likely to be introduced in the near future which may to affect the functioning of the university. Where some positive measures are being enforced by the government, the university might be able at the same time to take the opportunity to introduce some other change from its own agenda. An important point here is that any innovation may automatically trigger a series of others, and that strategy should determine how many such elements of change can be tackled at one time and how they may all

be phased in. This will depend on the management's ability to cope within the circumstances.

(iv) Use should be made of normal planning and administrative procedures as far as possible. Small 'task forces' to address particular aspects of the problem may be set up, provided their work is co-ordinated and that they are disbanded when their work is complete. New mechanisms may alarm the university and create the impression that regulations are being by-passed. Useful members of task forces have been found to be senior staff new to the university who can perhaps take a more dispassionate view. Those who have served for longer periods may find it more difficult to come to terms with the severity of the problem and its origins. External consultants (possibly from donor agencies) can help address some aspects of the problem, where university officers lack the professional expertise or are too closely associated with the current unsatisfactory arrangements.

(v) A stock of goodwill should be built up, fuelled by the publication of mission statements, write-ups in the press, and other public relations techniques. The purpose is to demonstrate that the institution is positively acting to meet not only its management problems but those of the region or nation, its students and its enterprises.

(vi) The role played by students and the finding of key allies among them has been found extremely important. In the Philippines case, students were enlisted to undertake the initial feasibility studies of the parameters of the trimester system. For the first study, a team of some of the best industrial management engineering students was carefully identified; it was suggested to this team that they study the management aspects of this change and present their findings as their thesis requirement for graduation. They agreed, and the institutional planning officer at the time was appointed as their thesis adviser. In subsequent years, similar teams of graduating students were enlisted for further technical studies of the trimester system, using these as thesis topics.

d. The implementation of change

(i) The design of strategies and their implementation requires experimentation. Pilot runs should be conducted to test the correctness of the direction taken. This is similar to practice at national level, where test runs of a reform measure are conducted to see if it works as expected and to identify unexpected negative consequences.

(ii) Efficiency of implementation requires that tasks and responsibilities be set out in detail. Periodic analysis and feedback should be incorporated.

(iii) The university should set aside some funds to strengthen key support functions for implementation. The ability to offer some incentives seems to be critical, particularly at points where planning or implementation may be getting bogged down. The incentives are preferably financial, but may also include time for research, facilities, cheaper total study fees and quicker degree completion, and prestige.

In any case, some uncertainty about the outcome has to be lived with however good the planning. The pragmatic approach is to convert uncertainty into risk and then minimize it as far as possible.

e. Evaluation

No reform is ever completely finished, since it inevitably results in requirements for further change. However, at a suitable point it is good practice to produce an evaluation showing the achievements so far in order to reassure students, parents and government of the capabilities of the institution to meet their needs and adapt to socio-economic development. Successful innovation must be followed by a new routinization to replace the old, with judicious control of the innovation-routinization cycles.

Finally, and very significantly, much has been said about the cost of change and innovation, as if an orderly change or innovation is invariably expensive. In this context, two questions are conveniently ignored: what would have been the cost of retaining the traditional methods and is the innovation necessarily expensive? In the earliest stages of innovation at BITS, for example, it was found that money was never a critical factor. In fact soft money tended to make the system flabby and non-enterprising. This was in general terms the criticism levelled at universities in the self-regulatory group prior to government reforms.

f. Overcoming problems

The most common problems encountered were:

(i) Staff resistance

Often this derives from fear. Strategies adopted have been:

- Open communication.
- Assurance of continued employment, status and salary levels.
- A new reward system, offering better pay to, say, the best 30 per cent. Where few monetary incentives can be offered, time for Ph.D studies via distance education, research opportunities, institutional workshops, and short-term secondments to gain experience may be arranged.
- Active and committed participation of senior management, i.e. leadership by example.
- Particularly vociferous opponents should be sought out for inclusion in the dialogue, in order, if possible, to win them over.

(ii) Lack of information systems

In some cases this may be due to lack of equipment, but more often it is due to lack of management expertise (as the IIEP Workshop in Ghana, 1994, found). Donor agencies are particularly active in this domain and developing country staff are increasingly computer literate so that it is more a problem of training and suitable software in the domain of management that needs to be tackled. Sophisticated systems have created enormous problems when attempts have been made to utilize them in African universities. However, simpler software produced in the region itself is now coming on line.

(iii) Lack of managerial expertise

Department heads have found, particularly where they are elected by their department, that they have problems in gaining acceptance as managers by their colleagues. They also often lack the time for their management duties and are reluctant to assess their colleagues.

Strategies adopted have been:

- appointment of heads of departments based on merit in teaching and research as well as attendance at management courses and belief in the job as an essential part of ensuring good academic work;
- a proportion of time allocated to management duties;
- a bonus, based on performance, paid to department heads.

(iv)   Adaptation of foreign experience

Foreign collaboration or experience is meant to quicken the process of transformation. Far too often developing country universities have used it as a crutch and a status symbol, and to acquire funds for studies and equipment. There is no desire to adapt the know-how, develop a synthesis and establish a two-way traffic of ideas and concepts. This state of affairs is harmful to both donors and receivers. Potentially useful ideas should undergo rigorous testing after local academicians and managers have examined their feasibility within the local context.

(v)   Maintaining the momentum of adaptation to changing needs

Change means additional work and is often resented for taking up time that academics would prefer to devote to scholarship, consultancies and research. There is a tendency to revert to old ways once the initial pressure has been lifted. Routinization of adaptation by means of strategic planning processes, information systems, and annual accountability procedures should eventually mean that change becomes an accepted part of academic life. Making the transition to this state of affairs requires perseverance and a core of staff dedicated to continuing improvement. Attitudes are deep-seated and do not change overnight, so such a process requires many years of continued effort.

Developed country universities are already hearing the warning signals which threaten their position in the socio-economic system; they are no longer the major knowledge producers, and new models of higher education delivery are increasingly being introduced. If they are not to become merely the purveyors of 'traditional' higher education, they must participate in the wave of innovation now taking place. Developing country institutions as a whole may not feel that they are implicated in this process, but such countries as Malaysia, Indonesia, and Singapore are already participating in joint courses and satellite links. Such changes require efficient management and receptive attitudes.

4. The implications for training and upgrading the quality of management

One major lesson, particularly from developing country experiences, is the lack of interest of academics in management and their unwillingness to assume responsibility for it. This stems from irksome bureaucracy and the low status of most middle-level administrators, in governments and in universities. Ministry officials are no better trained in management than their university counterparts; many countries have poorly developed grading, work measurement and job evaluation systems in public administration. Employment has been expanded but not accompanied by effective work organization. The differentials of civil service salaries in Africa, for example, have narrowed and have had adverse effects on the motivation and efficiency of the higher grades(6). In developing countries which have allowed public sector salaries to erode, there is more moonlighting in public than in private employment(7). University and government administrators alike look upwards for advancement, and consider time to be an abundant commodity; motivation is enhanced by a highly structured interpersonal relationship pattern and by centralized authority. There is little stability in the environment of most developing countries.

Such characteristics cannot be ignored, since one of the major features of recent changes in higher education in the developed countries is the importance of the human dimension. New structures and strategies will not be implemented unless they have the support of the people involved and are underpinned by programmes to develop the new skills needed, and in particular by changes in attitude. Training courses can achieve some of this, but the main influence on behaviour is *the wider work environment of an institution*, where the mission is clearly stated and supported and people feel some assurance that things are now different(8).

Training and changes in attitudes must therefore focus not only on Ministry officials and university administrators but also on some of those leaders who set the standards for the institutional environment. The problem is that it is not the leaders who actually carry out most of the types of management tasks which have been described in the foregoing chapters, though they need to know and support what has to be done. Forums for university leaders are being organised in the African region, for example, by the African Association of Universities, which conducts workshops for Vice-Chancellors, while the IIEP has organized sub-regional workshops in integrated resource management for senior administrators in the domains of finance, staff and space.

The IIEP has so far (1995) undertaken six training workshops and has, in the light of experience, adjusted its programme by concentrating on senior level administrators, with some parallel information sessions and policy discussions for university leaders and Ministry officials. The programme consists of preliminary analysis of problem areas in higher education and in resource management conducted in the countries concerned. The workshop itself then concentrates on giving information on the latest trends and analysis of the material, demonstrating in particular how computers can assist in this task. Follow-up and implementation of what has been learned during the workshop is encouraged:

(1) by studies applying techniques in specific domains;
(2) by course materials presented in distance learning mode so that participants may easily pass on their experience to others;
(3) by encouraging the establishment of national and regional networks of administrators to discuss common problems.

It is hoped that this will help build up the analytical and problem-solving capacity of the developing regions, increasing the flow of information, both inwards and outwards, which has been such a feature of the self-regulatory systems.

The process of sensitizing governments and universities in developing countries to the need for improved management in higher education has therefore already begun. The IIEP project, with its information base, research studies and training activities has directed part of its programme to this end; in addition, the Association of African Universities, the Commonwealth Secretariat, the Carnegie and Ford Foundations, DSE of Germany, the British Council, NUFFIC, SAREC and a host of others have been actively giving assistance in this field. and if universities fail to take their proper place as increasingly dynamic and respected partners in the social and economic development of their countries, it will not be for want of goodwill and help. The changes have indeed begun to take place, but institutions and those who work in them should understand that such changes must emanate from their own national and institutional contexts. There must be the will to change and the will to adapt to the needs and priorities set down in national plans and institutional missions.

References

1. Cornish, M.D. (idem.)
2. Akopov, P. " Financial Management Model of the State Higher Education Committee in Russia". Paper presented at the St Petersburg Workshop on Institutional Management in Higher Education, St. Petersburg, 27-31 March, 1995
3. DEET. *Highlights of Higher Education*, Report No. 22, Canberra, 1994.
4. H.R. Kells. *The development of performance indicators for higher education.* OECD, Paris, June 1993. .
5. Anthony, P. *Managing Culture*, Oxford University Press, Buckingham 1994.
6. Robinson, J. International Review of Administrative Sciences, Vol. 54, No. 2, pp. 179-281, June 1988.
7. Van der Gaag et al. "Age differentials and moonlighting by civil servants. Evidence from the Ivory Coast and Peru" *World Bank Economic Review*, Vol. 3, No. 1, pp. 67-95, January 1989.
8. Howell, D."Can change be managed in an academic community?" In *Higher Education Newsletter*, Price Waterhouse, September 1991.

IIEP publications and documents

More than 750 titles on all aspects of educational planning have been, published by the International Institute for Educational Planning. A comprehensive catalogue, giving details of their availability, includes research reports, case studies, seminar documents, training materials, occasional papers and reference books in the following subject categories:

Economics of education, costs and financing.

Manpower and employment.

Demographic studies.

The location of schools (school map) and sub-national planning.

Administration and management.

Curriculum development and evaluation.

Educational technology.

Primary, secondary and higher education.

Vocational and technical education.

Non-formal, out-of-school, adult and rural education.

Copies of the catalogue may be obtained from the IIEP Publications Unit on request.

Imprimerie Gauthier-Villars
1 bd Ney
75018 Paris
Imprimé en France